Père Lagrange
Personal Reflections and Memoirs

Père Lagrange
Personal Reflections and Memoirs

translated by
Rev. Henry Wansbrough

foreword by
Pierre Benoit, O.P.

PAULIST PRESS
New York/Mahwah

This book was originally published as *Le Père Lagrange: Au Service De La Bible— Souvenirs Personnels*, by Les Editions du Cerf, Paris.

Library of Congress
Catalog Card Number: 84-62153

ISBN: 0-8091-2678-8

Published by Paulist Press
997 Macarthur Boulevard
Mahwah, N.J. 07430

Printed and bound in the United States of America

Contents

Foreword

In March 1926, at the age of seventy-one, Père Lagrange set down in writing his recollections of the founding of the Biblical School. Four years later, in October 1930, he added to this manuscript a sort of introduction in which he recounted his childhood. From 1932 to 1936 he revised both these texts, filling them out with a few extra details here and there. He died in 1938.

These, then, are the texts which are presented here, in an order which corresponds not only to that in which they were conceived, but also to their respective importance. His childhood memories, besides having the charm of freshness and sincerity, are of interest because they both herald and throw light on his adult life. The latter is obviously what is most important, and it was right to introduce the reader to it at the outset.

It is clear from the first lines of his 1926 text that Père Lagrange had no intention at all of writing his memoirs. His sole wish was to explain to his brethren and "to them alone" his intentions in the campaign which he led. His brethren remained respectfully discreet for thirty years. Only after this period of decorous silence did it seem to them that the moment had come to make the testimony public; consultation with friends who were most closely involved confirmed them in their opinion. The life and work of Père Lagrange have become deeply embedded in the life of the Church, and with the passing of the years, can be seen to make up a page in its history. It is important to read that page again—or for younger people to read it for the first time—in order to appreciate all it has to teach us. The crisis in the development of the faith which Catholics experienced in Père Lagrange's time was to generate other crises which we are living

1

through today. The better we can understand the first crisis, the more able we shall be to come through the present crises; and so it will be to our benefit for us to listen to a man who, in giving us his testimony, provides us with an exemplary model.

Much has already been published on the Modernist Crisis. Père Lagrange himself devoted a book to it: *M.Loisy et le modernisme* (Les Editions du Cerf, 1932). The text which we present here—a few passages of which he incorporated into the other book—does not claim to retrace completely the historical events, nor is it an attempt to analyze the nature of the crisis. His intention is at once more modest and more precise: it is his personal testimony, and therein lies its value. Embroiled in every issue which arose, at that time, at the very center of each because of his work and the attacks to which it was subjected, Père Lagrange gives us a day to day account of his endeavor and that of the school he had founded. It is a limited testimony, but of exceptional significance given the personality of the man. Historians will find that they can glean from it much first-hand information which will fill the gaps in their knowledge. The reader who is less of a specialist will learn through the mind and heart of one of the principal actors the nature of those testing years. These were years in which our faith in our understanding of the Bible, thrown into confusion for a while by the sudden upsurge of uncontrolled rationalist criticism, found itself renewed, deepened and purified by the application of a criticism which was both scientific and cautious, and which taught us to accept the Bible for what it was: the work of men, with man's limitations, man's imperfections and all that these entail, but at the same time entrusted by God to the Church; the work of God in which absolute truth is surely revealed to those who look with the eyes of faith.

It is not for me to restate here Père Lagrange's approach to exegesis and theology. All his works bear witness to it, and several recent books have attempted an outline of it.[1] Moreover, the recollections which he offers us here are of a different order. They trace out for us the real background and the everyday vicissitudes in which that approach matured and was expressed. They take us into the room where he, the craftsman, carried out his work, the priory of Saint-Etienne which he helped to build, the Biblical School he set up there and where he trained followers for the promotion and prolongation of his own endeavor. They show us a development over the years of his career, at once restless and yet permeated with deep peace: restless because invitations or attacks from outside provoked him to make frequent journeys or swift refutation; deeply peaceful in his persistent endeavors which themselves ceaselessly brought more protracted, more intensive toil in their wake. Constant travel about Europe, made necessary either by entreaties or by events directly perilous to his aims, alternated with archaeological and epigraphical exploration of the Holy Land and its neighboring countries. No sooner did he return from a tiring tour, sometimes stricken with illness, than this learned man would zealously set about his research once more. Having had a narrow escape countering the accusations of his adversaries, he entered passionately upon the study of some new subject, or began a commentary of another book of the Bible.

From this daily witness of his struggles which he offers us, there arises, contrary to his wishes, the marks of a powerful and remarkably engaging personality. Firstly there is his penetrating intellect which exacts honesty in all things, passionately fond of the truth, never satisfied with close approximations nor with ready-made opinions, trying ceaselessly to accept only what it sees for itself. How many times did his followers hear his call for a return to the sources! It is this concern to find solid and carefully checked bases which explains his enthusiasm for studying the Bible on its home ground. As he states: "The combination of document with monument (i.e., archaeological evidence) is the most fruitful of methods." Was it not the thrilling experience of the Sinai desert which gave the impetus to his reflections on the presentation of truth in the Bible?

There is nothing worldly in his thirst for knowledge. He admires the classics certainly; it was his masters in Autun who gave him the taste for these, and later he will find pleasure in rereading some of them with his younger brethren beneath the pines of Saint-Etienne. Nevertheless, it is the Bible above all else which attracts him both heart and soul. This passion for the Word of

God which he received in the seminary at Issy, and which was
further developed in him by his Dominican superiors, will prove
to be the mainspring, the whole secret, as it were, of his life: the
better we understand the Word, the better we can live by it.

This attempt at better understanding the Word of God was
not only for himself, but also for the sake of others who could be
helped to understand better. His religious personality bore the
additional mark of an apostolic solicitude. As a boy he was drawn
to the idea of priesthood, and when he became a priest he chose
to be a Dominican in order to work for the salvation of his fellow
men. He once spoke to me of a plan of campaign which he had
drawn up with two of his friends at the seminary of Issy. They
were to share each other's ambition of serving the Church in areas
where its struggle was most real: Father Gayraud would devote
himself to social and political problems, Father Batiffol would
give himself up to historical studies, and Father Lagrange chose
the Bible. His clearsightedness was already showing him that
this was one of the areas in which the Church had most need of
support and help. He has remained faithful to this decision
throughout his life, and those who have known him will be able
to confirm what these "recollections" hint at: he did not study,
nor teach, nor write, nor struggle for any other reason, than to
ward off the threats to his brothers' faith, or to lead to the faith
those who were far from it.

His own faith, which was perhaps his most profound characteristic, inherited from parents whom he revered, he kept always intact through all the perils of youth, and drew from it zeal
for God's Word and for the salvation of others. Those who have
suspected him of having lost his faith, and of undermining its
very foundations, really have not known him, nor understood
him. They were judging him perhaps in the light of their own
faith, ill-informed and therefore fragile. His was a robust, demanding faith, unable to blossom out except in the full light of
knowledge: one should face up to the problems which faith
brings, then pay homage to God and to his Word with a submis-
siveness all the more pure because it is reasoned. For him it was
not just man's reason at stake, which must not be crushed by
heavy burdens (Mt 23:4), but the very grandeur of God, who re-

spects man to the extent that he will accept from man nothing but intelligent self-surrender.

At once critic and believer, Père Lagrange was always anxious to be theologically sound. He was justly proud that nobody was able to fault him on this. I remember being taken by him for the first time into the library of the Biblical School, where he told me in front of shelves filled with works of St. Thomas and their commentaries: "They have been able to attack my opinions as a critic; they have never accused me of theological error."

His faith, burning as it was enlightened, explains his constant, loyal submission to the magisterium of the Church. He always pledged the passionate attachment of an obedient child to the Church which, as he humbly wrote for his mortuary card, "he hopes he served." Even when he was pressing ahead with bold new schemes in an attempt to bring traditional instruction up to date, he did not cease listening to the directives of the Apostolic See, "for fear the course I was adopting . . . would not be allowed" (Gal 2:2). Moreover, his gestures of submission and obedience were just as sincere as his attempts had been at basing progress on criticism.

It is because he was profoundly humble that he showed himself to be truly obedient to the head of the Church and to his own religious superiors. This characteristic humility, which struck all those who were associated with him, is illustrated many times over in the following pages. His severe judgment of his youth—years which nevertheless were to yield a rich harvest—and his imputation of laxity in his own character—which the energy demanded by his life's work seems to contradict—can in no way be taken as affectations of modesty. He was in every way aware of those limitations in himself which prevented him from being fully competent in all of the things he was to undertake, and he would genuinely rejoice at seeing his followers become "his masters." He once said to me: "I have had to face things on all sides and at the same time; that is why I have never done anything which has been perfect." His humility was so simple of course, but from it sprang discernment, the scrupulousness, the respect for other people which made contact with him so engaging.

That faith of his which hungered after truth, his apostolic

zeal, his humility and obedience were all fed by a life of intense prayer. The exacting demands of incisive criticism blended harmoniously in him with simple, gentle, trusting piety. In moments of crisis or confusion, he would turn to prayer from which he gained peace and understanding. His devotion to Our Lady, whom he would readily invoke at each major turning point in his life, is a striking manifestation of his childlike piety, childish even, unless one remembers that in him it was associated with an adult's faith, finely balanced, the source of all the richness of his spirit.

The pages you are about to read are full of sincerity. At times animated and passionate, they remain nonetheless dignified, careful for truth, and tempered by a charity which is never tainted by base polemics. Then again, they are written in the manner which will be familiar to those who have already read him: brisk, elliptical, and in an animated style which, though bordering even on incorrect expression, is nevertheless abundantly compensated for by his conciseness and felicitous aptness with words, which are powerful servants of his thought.

To retain these aspects of form and substance, it was deemed unsuitable to change anything in the original draft. Père Lagrange's own wording is reproduced here without alteration, without cuts and without additions. There are also the notes and all relevant documents provided by him. We have allowed ourselves only to add a few brief notes which have become necessary in order to enlighten the reader about people or events so distant from us today. These notes are easily distinguishable from those of Père Lagrange: we have placed them in square brackets wherever they are added to his numerically ordered notes, and where they are entirely new, they will be found in alphabetical order. All titles and sub-titles are by the editor, but whenever Père Lagrange has himself qualified a year—such as "the terrible year" for 1912—his own expression has been retained.

Père Lagrange's remains, which had lain since 1938 in the cemetery of Saint-Maximin, have now been taken to Saint-Étienne de Jérusalem, where they are buried at the heart of the school which he founded. Professors, students, pilgrims, praying at his tomb, ask God to grant them just a little of his spirit. May the publication of these recollections rekindle the flame of witness which he so valiantly carried, and procure for the minds and hearts of younger generations understanding and warmth so that they too may triumph over the crises which they in turn will experience.

Pierre Benoît, O.P.
Director of the French Biblical and
Archaeological School
Jerusalem, May 8, 1967

The Biblical School
of the Dominicans in Jerusalem

Personal Recollections
(1889–1913)

Written March–April 1926

PREFACE BY PÈRE LAGRANGE

These are not the memoirs of Père Lagrange. Nevertheless I will often find myself speaking in the first person. On such occasions the "I" runs not much more counter to humility than would the letter "N." Why in any case should I decide to recount events in which I shall have to show that I had a certain role to play? My superiors, thinking that my state of health no longer allowed me to teach, have just told me to take things easy. I am no more than a witness here at Saint-Etienne, but they are now asking me for my own view of the past years. Since I am forbidden to do any serious work on this, let us try to set down these memories to which study has yielded its place. Perhaps too, having been much attacked, I have the right to explain to my brethren— and to them alone—what my intentions have been.

This history will not be written unless I do it, for according to Dominican custom, and contrary to the text of our constitutions, we have hardly ever taken the trouble to set down in writing what has happened in the priory. There is only a rather meager chronicle of these events; I myself never kept a diary of what was happening. Only during retreats did I detail a few dates, and in important circumstances I did jot down a few details. I have kept many letters sent to me here, but those I used to receive on my journeys have been lost more often than not. However, I shall say nothing I am not sure about. I have often reproached others for not having committed themselves to print; may I be forgiven for having done so myself.

1. Foundation and Development of the Biblical School

BIRTH OF THE PROJECT (1889)

On February 5, 1889, I received in Vienna, where I was one of the community of fathers of the Austrian Province, a letter from Colchen, provincial of the Toulouse Province. This letter, written on February 2, Feast of.the Purification of Our Lady, told me in substance that the provincial was transferring me to the community in Jerusalem, at least for a few years, in order to found a School of Holy Scripture. This was a call to my obedience, without any suggestion from me. What had happened—Jerusalem? Who was I to undertake the work in question?

I have recounted in *Saint-Etienne et son sanctuaire à Jérusalem* the beginnings of the foundation.[a] P. Matthieu Lecomte's death left things in great disarray. P. Maumas, appointed as his successor, had not been able to bear the climate and soon returned to France where he died. P. Paul Meunier, his deputy, had extremely poor health and had to spend weeks on his couch. P. Paul

---

a. It was in 1882 that P. Matthieu Lecomte, from the Dominican Province of Occitania (Lyons), conceived the idea of establishing a Dominican priory in Jerusalem. The Master General, P. Larroca, supported him. In the same year a small church was discovered in Jerusalem on the reputed site of the stoning of St. Stephen. P. Lecomte offered to purchase it as the center for the future establishment. With the help of P. Marie-Alphonse Ratisbonne and M. Langlais, the French consul, the land was bought on December 26, 1882, for 40,000 francs, a huge sum at that time. P. Lecomte was to die in Jerusalem on June 19, 1887 at the age of fifty-six. For the origins of the foundation, cf. M-J Lagrange, *Saint Etienne et son sanctuaire à Jérusalem,*, Paris, 1894, pp. 89–103.

13

Séjourné had excellent potential but he had not yet completed his theological studies in the Order.

The Idea of a Biblical School

How did the idea of a School of Holy Scripture originate in this setting? It is hard to say precisely. One can read in P. Paul Meunier's chronical for 1888: "It was also about this time that the thought occurred to us to create a School of Holy Scripture and Oriental languages. . . . It also tied in with the intentions which P. Matthieu had often revealed, to make this priory a center of scriptural learning as well as the place for living our rule, for our singing and our beautiful ceremonies. It seemed of great importance to us to have here, besides our conventual life and our few preaching commitments, a work of our own making which had not been done before, which could bring us to the attention of the bishops and the French government and which would warrant an annual grant for us. . . ." I do not conceal this last motive; but at the same time I wish to underline the tact shown in not intending to encroach upon someone else's territory.

Thus the idea dates from P. Matthieu, who in turn had it perhaps from Leo XIII himself, who esteemed very highly the teaching vocation of our Order.[b] I heard it said that the idea took on more shape, so to speak, during the presence in the priory, in March 1888, of the renowned M. Vigouroux[c] and of M. Le Camus,[d] who had both come to the Holy Land to seek assistance with their biblical studies.

---

b. P. Lecomte had obtained an audience with Leo XIII on January 27, 1883. The Pope had told him, among other things: "When the priory is established, there will be of course from within your Order men of learning, lecturers, who will find pleasure in retiring to Jerusalem to live and also to die there in sight of Calvary, and they may well be of great use through their teaching of sound theology" (M-J Lagrange, *op. cit.*, p. 99).

c. Fulcran Vigouroux (1837–1915), student of St. Sulpice, professor of exegesis at the seminary of Issy (1864), and at the Institut Catholique de Paris in 1890. To him we owe numerous works, in particular the *Sainte Bible polyglotte* in eight volumes (1900–1909). He was also editor of the *Dictionnaire de la Bible* (1895–1912). He was one of the most eminent representatives of conservative exegesis. In *M. Loisy et le Modernisme* Père Lagrange says of him: "M. Vigouroux was a man of amazing erudition, and impeccable in the accuracy of his quotations; the sureness of his criticism was astonishing" (p. 14).

d. Mgr. Emile-Paul Le Camus (1839–1906). Despite a heavy burden of ministry, he published a great number of biblical studies. His *Vie de Notre-Seigneur Jésus-Christ* (1883)

P. Guillermin of our Order, a most distinguished professor
in the theological faculty at Toulouse, who had been resting in
Jerusalem since the end of 1887, was very much in favor of the
idea too. Finally Mgr. Bracco, patriarch of Jerusalem, where his
memory remains blessed, did not merely approve of the plan, he
championed it during a visit to Rome (in the presence of Larroca)[e]
insisting that his diocese be given this distinction. According to
the chronicle, P. Larroca "greeted Mgr. Bracco's overtures with
extreme reserve. Mgr. Bracco later conveyed to us his surprise
at this." The fact is that the Father General was not unaware of
the difficulty he would have in removing from his provincials the
very few biblical scholars there might be in the Order. At the
time when he was asking them to make some real sacrifices in order to set up the University of Fribourg, he objected to the idea
of pursuing another similar project.

The chronicle continues: "Nevertheless, his reticence was
not a refusal. He gave us to understand that, without committing
himself to anything, he would let us go ahead, as long as we did
not infringe the rights of the provincials. Then P. Paul Meunier
wrote to each of the French provincials asking for lecturers. The
responses of the provincials of Paris and of Lyons were evasive.[1]
P. Colchen, provincial of Toulouse, was kind enough to promise
us P. Marie-Joseph Lagrange, who at the time was studying Oriental languages at the University of Vienna."[2] In the province of
Toulouse, P. Colchen had the reputation of a saint, but not of a
learned man. It was as an expression of his faith that he strongly
encouraged others to study, since this was also the vocation of
our Order. Perhaps too, being of Jewish origin himself, he had a
particularly soft spot for holy Sion. Together with his reply to P.
Meunier, he wrote me the letter of which I have spoken. I was ut-

---

was considered in its day to be the best of the lives of Jesus done by a French Catholic.
He was the assiduous collaborator of M. Vigouroux for the first three volumes of the
Dictionnaire de la Bible. In 1888 he traveled east with M. Vigouroux and published three
volumes under the title of *Notre voyage aux pays bibliques* (1890). Between 1891 and
1905, his work *Origines du Christianisme* appeared in three volumes. In 1901 he was appointed bishop of La Rochelle where he strove to develop the study of the Bible in his
seminary. At the beginning of the Modernist Crisis, he tried to exert a moderating influence.

e. 74th Master General of the Dominicans, 1879–1891.

terly crushed by the news. At this point I feel obliged to relate
the extent to which I could be of use to the project.

Biographical Review

I was born in Bourg, in the department of Ain,[f] on March 7,
1855. The town was placed under the patronage of Our Lady,
and my birthday coincided with the first feast of St. Thomas
Aquinas after the proclamation of the dogma of the Immaculate
Conception, a most happy event, and one that filled the heart of
my devout mother with deep joy. I was sent to school at the minor seminary of Autyn. I was a fairly unruly child, working
when I wanted to and at whatever I chose, which was mostly
Greek, but also German and English. During my last three
years, I was often obliged to return home for reasons of health,
quite apart from the enforced interruption of 1870–1871. My legal studies in Paris were even more neglected. However, I had
noted the scientific superiority of the practical classes instituted
by Duruy at the Sorbonne over the literary classes which had
made Guizot, Cousin, Villemain and Saint-Marc Girardin illustrious. I attended a few of these for the sake of the Greek, but
hardly more than ten: one had to be up so early! When I was seventeen I still believed, as I had from my childhood, that I had a
vocation to the Order of St. Dominic. When God in his mercy
renewed this call, at the time when I had made myself most unworthy of it, I at once desired to drop everything and follow it.
My father was not opposed to it, but he advised me to complete
my doctorate in law.

It was thus not until October 1878 that I entered the seminary at Issy to study God's ways. It was only at that moment that
I started working seriously, and that I acquired among my brothers of St. Sulpice, masters whose memory I venerate, a passion
for the Word of God. Toward the end of my novitiate at Saint-
Maximin I had been allowed to read hardly anything else. Having successfully concluded my studies on October 7, 1880, I was
immediately transferred to Salamanca as a result of the decree

---

f. Père Lagrange describes his early years in greater detail later.

which had dispersed us. It was there that the good P. Gallais, first as prior then as provincial, encouraged me to start Oriental languages. I even attended the course in Hebrew at the once famous University of Salamanca. But it was evidently too late, since I have never been really competent in Oriental langauges. Besides I had to devote myself before all else to Thomist theology, since I had been exempted from philosophy, which I had already studied at Issy; it took a great deal of dogged effort to work at theology. After four years I was asked to teach Church history for two years, and it was only when back in Toulouse that I was able to devote myself to studying the Bible, aided by that charming scholar, the Abbé Thomas, condemned to inactivity by the chest complaint which was to bring about his early death. They also made me teach philosophy, as there was no one else; I would find it very useful according to dear P. Colchen. On top of this I heard confessions, preached and gave lectures. I accepted it all in obedience, but there came a time when I had to tell P. Colchen that my grounding was incomplete, and that therefore I would never be the biblical expert they had dreamed of, and that they would have to give up their dream. It was at that precise moment that P. Colchen told me he was about to designate me to that end alone. At first he thought of sending me to Paris; then, at the beginning of October 1888, he sent me to Vienna where I received the warmest hospitality from the Dominican Fathers.

Studies in Vienna

My time was all planned for me. I did not follow any course of theology, only languages. I had done some studies on my own of Syriac and Arabic, and started Assyrian. Professor David-Heinrich Müller was my teacher for Arabic and Assyrian, Professor Reinisch for Egyptian, both hieroglyphic and hieratic, and I also studied Arabic under M. Wahrmund at the Commercial School. M. Müller was kind enough to give me instruction on some particular aspects of rabbinical exegesis and the Mishna. He gave me the impression of being a very good Jew, and it was at his home that I met Professor Euting who taught me how to take impressions of inscriptions. I was not intending to make myself expert in all these fields, but to form later on in Toulouse a body of biblical teachers; I was in fact already outlining syllabuses. P. Colchen's letter appeared to put an end to these hopes of mine. What would there be to do, so far from the world of learning? Would we have any books there? Would it be possible to work in that burning climate? I was full of uncertainty, but obedience bade me keep silent. I made some very indirect inquiries of a Canadian pilgrim who had seen our priory at Saint-Etienne: there was no library, no priory as such. The brethren were poorly lodged in the former town slaughter-house, with a few cells added upstairs; there was a single tree in the garden, and the heat was stifling. My bewilderment increased.

The holidays arrived. Should I stay in Vienna or leave for the East? P. Colchen invited me to return to France just in case. I met in Pont-De-Beauvoisin, on his home ground, P. Paul Meunier. What he told me turned my suspicions into firm conviction that my life of serious study was at an end. He said that in order to overcome the problem of the heat, they would open up a basement and light it with gas—a commodity which we are still waiting for in Jerusalem! There could be no resources, no hope of finding properly instructed teachers nor indeed teachers to instruct, otherwise why would they be sending us so far away? It was agreed with P. Colchen that we should wait to see what happened. I would do a third term in Vienna and leave in the spring for Palestine in order to finish my training by seeing the country. Providence would see the rest.

Arrival in Jerusalem

I left Vienna on February 11, 1890, and stayed in Cairo for a fortnight. On Sunday, March 9, I disembarked in Jaffa; the weather was very bad. I spent the night at the Amwas hermitage with the Abbé Viallet,[g] and Brother Thomas Tabin,[h] who had come to meet me off the boat, because he feared I would not be

---

g. Former officer who had become a priest. He brought a community of Trappists to Palestine, from which arose the Abbey of Latroun.

h. Dominican laybrother, of Swiss origin, who helped P. Lecomte to found the priory of Saint-Etienne. He died on April 5, 1940, at eighty-six.

brave enough to get off it. We were in Jerusalem on the evening of March 10.

I have never had the gift of being able to describe landscapes whose beauty leaves a deep impression upon me; therefore I have never tried. I must say here, however, that I was moved, seized, gripped by this sacred land, and I abandoned myself to the delightful appreciation of distant and historic times. I had so loved the book, and here I was gazing at its setting! Not a single doubt remained in my mind about the aptness of pursuing biblical study in Palestine; I was told too that the climate was no obstacle. But would students come? Yes, they would, because there would be an obligation to send them.

A Providential Piece of Legislation
At this time, three years of military service had been introduced by law into France, for everybody without exception. But the foreign ministry, anxious to maintain and increase French influence abroad, had obtained a dispensation for anyone who would spend ten years outside Europe, provided he went abroad before he was nineteen. P. Larroca, realizing what this measure could mean for the level of recruitment into French novitiates, had offered his house in Jerusalem for novices of the three French provinces. This house was thus bound to become a center for studies. The province of Lyons was already prepared to accept the offer. This was, to my mind, a decidedly providential turn of events. I sent to the Father General an enthusiastic report on the setting up of the Biblical School, an undertaking to which I now considered myself bound. I then left with Abbé Heydet, resident in Jerusalem for the previous nine years, and P. van Kasteren, S.J. for the lands beyond the Jordan.[3] I was lucky enough to take an impression of a fine Nabataean inscription at Mâdaba.[4] I was eager to return to Jerusalem and read the Father General's reply. It had not arrived. I wrote again. No reply. Since I had come out as a guest, as part of my studies, I could not ask for an extension of my stay. I left Jerusalem July 15, together with P. Ollivier. When I reached Marseilles, I learned that the problem had been resolved, and that I was to go back to Jerusalem.

THE SCHOOL IS FOUNDED (1890)

Nevertheless there was still some doubt. Fribourg University was to open in the autumn, and P. Berthier[i] had entered my name on the list of lecturers, next to the course he thought I would be giving on St. Matthew, if I remember rightly. In addition to this, P. Gallais, who had succeeded P. Colchen, had singled me out to give the course on Thomist dogmatics. I was very fond of my Toulouse Province, but the thought of thus abandoning my biblical studies saddened me and many others besides. I took a totally passive line, and submitted myself to the decision of the Father General.

The Solemn Opening

At this point, P. Séjourné intervened in what was perhaps a decisive way. The Father Provincial, whom he had followed to Biarritz, finally got rid of him. He was happier than in Rome, most of all, I think, because P. Chatillon, the Father General's companion, showed himself not in the least bit keen to support the plans of P. Berthier in Fribourg, nor indeed the wishes of a province which he had left. Or was it perhaps that his official title of Provincial of the Holy Land inclined him in favor of Jerusalem? This good father hated writing letters, and had a nice way of saying: "Just think of all the things you can settle by not replying!" But then he changed his habit and wrote me four long letters urging me to leave. I was bound by obedience, but precisely because of this, I did not want to take the initiative in a difficult project, which I did not feel competent to carry out to the credit of my Order. I asked for an official directive. P. Chatillon replied on behalf of the Father General: "Go! You will find our directive when you get there."

The directive came, in fact, in the form of my appointment as *lector primarius*[j] to the priory in Jerusalem. This modest title, which had passed into disuse, was just what was needed for our

---

i. Joseph-Joachim Berthier (Dec. 31, 1894–Dec. 24, 1924), a Dominican, shared in the founding of the University of Fribourg, Switzerland (1889) where he taught in the Faculty of Theology run by the Dominicans (1890–1905). Afterward he lived in Rome, where he restored the former basilica of Santa Sabina.

j. Principal director of studies in Dominican priories which do not have a "Regent."

embryo college. Embryo it may have been, but nonetheless, on November 15, feast of St. Albert the Great, we performed the solemn opening ceremony of the School, attended by M. Ledoulx, the French consul, but without Mgr. Piavi, patriarch of Jerusalem, who was out of town. The solemnity was just a little restrained, since the ceremony was performed in the old abattoir, in which one could still see the rings set along the walls for tying up oxen.

Teachers and Students

What sort of teaching body did we have? I have spoken too much of myself. My collaborator was P. Paul Séjourné,[k] who had had to take his examination as lector in the French province. Having proved an excellent student at the minor seminary of Séez, and become one of the clergy of that diocese, Abbé Séjourné had gone on pilgrimage to Palestine, and devoted himself to the work P. Matthieu was doing. He entered the Dominican novitiate in Italy since he would come under the Father General's jurisdiction. However, the future of Saint-Etienne had become so uncertain that he made his profession in favor of the French province, which in turn showed how sympathetic it was to our work in the early stages by sending him back to us. He was my most devoted friend, my most zealous and accommodating collaborator. We shared the task between us. He was marvelous at leading us out on journeys, with his instinctive certainty about paths to take and geographical locations. He started by teaching the New Testament, but his task was to give instruction above all in topography and geography. His natural optimism was sustained by a very firm will. Nothing was too good for our work at Saint-Etienne, which he loved faithfully until his death. Future generations will not forget what they owe to his self-sacrifice, his generous heart, to the approach which he cultivated at Saint-Etienne of resolutely upholding the true traditions, and rejecting without question those which are, frankly speaking, founded on nothing but error. We also remember with gratitude the unselfish way in which Abbé Haydet kindly placed his knowledge of the country at our service in the early days.

---

k. June 6, 1857–November 7, 1922.

P. Doumeth, a Maronite priest, respected by all in Jerusalem, had been clothed as a Dominican at Saint-Maximin. The Father General kindly assigned him to us in Jerusalem immediately after his year as a novice. He taught Arabic, which he knew well.

We had three student novices from the Province of Lyons, two of whom had arrived a few days before my departure, and I had set them at once to learn Arabic. One of these is P. Jaussen.[1] The third had come back with me from France. P. Luc Marquet, of the same province, was appointed to teach them theology.

Thus from the outset, the three French provinces contributed to the founding of the Biblical School.

Choice of Syllabus

What should our syllabus be? We could have hesitated between two possible courses of action. The first, and most simple, would have been for P. Séjourné and me to consider ourselves on permanent mission to study the country, excavate sites, and play host to learned men on their journeys to the Holy Land. This was the opinion of Abbé Thomas, who wrote to me on August 16, 1890, as follows: "Nobody has yet been able to tell me what the plans are for the study center in Jerusalem. I have met only skeptics and zealots. As I listened to the skeptics, I said to myself: But there is serious work to be done, and a house in Jerusalem capable of directing scientific excursions and centralizing information would render valuable service. Then I heard what the zealots had to say, and I thought to myself (in secret): That's marvelous, but it could never work. They won't have resources to create a study center equipped with the necessary tools; by that I mean a library. They just will not get the students willing to spend two or three years in such a place. . . ."[5]

---

1. Marius Antonin Jaussen (May 27, 1871–April 29, 1962), a Dominican, the oldest of Père Lagrange's disciples. He studied, then taught at the Biblical School until the First World War. He was a fine Arabic scholar, and wrote the *Coûtumes des Arabes au pays de Moab* (1908) and collaborated with P. Savignac in writing *Mission archéologique en Arabie* in three volumes (1909, 1914, and 1922). After the 1914–18 war, in which he served as naval chaplain, he settled in Egypt, where he established the *Institut des Etudes Orientales* of the Dominicans in Cairo.

His argument was sound; the students would never have come—but they had been forced to come; they were here!

On the other hand, P. Berthier had taught me that one should never avoid looking boldly at a problem, thinking that what Providence authorizes us to do is limited by the situation in which it puts us. We should rather look ahead and see the situation as an invitation to act. My old plan of training biblical scholars could be realized; more than this, we had a duty to educate fully these students who had left their own country out of loyalty to their vocation. Our uncertainty was being dispelled by the course of events. What we still feared was that our exploration of the country would be hindered by having to hold regular classes. Yet this is just what we resolved to do, and what we have always adhered to: exploration and teaching. The combination of document with monument (i.e., archaeological evidence) is the most fruitful of methods. Moreover, as Dominicans, who are inclined both by vocation and education to speculate, we could not remain uninterested in any historical or even theological conclusions which might be drawn from research on the ground, or indeed beneath the ground. Then again, our poverty prevented us from opening up excavations, but thanks to the generosity of those who did open some, we always had sites available to us. One can say that we profited from them without having responsibility for them.

What was difficult was the prolonged period away from the homeland—but this does not frighten religious in the slightest. We were right in deciding to set up a permanent school, and it was to this end that our efforts had been directed, together with that of acquiring a deeper knowledge of the country. Research has not played an insignificant part, as others have been kind enough to recognize. However, alongside our speculative studies, we had to fit in an amount of archaeology. Now, I did understand just enough about archaeology to know that excavation is not simply hacking about with a pickaxe in order to find ancient objects—which was still more or less M. Clermont-Ganneau's approach at Aswan. I was also careful to have a professional, M. Sandel, architect to the German colony, record the results of the searches done at Saint-Etienne before I arrived.

This was a recognition of my total lack of competence. Even he was not much more capable than I at sorting out the material with a view of restoring the ancient basilica. This was kept for P. Hugues Vincent, but it took thirty years of study.

Archaeology in Palestine

The Catholic Church's archaeological representative in Jerusalem at the time was P. Germer-Durand,[m] of the Augustinians of the Assumption. Born in Nîmes, and brought up by his father, who was a very distinguished man of letters, in an environment full of Roman relics, P. Germer had a passionate interest in Graeco-Roman epigraphy. Whereas pilgrims, tourists and even learned people sought for little more than biblical remains in Palestine, he had realized the importance of the Byzantine tradition, a knowledge of which was necessary in the investigation of ancient sites. He was such a good Greek scholar that restoring a text was child's play to him; however, he was not always at pains to confirm his interpretation by an exacting study of points already established. With exquisite benevolence, he initiated us into the hunt for milestones with even the slightest trace of engravings. He soon started regular meetings at Notre-Dame-de-France at which we used to discuss freely the question which most agitated the clergy, that of local traditions. There was a great row when I spoke out resolutely in favor of the theory that Sion used to be the little hill to the southwest. Nevertheless, P. Germer soon came around to this view, and he even took it a little too far. I even went against the very firm and exclusive view of the Society of the Palestine Exploration Fund by taking the lead in Catholic circles with this theory. An article on it in the very first number of the *Revue biblique* caused some fairly animated booklets to be published in France. I was not sorry for having set our school off to such an accurate start, for we did not have to change our tune when the excavations had revealed everything. But I am bound to say that, from then on, the question of local

---

m. Joseph Germer-Durand (September 23, 1845–September 27, 1917), an Assumptionist, founded in 1886 the guest-house and theological college of Notre-Dame-de-France at Jerusalem. He was one of the pioneers in the fields of exploration and Greek epigraphy in Palestine. We owe to him the excavation of the Byzantine shrine of Saint Peter in Gallicantu.

traditions and shrines aroused no less animosity against the school than its approach to exegesis. Today this touchy point is the cause of just a very few sparks, which all come from the same quarter, but they are too weak to rekindle the war.

Since he was there before me, I let P. Germer-Durand continue in charge of archaeological and topographical discussion—I mean that he himself had been out there before I was, whereas the meetings had not taken place, I believe, before I arrived—while we went ahead with a new series of lectures, at first based solely on the Bible. These too were given in that wretched room I have already spoken of. P. Germer subsequently became one of the lecturers whom people most enjoyed hearing.

Building Work

Since we had founded a school, we had to have a few classrooms. It was my duty to see to this, as I had been appointed superior of the priory on April 7, 1891, by P. Laboré, vicar general of the Order since the death of P. Larroca. My idea was to have a large main hall for lectures, with ordinary classrooms around it. Above it would be a small cloister, with cells around that. The first stone was laid on June 5, Feast of the Sacred Heart, to which P. Matthieu Lecomte had dedicated his original foundation. A parchment bore the information that the purpose of the school was to further biblical studies, under the patronage of Our Lady of the Rosary. Future generations of diggers are advised that they may find there medals of the Sacred Heart, Our Lady of Lourdes, Our Lady of the Rosary, St. Benedict, St. Mary Magdalen and of Pope Leo XIII gloriously reigning. The student novices took possession of the School on December 7 of the same year, and the school was placed under the further patronage of the Immaculate Conception. Each year on December 7 the novices used to hear Mass at the altar of the crypt of St. Anne. Among these students was Br. Hugues Vincent,[n] who had come

---

n. Born August 31, 1872, Louis-Hugues Vincent came as a novice to the priory of Saint-Etienne and dreamed of becoming a missionary. Père Lagrange persuaded him to devote himself to the Biblical School. In fact, until his death on December 30, 1960, he gave long and fruitful service as an archaeologist. Having closely followed the progress of the excavations in Palestine for some sixty years, he wrote numerous articles, chronicles and reports for the *Revue biblique* and published several works, of which the most

out to Jerusalem in August 1891, a few days before his nineteenth birthday.

THE *REVUE BIBLIQUE* IS LAUNCHED (1891)

The Idea of a Biblical Periodical

I was at that time in France to organize the launching of the *Revue Biblique*. The result far surpassed what I had intended. I found it difficult° to start even a news-sheet, since I found little to attract me in the idea of a thin pamphlet for our own consumption, in which excursions were recounted, courses outlined and news given of excavations and pilgrimages. A real periodical, printed in Paris and directed in Jerusalem, seemed sheer fantasy. With determination, stubbornness even, P. Séjourné gave me no peace. I consulted M. Vigouroux and M. Le Camus, who were markedly in favor of a large-scale periodical and promised me their assistance. At last, in great agitation, I sought advice and permission from P. Laboré. He was quick to give his consent, but on condition that advance subscriptions should cover our costs. This was a very kind way of putting us off indefinitely.[6] People do not subscribe to a periodical which has yet to appear. P. Faucher knew a way of getting round the difficulty. A close and loyal friend of P. Matthieu, he always cared a great deal for his foundation. An annotated edition of the *Summa* of St. Thomas gave him access at the time to the Lethielleux publishing house, whose founder was still alive, and who undertook to cover all our costs. We would thus be running no risk. P. Laboré, gentleman that he was, gave his assent immediately.

The Search for Contributors

We could not dream of providing enough material of our own for an important periodical. We had to find other contribu-

---

important are: *Canaan d'après l'exploration récente* (1907), *Jérusalem sous terre* (1911), *Jérusalem antique* (1912), then in collaboration with P. Abel, *Jérusalem nouvelle* (1914–1926), *Bethléem* (1914), *Hébron* (1923), *Emmaüs* (1932), and finally *Jérusalem de l'Ancien Testament* (1954 and 1956).

o. Almost this entire section has been taken by Père Lagrange from his book *M. Loisy et le Modernisme*, pp. 69–78.

tors. Moreover, the spirit of Christianity seemed to me to demand that this new organ be open to every Catholic exegete. I turned first to those at St. Sulpice, my dear and venerated masters of Issy. M. Vigouroux, still very much in favor, gave me hope that other willing souls would lend their support; however, M. Fillion, protesting himself sympathetic, preferred to remain in the background. Obtaining the cooperation of the Society of Jesus was of supreme importance on many grounds. M. Lethielleux intervened with the fathers of the *Cursus*, published by his firm, and we acquired among our contributors Pères Corluy, Cornely and Knabenbauer, not to mention my traveling companion P. van Kasteren. Subsequently we had fourteen Jesuit fathers from various provinces as active contributors. From within our own Order, P. Didon lent his name, Pères Faucher, Lacôme, Ollivier and Scheil their support. Of my friends, M. Batiffol and M. Hyvernat, my colleagues at Issy, M. Thomas, M. Jacqier; Abbé Lesêtre was co-opted by M. Vigouroux.

Not one of these names stood out as much as did the absence of M. Loisy's. With his two works on the Canon—which have not been censured along with others[7]—he had placed himself in the forefront of biblical scholarship. Because of his insight, his critical genius, his lucid, almost incisive manner of expressing his views, and his extensive knowledge, I hoped very much to enlist him, and thereby co-opt a vigor which could only increase. However, not everyone was in favor of him. Some said his views were rash. I did not wish to make any decision without having talked it over thoroughly with him. I could not find him at home when I made a fleeting visit to Paris, and I could not bring myself to suggest anything in a letter. This then is why I did nothing. Would he have accepted? Was it only in order to have the outlet which he lacked that he founded his own periodical? I am inclined to believe that once he had, he would, given the choice, have preferred to stay with his own publication. Hardly had the first number of the *Revue Biblique* appeared—toward the end of December 1891—than he launched the *Enseignement Biblique*.[8] On its first page stood the following: "It is our wish that the *Revue Biblique* should receive everywhere the welcome which it merits.[9] It will achieve the noble goal which it has set itself, and will prove that there are Catholic exegetes, that these exegetes are aware of the needs of their time, that they are capable of advancing our knowledge of the Bible, that they are qualified to understand and defend Holy Scripture. If we had set our sights as high, we would have abandoned the scheme when we saw others carry it out much more surely than we, and we would take good care not to circulate a publication which would duplicate that to which the Reverend Dominican Fathers M. Vigouroux, M. Le Camus and other learned Catholics lend their name and which they will support with their own works." M. Loisy went on to present his own periodical as a work with popular appeal. But a master such as he could not avoid tackling the loftiest and most difficult questions, whether in his monographs or in his reports. Obviously the two periodicals followed the same course, at least at the start— and was there not a touch of irony in what he outlined as our program?

The Scope of the *Revue Biblique*

What were we trying to do? I must first say that we never spoke about having a management committee, half in Paris, half in Jerusalem. M. Vigouroux and M. Le Camus, who undertook to promote the work to a public to whom I was a total stranger, never once thought of telling us what to do, nor even of coming to some agreement about our terms of reference. I had not wanted my name to figure in the title, but it read as follows: "*Revue Biblique*, published quarterly under the direction of the professors of the school of practical biblical studies, established at the Dominican Priory of Saint-Etienne in Jerusalem."

None of the other contributors was committed to anything in particular, at least in principle. They were always free to back out, and therefore could not be compromised by any particular form the *Revue* might take on. Our occasional contributors could be reassured about the paths we would take by the fact that in the Dominican Order nothing may be printed unless it has first been scrutinized and been given assent by the superiors. Those who knew me knew also that I would never seek to elude this rule, which in fact was always rigorously applied in one way or another.

It has often been said that the *Revue Biblique*, at first very conservative, went on to abuse the trust it had inspired. Yet from the outset it was proposed to proceed resolutely in opposition to a certain well-meaning but badly informed tutiorism, which, as we saw it, considered unprogressive views as assertive statements in Scripture, thereby compromising the truth. The Order's most illustrious lecturer, P. Monsabré, defining his distrust of one of Père Lagrange's articles, expressed himself thus: "Instead of drifting into an easy acceptance of certain concessions, one should call upon the natural sciences and history to prove that this or that statement in the Bible is a *manifest* contradiction of absolutely *incontestable* laws and of facts *as clear as daylight*. Someone who had the time could do very interesting work under the title of: 'Biblical Difficulties.' I believe the Church's definition of the original statement would come out of it all unscathed."

To say this leaves intact a personal conviction that the veracity of the Bible will remain triumphant, but also comes close to proposing the opposite hypothesis. In the case of the natural sciences, answers would be found, but an historical fact cannot be a contradiction of a "statement in the Bible." The real hypothesis is thus the contradiction between an historical fact and an accepted explanation of the sacred text. Therefore, what need is there for the fact to be manifest, as clear as daylight, before it can be set down in opposition to an exegetical judgment? According to the ordinary laws of psychology and logic, the more probable a fact appears, the less certain will be an opposite explanation. If one never yields until forced by the weight of evidence, one leaves to one's adversaries the advantages of attack, with all the attendant and long-lasting acclaim, to the detriment of souls made anxious at seeing the defenders limit themselves to parrying the blows. What is more, these defenders are placed in a situation contrary to the laws of logical thought.

The Spirit of the *Revue Biblique*

Obviously, a Catholic theologian would never dream of revising the Church's judgments in matters of dogma and morals. Moreover, the well-informed theologian can be easy in his mind, since he knows that the inconsistencies of heresy have been recognized, each in turn, as breaking the rules of exegesis itself. At this level, one is dealing only with facts whose historical nature is in doubt, with philological explanations, with literary criticism, all of which deal not with the overall biblical authenticity of a given passage, but with its own inherent authenticity.

In these conditions, and with his faith quite safe, why would the conscientious Catholic student not simply seek out the truth, with as much zeal and, if possible, as much competence as anybody else, without having to consider as sacrosanct the current views of Catholic writers, views which one day may well be corrected? Will he not inspire a more certain confidence in those who see him—his faith unshakably based on divine authority—resolutely tackling problems to which theology gives no solution, with the simple purpose of saying what appears most likely to him, after the experts have had their elaborate discussion? This is what I had expressed very simply in a few lines of the preface which served as a program for the *Revue Biblique*: "The right step seems to be to seek out the truth, and then, after close consideration, and having taken into account the long-standing tradition of exegesis as a highly valuable element of the whole process, pronounce oneself in favor of the most likely opinion. Here again I am assuming that the Church's authority is not at stake. My answer to the first question is therefore: The *Revue* will be approached in a spirit of orthodoxy and in a spirit of science."

Dogma versus Opinion

Nevertheless, I felt my lack of authority too deeply not to cite someone of unquestioned importance. I had recourse to the recently published book by Cardinal Gonzalez, theologian and philosopher—there can be no distinction between the two in the Order of St. Dominic—*The Bible and Science*.[10]

How intensely he feels the need for progress! How firmly he distinguishes betweeen dogma and evasive opinions! His sincere account of the peril we faced will continue to be of benefit for a long time to come: "The distinguished and real friends of the Catholic faith and of Christ's Church must bear in mind that, if the circle of truths of dogmatic theology is so to speak relatively complete and closed—which means that it has nothing to fear and little to hope for from scientific progress—it is not the same with exegetical ideas and questions, where the field is being invaded at different points by modern science. Radical changes are being introduced into biblical exegesis, important modifications, new an-gles totally unsuspected by those who, in earlier times, gave up their night's rest in order to compose commentaries on certain biblical texts, attempting to reveal and fix their meaning. . . . On the other hand, we would do well not to forget the Christian exegesis, taken on its own, is not necessarily the truth, but the search for truth. In this it resembles other branches of science, and because of this a degree of independence in the selection of exegetical criteria is implied. In truth, this widening choice of criteria, this relative freedom in exegesis, has never been so appropriate nor even so necessary as it is now."[11]

The old routine approach, so smugly entrenched, is being replaced by this new *conquistador* spirit which is still not universally appreciated. At that time it was appreciated even less. My preface was examined in Rome and accepted, but it had to go without the approval of the Master of the Sacred Palace, a position not yet held by P. Lepidi.[12]

However, I have no recollection that the first volume of the *Revue* aroused any protest from the conservatives. The Jesuit Fathers, as we have shown, had collaborated with complete good will. I tried to secure further the cooperation of P. Delattre.[p] At that time he had a certain reputation as an Assyriologist. I sounded him out through the good offices of Mgr. Lamy, who was kind enough to give me this reply:[13] "I have spoken on your behalf to P. Delattre, in order to obtain his collaboration. He refused point-blank, and told me that no Belgian Jesuit would collaborate. The reason is not that he and his brethren have anything to reproach the *Revue Biblique* with; but it is the question of Thomism which displeases them."[14]

In fact the first number of the *Revue Thomiste*, which was founded in 1893, contained a fairly sharp article by P. Berthier in response to a volume of Fr. Frins, S.J. on the subject of grace. Several fathers of the Society lost no time in demanding that their names be deleted from the list of contributors, among them Fr. Cornely (in a letter dated March 30, 1893): "In view of the article published by the *Revue Thomiste* against my friend Fr. Frins and against *our Society*, I must now ask (and if necessary demand) that

---

p. Alphonse Delattre (1841–1928), a Belgian Jesuit. For his subsequent attacks against Père Lagrange, see below.

you delete my name from among the contributors to the *Revue Biblique*. You will understand that my honor, or rather the honor of the Society to which I am fortunate enough to belong, allows me no alternative course of action."

From Fr. Knakenbauer we received the following (April 6, 1893): "Having read the article in the *Revue Thomiste* wherein are debased not only some of my brethren, but the Society" and so on. P. Corluy (April 3, 1893), knowing full well that the *Revue Biblique* was not at fault, thought nonetheless that "the public will see in this only Dominicans on the one side and Jesuits on the other. . . . This is why I consider that for a member of our Society to be involved in the work of the Dominicans at this time is no longer right" and so on. Unfortunately I could do nothing about it. But it had not come so far simply to start telling our contributors never to attack any community, religous order, country or province.

At this point I have felt bound to give the real reasons, which had nothing to do with our orthodoxy—neither do I suspect they had anything to do with the orthodoxy of the good fathers, since I do not consider Molinism to be a heresy—as I was saying, I have felt bound to explain this rebuff which the *Revue Thomiste* won for us, and the first secession of the fathers of the Society.

The Encouragement of Leo XIII

Even before this unfortunate event, we had received the most effective of encouragements, and that most dear to a Catholic heart, a very significant letter from Leo XIII.

I would never have dared to hope, especially so early on, for such high favor. But having gone to Rome, I had been presented to His Eminence Cardinal Zigliara.[q] For the first time I learned just what the great charm and smiling indulgence of a prince of the Roman Church can be. This illustrious Thomist scholar enjoyed the complete confidence of the Pope. He offered quite

---

q. T. M. Zigliara (1833–1893), Dominican, Principal of St. Thomas's College in Rome from 1873 to 1879, made cardinal in 1879, Prefect of the Congregation of Studies in 1888. He worked on Thomist renewal and was the first director of the Leonine edition of the writings of St. Thomas.

spontaneously to ask of him not only his blessing for our work, but also an early statement of his satisfaction with it. I expressed my fear that it was too soon for this, since we still had done nothing to merit the attention of His Holiness. "Leave it to me," he said, with an authority which put an end to my resistance and pleasantly gratified the wishes he had aroused in me. The Pope's letter, dated September 17, 1892, appeared in the *Revue* in 1893. It conveyed approval for what seemed at the time, as the Pope said, an exceptional plan—which has been faithfully followed ever since—namely, the exploration of the Holy Land, courses and lectures, open even to non-Catholics,[15] and the founding of the *Revue Biblique;* the letter bore a command to increase our zeal, "augere to animos . . . tuosque jubemus auctoritate fretos et comprobatione Nostra. . . ."

Father Frühwirth, Father General

I have been speaking so far with reference all the time to the beginnings of the *Revue Biblique.* Yet during the year 1891, the founding of Saint-Etienne itself had very nearly been put in doubt again with the election of P. André Frühwirth as Master General[r] (September 1891). This successor to P. Larroca had been Subprior of their priory in Vienna when I was sent there. The great affection which P., now Cardinal, Frühwirth, showed me, together with that of P. Cormier who in receiving me into the Dominican Order at Saint-Maximin had put on me his own cincture, I consider to be one of the most tangible proofs of God's providential goodness to me. I do not doubt that in everything they simply followed their consciences, but our long intimacy in the past, the habit I had acquired of sharing my thoughts with them which always allowed them to see into my soul, the self-confidence which was inspired by their kindness to me, all served to create between us a closeness, almost a special relationship, despite the separation of both place and rank. Explanations were thus much more easily made. They knew my faults and never made any secret of them with me, but I dare say that they counted on my openness, and this was always of fundamental importance, as we shall see later.

---

r. 75th Master General of the Dominicans from 1891 to 1904.

Frühwirth, having become prior in Vienna, then provincial of the province of the Empire, which covered at that time Austria, Hungary and Bohemia, spoke very good German, Italian and French. Fond as he was of his Austrian House, yet a sincere friend of France, he seemed to bind the whole of the Order together in charity. Rarely have I met a man of such real compassion and goodness. At first, our friendshsip almost prevented me from being transferred finally to Jerusalem. He was fearful of the effect of the climate on me, and of the difficulties of the foundation about which I had finally told him, not without a certain dread and reluctance. The celebrated P. Weiss[s] certainly would not have encouraged him with his tongue-in-cheek eulogy of the scheme, which he certainly considered very useful for getting rid of recalcitrant religious, and perhaps also for finding out in situ how St. Peter's cock crowed. On the other hand, Fribourg was very close to P. Frühwirth's heart. It was where Austrians and Germans were working side by side with the French, a fact which both symbolized and provided the basis for his influence on the entire Order. Therefore he suggested with affection that I should go back on P. Larroca's decision and accept the tranquility of a chair at Fribourg. I did go to the Council of the Order being held at Oullins, but it was to get him to accept the idea of the Biblical School. While protesting my obedience, I told the Father General in all simplicity that Fribourg would get along very well without me, whereas I could not think—nor surely could he—of anybody who would want to take on the difficult mission in Jerusalem, especially the biblical studies aspect of it. Meanwhile, the Council to which I had submitted a written report[16] showed itself very sympathetic to the foundation in the Holy Land. Having recommended the study of Holy Scripture and Oriental languages, it added: "Huic autem intentem plurimum juvare poterit coenobium quod Hierosolymis, sub titulo S. Stephani, nuper fundatum est, et quod paternae curae Rmi. Magistri Ordinis specialiter commendamus."[17]

---

s. A.-M. Weiss (1844–1925), Dominican, professor of sociology (1890–1892) and apologetics (1895–1910) at the University of Fribourg in Switzerland. A man of vast learning, he wrote numerous works on social and religious questions.

Prior of Jerusalem

I therefore came back to Jerusalem as superior, a title which had been conferred on me in April by P. Laboré, and on the eve of Easter 1892 I took up my duties as the first prior of the convent, canonically instituted by P. Frühwirth. That year there were numerous lectures to inaugurate the new main hall of the school, sixteen in all, a figure which has never been exceeded. The school's program for this starting point can be found in the *Revue Biblique* (1892, pp. 126ff) which has often published the main results of our travels. Let it be enough here to refer the reader once and for all to this information.

THE REBUILDING OF SAINT-ETIENNE (1892)

Journey to Constantinople

The year 1892 was marked by a great step toward the rebuilding of the sanctuary, namely the obtaining of the firman. A word here about the method, now superseded and soon to be forgotten, by which things were done in Turkey. Our request had long since been deposited at the Sublime Porte by courtesy of the French Consulate in Jerusalem and of our embassy in Constantinople. We were first on the list, yet others were being dealt with before us. In the end M. Ledoulx, our excellent consul, and a true friend, told me that he would not take it amiss if we set about sorting things out for ourselves. This was the official opinion of M. de Noailles, our ambassador. I therefore lost no time in availing myself of the services of His Beatitude Mgr. Azarian, the Armenian Catholic patriarch, who had the reputation, and rightly so, of being very influential at the Sublime Porte and at the Palace. Things were now beginning to move, so I went to Constantinople toward the end of August. Shortly before this, M. Paul Cambon had taken over as our ambassador. He was an alert and shrewd diplomat in the great tradition of our representatives in Constantinople, as he went on to prove in London before and during the Great War. He had not been slow in finding out about our activities and his welcome was more than stern. How could we dare to enter into direct negotiations with the

Turks, eluding the prerogative of the French government, and denying him the honor of obtaining the firman?

The Firman Obtained

Somewhat taken aback by such a direct attack, I asked leave to reply with absolute frankness, and I did not hesitate to cast responsibility onto the suggestions of the previous ambassador. There was no mistaking my complete good faith, and M. Cambon, having immediately recovered his composure, took the matter in hand, presented me to the Grand Vizier who granted the request, "being more sympathetic to the building of a church than to a commercial and industrial undertaking." My stay in Constantinople lasted a fortnight, and was a continual delight. Scarcely had I returned to Jerusalem, when I received a telegraphed message saying that the firman had been obtained: we had a license to rebuild the sanctuary of Saint-Etienne in Jerusalem, the basilica first put up by the Empress Eudoxia and the patriarch Juvenal on the site of the stoning of St. Stephen.

Who Would Help Us?

In our indigent state, this license was but a useless instrument. I could not go begging alms, as I had to stay in Jerusalem, fully committed as I was to the classes on the Old and New Testaments. Anyway, to whom could I have gone, having no links with anyone outside the academic world? I therefore thought of resigning immediately from the priorship. P. Etienne Le Vigoureux, several times prior in the French province, was at this time inspired by Providence with the charitable thought of coming to our aid. His reply to my entreaties was that he hoped to bring the work to a successful conclusion. However, the Father General wanted me to complete the statutory three years as prior. All I had to do was to make the public see that we deserved to have our sanctuary, and tell them how the restoration work would create a center of piety and study in the spirit of the first deacon and martyr. He said that the new prior could appeal with a clear conscience to the charity of Christians, and above all to those people who wanted to show him their gratitude for the way he had served them spiritually.

Saint Stephen and His Sanctuary

As soon as the classes finished (July 1893), I hastily wrote *Saint Stephen and His Sanctuary in Jerusalem*. P. Ollivier was kind enough to write a Foreword. He had an incomparable ability to extemporize, a great love of evangelical studies and a concern to place the Gospels in their Palestinian context; he was always our warmest friend. P. Rouillon, who did all his studies at Saint-Etienne, has set down in a booklet how grateful we were to him.[t]

Saint Stephen and His Sanctuary in Jerusalem came out in the autumn of 1894. In the following spring P. Le Vigoureux was unanimously elected prior of the house, and on December 10, 1895, the first stone was laid by His Beatitude Mgr. Piavi, Latin patriarch of Jerusalem. But we must investigate from a point earlier in time the matter of the doctrinal question.

PRELUDES TO THE CRISIS (1893)

The Biblical Teaching of Loisy

It is not necessary to relate here how the biblical crisis broke out in Paris. In his *Enseignement Biblique* M. Loisy made quite a sharp attack on the authenticity of the Pentateuch. Much of what he wrote, and even more of what he implied, was causing public anxiety. Mgr. d'Hulst intervened, with the obvious intention of doing him a service, but without a precise understanding of his work. His article in *Le Correspondant* of January 25, 1893 had all the appearances, so avoided by M. Loisy, of a coherent system, practically irreconcilable with the traditional view of the inerrancy of the sacred texts.[18]

The Encyclical *Providentissimus Deus*

Urged to utter a condemnation, Leo XIII declined, but he did enlarge on the traditional doctrine in the famous encyclical letter, *Providentissimus Deus* (November 18, 1893), which was published immediately in *Revue Biblique* (January 1894), and followed, not by a special act of submission, since the *Revue* felt in

---

t. A. M. Rouillon, O.P., *Le Père Ollivier (1835–1910)*, Paris, Lethielleux, 1911.

no way a subject of attack, but by an exhortation to agree with the views of the Sovereign Pontiff: "To preserve the doctrine of the inerrancy of the Bible, and to seek to solve the difficulties by traditional, but at the same time progressive exegesis" (p. 29).

Moreover, the *Revue* had almost nothing to say on the questions about which objections were raised. There were only two articles by the Abbé Robert, of the Oratory at Rennes, on Genesis.[19] Some people might be astonished. Perhaps they were astonished in Paris and Rome. The fact is that in Jerusalem we were completely engrossed in the discovery of the Oriental and Palestinian environment, spellbound by these new horizons which were throwing light on so many things, making possible even more. Without any trace of contempt, we were quite naturally remote from pure Scholastic and bookish disputation.

Journey to Sinai

In the winter of 1893 we had been to Aqaba in Sinai. In 1874 we had been just as impressed by the southern shores of the Dead Sea. Attendance at the Orientalists Congress in Geneva (September 1894), journeys to France, Rome, Constantinople and in Palestine, not to mention the regular task of teaching, all this was quite enough to overwhelm and occupy our minds.

I must here admit, however, that the journey to Sinai (1893) made a deep impression on me, which I shall even call a secret and painful anxiety. Since hardly any mention was made of it at the time in the *Revue*, except in order to clarify a point of epigraphy,[20] I must say something about it now.[21]

With P. Séjourné, we shipped a load of camping equipment from Jaffa to Suez. The French consul, who had been informed, was kind enough to send for two bedouin sheiks, and with his help, agreement was quickly reached. We could go wherever we wanted, for as long as we wanted, on payment on one megidi (approximately 4.25 francs) per day for each camel. It turned out that we had to restrict ourselves to the route from Suez to Sinai via Mount Serbal, at the top of which we enjoyed the splendid view of the peninsula spread between the two gulfs. We had three days in Sinai, before going back to Petra via Aqaba. But in Aqaba we could not find Abu Jad; we had to keep our bedouins and pay them for three days. The Turkish commander was suspicious and hostile. A slight graze on my leg which I had not properly tended had developed into an abcess and I was running a temperature. At last we got out of that hell-hole, and when, having abandoned the idea of going to Petra, we reached Gaza, I was exhausted. They carried me back somehow and I had to stay in bed for a long time.

Reflections on the Pentateuch

I have mentioned my low physical state because it perhaps contributed to the intensity of the impression on my spirit. I have contemplated the beauty of Sinai—the arid desert, the oases, the colored sandstone, the pink granite, the majesty of God's mountain bathed in celestial light; I could not begin to describe it. One should read *Le Desert* by that marvelous writer Loti, who followed closely in our footsteps, and, like us, failed in his attempt to see Petra. But what I was searching for above all was the trail of the Israelites, the confirmation of the Pentateuch. It was as though, in my mind, I began to see through a complex question: it seemed to me that the earth itself had a contribution to make to literary criticism of the Pentateuch. Substantial reality as related in the last four books appeared to me to be in perfect harmony with the nature of the country, its appearance, its culture, its traditions. The bold attempt by some critics to resite Mount Sinai in Midian or at Kadesh seemed fanciful to me. Moses arose for me against the skyline in each valley and especially at the summit of Mount Horeb, and I have never doubted that there and subsequently at Kadesh was where he formed the people of God with a revealed moral law.

On the other hand, is the Pentateuch, such as we have it, in all its aspects, the historical account of these facts? How was it possible to move the millions of people referred to in the actual text around, not a limitless desert as flat as a sheet of paper, but those steep waterless valleys? And if one alleges that errors in transcription are to blame, how does one explain the solemn ordering of the tribes, drawn up as if on parade, according to the Book of Numbers? P. Julien, S.J., an attentive traveler, admitted to me that he had been struck, even distressed, by these difficulties. Was it not necessary, therefore, to conclude that perfectly historical facts had been as it were idealized in order to become symbolic of God's people, and of God's Church in the future—especially since the two aspects, the historical and that which we can call juridical or figurative, seemed to tally with each other and throw limit on each other if it was accepted that two main documents were the basis for the composition of the three central books of the Pentateuch: the one which critics said was drawn up by the Elohist and the Yahwist, and the Priestly Code of Wellhausen.[u]

Thus a basic distinction thrown up by literary criticism confirmed, rather than disturbed, the reality of the facts. It was necessary to accept a method of narration which was unlike that of sober history such as we understand it. When we read in Exodus (8:13): "Throughout the land of Egypt [the dust on the ground] will turn into mosquitos," the most obstinate literalist will no doubt accept the view that this is an extension, an "oriental" exaggeration, a generalization which must not be taken word for word. In this is laid down the principle that history was written in the Old Testament in a way which is not our way.

Those who are never at a loss for arguments to counter other arguments may well think these considerations are futile. I am not trying to claim they are superior, but merely to explain how a lengthy study of the texts in the field finally led me to imagine a mode of writing which was not at all meant to go with the terrain, but which was pursuing a different object.

CONSOLIDATION OF THE SCHOOL

Anxieties and Difficulties

I resolved to continue thinking along these lines, but at first to keep my thoughts to myself. My dealings with the Master General, in which P. Cormier, Procurator General, took an active part, were concerned most of all in 1894 with serious diffi-

---

u. J. Wellhausen (1844–1918) is not the first to have perceived several documents in the Pentateuch, but he went on to distinguish sources, and tried furthermore to integrate this information into a scheme for showing the development of the Israelite religion. This synthesis of his was to have considerable influence. Cf. H. Cazelles, *Le Système de Wellhausen*, in A. Robert and A. Feuillet, *Introduction à la Bible*, Vol. 1, Tournai, 1957, pp. 296–314.

culties of a quite different nature. Our financial position was still causing many problems: the Master General was never able to make us any donations; the sum of one thousand francs when he named me prior was one happy exception. He spent much time in making it easier for us to borrow money, often just to repay a previous loan. I forget now by what turn of events we found ourselves in debt to the Fribourg house, for a capital sum on which the Master General paid the interest. Professions and ordinations of the novices also caused special complications, which we feared less, however, than the prospect of the departure of the students from the province of Lyons. This province had decided to set up a novitiate and study center at Rosary Hill near New York, intending to care for all its religious there. However, to show its good will to the priory in Jerusalem which had taken in several of its students, P. Laboré agreed to leave us two. Although the main aim of the project was no concern of mine whatsoever, the interests of Saint-Etienne were at stake and I ventured to send a note to the definitor of that province, and even to predict that the experiment would last no longer than ten years. In fact it was over in six. What was of the greatest importance to us was the choice of the two brethren whom Lyons seemed to regard as being its participants in our biblical work. They were absolutely set on having Br. Hugues Vincent; but I already looked upon him as our best hope for the future. As I was not able to deal easily at a distance with such a delicate matter, which was moreover considered settled, I bade farewell to the students who were due to set sail while I was away, and I left for Rome in the spring.

The Theological College

Yet another difficulty called me to Rome. With the departure of the students from Lyons had come the contingent from Toulouse. At Jaffa, on my way back from Sinai, I had found P. Raphael Savignac,[v] now prior. We had also P. Sebastien

---

v. Antoine M. Savignac (July 21, 1874—November 27, 1951), a Dominican, spent his whole life at Saint-Etienne in the Biblical School, first as a student, then as a teacher. As a specialist in Semitic epigraphy, he went with P. Jaussen on some fruitful exploratory journeys, the results of which are recorded in the three volumes of his *Missions archéolgique en Arabie* (Paris, 1909, 1914, and 1922). His wisdom and his piety were felt in his administrative tasks and in his wide spiritual ministry.

Thomas, now a bishop in Brazil. So the theology course had to
continue. From the autumn of 1892 to the summer of 1894, the
teachings of St. Thomas were presented by P. Zanecchia, former
regent at Minerva, who had been very kind in coming back to
teaching. At first he was astonished, almost dumbfounded, by
the things he heard, even to the extent of writing a very hostile
letter about me to the Master General. But then he formed a great
attachment to practical studies, and he could be seen beating
himself about the head with a Greek grammar, complaining that
nobody had ever taught him anything. The result of this reversal
in his attitude was a work on the geography of the Holy Land,
written in French, and an account of inspiration in the Bible,
which caused this five-star Thomist to be ranked among the innovators. In the summer of 1874, he asked leave to return to
Rome. Thus the college found itself disorganized on the teaching
side.

The truth was that it did not have the status of a proper theological college. We hesitated to ask the Master General to grant
us this favor. Many of our friends in the Order advised caution.
Our raison d'être, our novelty, wherein was recognized our usefulness, was the Biblical School. To give theology courses was
perhaps necessary for a short while. But to set up a college, with
the principal, graduates, a director of studies, meant granting
pride of place to the teaching of Thomist doctrine, or even making it our essential purpose. Was there not a risk that biblical
studies would slide back down to the more than subordinate position which was allocated to them in the colleges of the Order?
What would be the situation of the director of the Biblical
School? In a Dominican college there can be but one man at the
top.

However, I had come to believe, as also had P. Séjourné,
that our standing within the Order would be greatly enhanced by
entering into the traditional mold, as official depositaries of the
teachings of its undisputed Master and placed under his inspiration. We would no longer be anomalous, and thus distrusted. For
our position vis-à-vis the Church authorities the advantage was
obvious. We had therefore decided to ask the Master General if
he did not think it proper to establish the college canonically. He
agreed, or perhaps asked, that I take the examination which

would admit me as a graduate. We went through this formality in Rome, and the Master General immediately approved in Council the foundation of the college. I assumed that the problem of having two heads would be resolved by the appointment of a regent. At the same time I got P. Frühwirth's permission to keep P. Vincent and P. Jaussen in Jerusalem. As has often happened for our beloved house, the initial disturbance had led only to a consolidation of our position.

Editor of the *Revue Biblique*

It was exactly the same with the *Revue Biblique*. M. Lethielleux had not resigned himself to the fact that it was hard to read, and, without vivid descriptions and picturesque accounts, was no help to the general public. He envisaged it as a periodical with a wide circulation. We were determined to be as scientific as our resources permitted. His contract with us allowed him to cease publication of the *Revue*, and he informed me that this is what he would do. Personally I found him not very eager to take care over art work of a technical nature, and I merely requested him to put in writing what he had told me. Having obtained his written withdrawal,[22] and on the advice of my friend M. Batiffol, who went with me to introduce me, I offered the business to M. Victor Lecoffre, who showed himself to be a perfect gentleman. He told us with a smile that the *Revue Biblique* had a home waiting for it, since he had been hoping to publish a periodical compilation under that title, which would be the organ of a *Société d'études bibliques pour l'interprétation et la défense des Saintes Ecritures*. The prospectus which he produced[23] is dated 1886, and is the result of a wish expressed at the Congress of Rouen Catholics. The organizing committee was headed by the Marquis de Beaucourt[w] and the Abbé Lesêtre.[x] As the committee had so far not done any-

---

w. Director of the *Revue des Questions Historiques*.

x. Henri Lesêtre (1848–1914), priest of the Paris diocese, author of numerous works on Holy Scripture, in particular *Notre Seigneur Jésus-Christ dans son saint Evangile* (1892), which is an historical life of Jesus and his teachings; he was co-director of the *Revue pratique d'apologétique* from 1905 to 1914. A disciple of M. Vigouroux, he always followed the conservative line, although possessing a more liberal mind. His authority won for him in 1903 the title of consultant to the Pontifical Biblical Commission. He was to write but one article for the *Revue Biblique:* "La méthode historique de Saint Luc" (Vol. 1, 1892, pp. 171–185).

thing about its periodical, it had not been able to object to the setting up of our *Revue Biblique*. I was totally unaware of the endeavor to which M. Lecoffre referred, and without in any way uniting ourselves to it we easily reached agreement. In order to avoid any future misunderstanding I expressly stipulated that he should never ask us to relinquish our scientific aims for the sake of attracting a wide public. This clause was observed religiously, and the most courteous and obliging relationship established by M. Lecoffre has also been continued by his son-in-law, M. Gabalda.

M. Lecoffre wished the *Revue* to have a secretary in Paris. M. Batiffol[y] was kind enough to take this on. It was he who arranged so lucidly the first number in 1895, an arrangement which the *Revue* has kept ever since: leading articles, miscellany, reports from Palestine, textual revisions and summary. With what consummate skill, what tact, what alacrity in anticipating our wishes he carried out his task, only I can say, and do attest publicly. These totally disinterested services have not always been valued within our Order. Esprit de corps is too often exclusive. There can be no doubt that a great deal of the success of the *Revue Biblique* is due to the most assiduous efforts of this friend. Ever since we became priests together, in that first delightful fervor of the seminary at Issy where our friendship was established, that friendship has never wavered.

Father Azzopardi, Regent

With the future of the *Revue* assured, and under more favorable conditions, I returned to Jerusalem, where I soon received Alphonse Azzopardi, sent to us by the Master General in order to teach dogmatic theology. His position was that of regent, which by right gave him the directorship of the Biblical School. I admit I was a little put out by this, despite the title of graduate which

---

y. Pierre Batiffol (1861–1929), one of the most remarkable figures of the French Church. Rector of the Institut Catholique at Toulouse from 1891 to 1907, the life and soul of the *Bulletin de littérature ecclésiastique*, author of numerous historical works, in particular, *L'Eglise naissante et la catholicisme* (1909) which marks an epoch in ecclesiastical history. Outside the Dominican Order, Père Lagrange had no more loyal friend than Mgr. Batiffol. Cf. the account which Père Lagrange published in *La Vie Intellectuelle* in March 1929, pp. 398–423.

had been conferred on me. Nevertheless I volunteered to give up my position as director of the *Revue Biblique* in his favor. The Master General had the kindness to reply to me that it was precisely so that I could better continue as director that he had not wanted to give me "the often all too absorbing anxieties of the position of regent."[24] Moreover, P. Azzopardi told me straightaway that, in accordance with P. Frühwirth's verbal instructions, he had no intention of taking over the biblical studies. Our relationship was indeed always excellent, without even any appearance of conflict in relation to the studies. I was often sorry even, *pace optimi viri dixerim*, that the teaching of St. Thomas did not enjoy greater standing. I have always been convinced that his *Summa* is an incomparable monument of Christian theology. St. Thomas depends on Aristotle's logic, to which philosophy is still indebted, and also unfortunately on a few weak points in his cosmology. For his religious teaching St. Thomas borrowed hardly more than on Aristotelian argument for the existence of God, which he transformed and set on its true basis. The Angelic Doctor is rather the faithful echo of the Catholic thinkers who went before him, of St. Augustine above all, although we still have St. Thomas to thank for toning down some of his theses. Thus, whenever I wanted to strive after greater insight into the notion of inspiration, it was to St. Thomas that I turned for the light of guidance.

BIBLICAL MATTERS (1895–1896)

The Problem of Inspiration

Was it right to approach biblical matters from first principles? Comfortable opportunism would have replied no. By merely noting facts, without trying to classify them within a theological framework, we would save ourselves much trouble, since theologians care little for stepping outside their domain, but they are on the other hand little disposed to let it be invaded. For me, such ingenuity would have implied a lack of faith. The watertight division between exegesis and theology would not have held in the end. How could intellectual acceptance be given to such an outlook? I was in all sincerity not willing to accept any critical so-

lution which was contrary either to dogma or even to the principles of theology; I was willing to appeal to the real theologians,
but on condition that they were not of the routine variety of exegetes, used to sheltering comfortably under the authority of so-
called traditional thinking. To cut the matter short, it was necessary to find out exactly what theology demanded and what it
allowed, or, in more concrete terms, to get to the bottom of what
the theologians would at least consent to tolerate whenever difficult points were being examined. The time seemed right, since
the encyclical of Leo XIII had drawn attention to the doctrine of
inspiration, while attention was also being focused on the literary
criticism of the Pentateuch by the activities of M. Loisy. I personally had more time to devote to study, P. Le Vigoureux having taken over as prior in the spring of 1895, as well as taking
charge of the building of the basilica and the priory. Thus, 1895
was a year of hope. A journey to the Golan in April-May had
highlighted the special talent of P. Hugues Vincent for scientific
observation of sites and monuments. The October issue of the *Revue* contained a first article on inspiration.[25] This was the beginning of the period of difficulties.

The *Revue Biblique* Under Censure
Up to this point, the *Revue Biblique* had been attacked only
for the novelty of its views on the topography of Jerusalem and
on a few Palestinian traditions. This seemed insignificant to the
theologians. It is true that we were often criticized for our tendency to take too much notice of work being done by non-Catholics, especially Germans. People were very quick to criticize.
However, just try to imagine for a moment the almost insur-
mountable difficulties posed by a periodical that was produced in
Jerusalem, printed in Paris, and censored in Rome. Because of
this, Father General had made a few allowances which rendered
things a little easier. Articles could be printed in advance, subject
to their being scrapped later if it was deemed necessary. This is
why an article of mine on a book by Lods could not appear. I
have kept in our archives a good number of articles, reviews and
reports which suffered the same fate. As for articles with a purely
factual content, epigraphy, topography, travel, and so on, Father
General relied on our own discretion. It was an amusing parallel

of the young girl who promises her mother that she will skip over the naughty bits in the novel. It was well known at the Mother House that I did not fail to submit to them anything which could give rise to complaint. People will say it would have been better for me to have suppressed this sort of material myself, if I sensed it could cause trouble. I can only tell how things were. I was absolutely determined not to rebel against restraint, but nevertheless I was forcing my superiors to impose it because of my aim of forging ahead, even if it meant defying the most widely held opinions. They knew full well that I would never at any price abuse their good faith, but having to apply restraint was causing them much distress—above all P. Cormier.

For my explanation of the doctrine of inspiration I was eager to obtain the approval of the most qualified theologians, such as the regent of the Minerva, at that time, P. Buonpensieri, whose notes I have kept. Conciliar teaching that God is the author of the inspired books was the first rule. But how should we take this? The Molinists regularly resorted to the human analogy: *duo trahentes navim*. In the same way Cardinal Franzelin had arrived at his theory which considered as inspired all the ideas in the sacred books, but not the terms in which they were expressed. This was the opinion of conservatives, but it did not find favor with M. Loisy,[26] nor with P. Pègues,[27] an already eminent Thomist, nor with M. Lévesque.[28] I too set myself to attack it.[29]

Articles on Inspiration

A new article on "L'Inspiration des Livres Saints" appeared in April 1898 in reply to P. Gardeil.[z] I am not aware that this theory, which I do not need to restate here, has ever been attacked by Thomist theologians. They recognized rather that it came from St. Thomas himself, according to the way Cardinal Zigliari

---

z. In these articles, Père Lagrange showed that if the sacred writers were the instruments of God, they were not so as passive machines, for God moves each of us according to our nature. The Scriptures therefore are possessed of indisputable authority, since they were written entirely under the inspiration of the Holy Spirit. But they are just as much an expression of human thought in human style, and subject to the laws of interpretation which are applicable to any other writings of antiquity. See the presentation of his ideas about this which Père Lagrange made in *La Méthode historique* (*Foi Vivante*, No. 31), Chap. 3.

had understood him. A few of them[30] have gone over these points again, developing and completing them; I cannot see any difference in their understanding of it.

But in the liberal camp, people wondered how, with such a system, anyone could answer the objections of the critics, M. Dick, an excellent friend whose real name I shall not divulge, asked the question in the *Revue* in October, and I answered it as best I could.[31] Let me stress the main point, a source of so much difficulty (pp. 15ff): "There exists in the Bible a primitive history, whose basis is guaranteed by divine truth; but certain circumstances can be considered either as metaphors or allegories, or as a Hebraic adaptation of the oral tradition, etc."

Loisy's Status

I must here explain the presence in our *Revue* in 1896 of two important articles by M. Loisy on the "Apocalypse Synoptique."

Mgr. Baudrillart has recounted in the life of Mgr. d'Hulst[32] how difficult it was for the rector of the Institut Catholique to get the bishop of Châlons to let him have the young Abbé Loisy as a professor of Holy Scripture; at Châlons they wanted to make him professor of theology at the seminary.[33] This was in 1882.

In 1890, M. Loisy was professor at the Institut Catholique de Paris, at the same time continuing to hold classes in Hebrew and Assyrian. But for the new academic year 1892–1893, M. Icard, superior general of Saint-Sulpice, had forbidden his students to attend Loisy's classes. He had started to publish *L'Enseignement Biblique* early in 1892, and it was this which gave a wider public the opportunity to appreciate the more audacious aspects of his teaching. It was to justify him that Mgr. d'Hulst had published his article in the *Correspondant* (January 25, 1893), for he was convinced that M. Loisy had secretly been denounced and his works put on the Index. The assertion was being made "rightly or wrongly," writes Mgr. Baudrillart (p. 479), "that the people behind this denunciation were the Dominican Fathers of the *Revue Biblique*." We shall come back to this point. Was M. Loisy really denounced? I simply do not know. What is certain is that no condemnation was issued at the time. Mgr. d'Hulst thought it possible to write from Rome itself: "I entirely agree with you that the risks arising from Loisy must be warded off. In

France they are more of a threat than in Rome."[34] He thought at
first that he had saved the situation by asking M. Loisy—who apparently accepted—to restrict himself "to teaching exclusively
the philology of Hebrew, Assyrian and Aramaic at which he excels." M. Fillion would replace him as professor of biblical exegesis. But before he fell silent, M. Loisy decided to speak out. He
did not see where he fitted into the picture painted by Mgr.
d'Hulst of the liberal school, and it was of course his right to state
his own position. His statement could quite well have been considered as belonging to the past, since he was not to teach any
longer. But his article on "La question biblique et l'inspiration
des Ecritures," which appeared five or six days before the general
assembly of the founding bishops of the Institut Catholique, was
held to be a sort of challenge to the rector and to the bishops. The
bishops were unanimous in asking for his voluntary resignation,
as the gentlest way of dismissing him, and the *Enseignement Biblique* had to cease publication. The official minute of the assembly
is dated November 15. The encyclical *Providentissimus Deus* was
promulgated in Rome three days later. The theology faculty of
the Institut de Paris was quick to show its approval of it, and the
Bulletin announced: "We know, besides, that the Abbé Loisy had
written, on his own behalf, to the Sovereign Pontiff to express his
filial attachment to all his teachings. He received from the Cardinal Secretary of State a letter full of the expression of the Holy
Father's benevolence."[35]

Loisy and the *Revue Biblique*

It was against this background that I made M. Loisy the offer of collaborating in the *Revue Biblique*. I recognize that this was
an imprudent step, but it was one which proves conclusively that
I had nothing to do with the alleged denunciation. If I had made
that denunciation from some qualm of conscience, why would I
withdraw it after the verdict of the bishops? If it had been to
make a political point, all I needed to do would have been to congratulate myself on my shrewdness and leave it at that. Opening
the *Revue* to M. Loisy, on the contrary, was it not a gesture of sol-
idarity with his teachings? However, I was not intending it be so.
It seemed to me sad that the greatest critical mind among Catholics should be removed from a struggle for which we needed all

our forces mustered, and it had of course to be agreed that if M. Loisy was going to collaborate with us, it was to be along the lines we set down, and not along his own, which he seemed to have renounced by his "filial attachment" to all the teachings of the Pope. The whole business was rather delicate to deal with by letter, especially given the distance between Paris and Jerusalem, and I asked M. Batiffol to see M. Loisy and come to some arrangement with him by word of mouth.

After their first meeting, at which sympathy was expressed and Loisy showed little inclination to collaborate,[36] he sent us two reviews (1895, p. 270;[37] 1896, pp. 128–129) and his study of the Synoptic apocalypse in two articles (1896, pp. 173–198; 335–359). The first did not worry me at all, at least not after M. Batiffol had obtained a few modifications. But the second was obviously a fairly sympathetic exposition of the theory which limited Christ's knowledge. People would have the right, would they not, to accuse the *Revue Biblique* of abandoning a thesis of St. Thomas held by the whole Thomist school? I was greatly troubled, for after having asked for modifications, I received the proofs of the article in Suez at the moment of our departure for Sinai. If I refused to take the second article, I would also have to refuse the first, and be left with an incomplete publication. I passed an anxious night. P. Coconnier was a member of our party, and his standing as a theologian was undisputed.[a] He advised me to disclaim responsibility on behalf of the editorship by means of a note, the least offensive possible for M. Loisy, since it would merely indicate that we shared his own reservations.[38]

However, the author was not at all satisfied with this arrangement. In addition, he no longer needed the shelter we had offered him, since he was engaged with M. Lejay in founding the *Revue d'histoire et de littérature religieuses* (1896) in which he would have a free hand.[39] But surely, if at that time M. Loisy had been convinced that we had denounced him, would he have agreed out of jealousy to give his help to the very publication which was sup-

---

a. Henri Coconnier (1846–1908), Dominican, professor at the Institut Catholique de Toulouse, then at the University of Fribourg, Switzerland, of which he was also rector. Cf. M-Fr Cazes, O.P., *Le T.R.P. Coconnier, des Frères Prêcheurs, Quelques notes sur sa vie, ses oeuvres et sa mort*, Toulouse, 1908.

posed to have killed off his own? His independence of character, his concern for his dignity—which must be acknowledged— would not have allowed him to. This argument is conclusive for everybody. I add my own testimony to it. When I saw him in Neuilly,[40] where he was chaplain at the boarding school run by the Dominican sisters—who were most pleased with him—he told me that he had in fact suspected us, but he had come to realize that this suspicion was based on false assumptions. Therefore I was very surprised when, in 1912, Mgr. Baudrillart repeated an absurd rumor, without declaring his own view, but with the interpolation "rightly or wrongly." As regards the editorship of the *Revue*, my rejection of the charge was formal; I issued it immediately.[41] Could tongues have wagged in Paris? I have no indication that this was so. Letters from the Master General contain nothing about it. If M. Loisy really was denounced, those who did it will perhaps have judged it prudent to attribute the denunciation to others.[42] Only the Index could cast light on this affair, and the Index is never eager to attract publicity to itself.[b]

In any case, neither the articles on inspiration and Hexameron nor the presence of M. Loisy among the collaborators had harmed the good reputation which the *Revue* enjoyed in Catholic circles. It will be enough to quote the *Ami du Clergé* of November 26, 1896: "Beyond all question, for all matters touching on Holy Scripture the *Revue Biblique Internationale* is the most authoritative organ we have in the French language. It strongly emphasizes the requirements of modern criticism, but we can at least be sure that we are dealing with well-balanced, conscientious minds possessed with a desire for precision and clarity, whose only care is to serve truth and, through truth, the Church. It uses all liberty permissible within current opinions, and a number of our readers will find this liberty far-reaching. But if it is used in Jerusalem, it is because it is justifiable."

---

b. These pages, from the sub-heading "Loisy and the *Revue Biblique*" up to this point, were used again by Père Lagrange in *M. Loisy et le Modernisme*, pp. 79–84, with some alterations caused in particular by Loisy's *Mémoires* which had appeared meanwhile and in which Loisy again gives some credence to the rumor of a denunciation by the Dominicans of the Biblical School.

Director of Studies

The Master General, for his part, had sent me his patent as regent of studies, and wrote to me on November 26, 1896:[43] "It is not enough to start something; it must be followed up and supported. The devotion which you have lavished on Saint-Etienne in its infancy has not only proved your worth to me, but has convinced me that the man most suitable to complete the establishment of our college is the one who first had the idea and then made it a reality. Therefore I thank you for having accepted your patent as regent of studies with completely filial submission, and I undertake to do all I can to further your decisions."

The School received at the same time useful reinforcement in the person of P. Rhétoré who had been a missionary in Mosul for many years, and whom the Cardinal Prefect of the Propaganda was letting us have only for three years and at the request of the Master General. His knowledge of Syriac, Aramaic and Armenian enabled us to complete the department of Oriental languages. That year, 1896, we were visited by three very distinguished members of the Society of Jesus, P. Leroy, P. Fonck and P. Condamin. P. Fonck wanted to attend my class, after which we chatted under our fig tree. This father defended with a smile the authors of the *Cursus*, whom he found a little too "conservative," but who were so charitable, such good priests—P. Knabenbauer for one. Since then P. Knabenbauer has modified his initial posture, although less acutely than P. de Hummelauer, and adopted broader views, whereas—but let us not anticipate matters.

2. From Leo XIII to Pius X

THE BUILD-UP TO THE CRISIS (1897)

The crisis loomed in 1897. That year was a very busy one. I shall follow the order of events, which will have both the disadvantage and the advantage of reproducing the interlocking structure of our work of exploration and our work on biblical theories.

Archaeological Expeditions

In the previous autumn, a party from the School had visited Petra and spent three days in a vain search for a large inscription which we had been told existed there. At the very last minute, P. Vincent, who had alone refused to give up the search, found the inscription in a remote valley. The baggage was unpacked. A makeshift ladder was constructed, and an impression of the inscription made. He later produced a copy of the inscription which was so perfect that from then onward he was the one of our number appointed to do this type of work, and also to draw up the maps. Thus he became my inseparable companion, and while it was I who continued to negotiate with the scientists and scholars as the person in charge of expeditions, yet it was he who did all the hard work; the only useful service I could give him was in philology and history, although it would not be long before he surpassed me in these two fields as well. Thus we both set off for Madaba at the beginning of February, in order to study the mosaic with which P. Cleophas, librarian of the Greek Orthodox monastery in Jerusalem, had made the briefest of acquaintances, leading to some strange interpretations which greatly aroused our curiosity: there was talk of a hand stretched out over the Dead

Sea, etc. Since he willingly agreed to our publishing his discovery, we presented our own work as being in collaboration with him. It can be found in the *Revue Biblique*.[1] The drawings and maps are by P. Vincent. As we have always decided to make public our documents as soon as possible, I quickly drew up an initial interpretative survey, and sent it all off to M. Batiffol. His friend, M. Etienne Michon, having been acquainted with the facts, managed to interest M. Héron de Villefosse, who in turn gave a paper to the Académie des Inscriptions et Belles-lettres on March 13.

M. Clermont-Ganneau was at the time a sort of superintendent of Palestinian archaeology, and justifiably so.[a] He was cut to the quick because nobody had informed him, and sent a telegram to P. Paul de Saint-Aignan of the Province of the Holy Land, whose zeal needed no spur, and obtained some mediocre photographs of the mosaic. A short work was printed in Jersulam, attributed to P. Cleophas alone. But this scheme bore little fruit. Later we returned to Mâdaba, P. Vincent and I, in order to take an impression of the mosaic as best we could by coloring the cubes *in situ*. Lack of money made it impossible for us ever to publish our copy in color as we had dreamed; it has been done fairly well by two Germans.

The Decree from the Holy Office

While the Madaba discovery was filling us with joy, I was crushed by a measure taken by the Holy Office. A resolution of January 13, 1897, approved and confirmed by Leo XIII, ran thus: "*Utrum tuto negari aut saltem in dubium vocari possit esse authenticum textum S. Joannis in Ep. I. c. V, v. 7 quod sic se habet: . . . Omnibus diligentissimo examine perpensis, praehabitoque DD. Consultorum voto, iidem Emi Cardinales respondendum mandarunt: Negative. . . .*"[b]

---

a. Charles Clermont-Ganneau (1846-1923), an expert in Oriental languages, worked as such in several diplomatic posts in the Near East, before devoting himself totally to a scientific career which took him to the Institut in 1889 and to the Collège de France in 1890. Gifted with remarkable intuition, he made numerous archaeological and epigraphical discoveries, notably in Palestine.

b. "Is it possible to deny with certainty or even to call into doubt the authenticity of St. John's First Letter, ch. 5, v. 7 ("There are three . . .")? Having fully deliberated, and

News of this reached Jerusalem on April 9. My distress was great. If the Holy See was setting up such barriers in the way of textual criticism, which had been a fairly clear field hitherto, and if the Holy Office was making pronouncements so clearly counter to the opinion of so many learned Catholics and all other scholars, what were we to think of its views on matters reputedly much more serious? I took to the olive groves of Gethsemane and immediately began a week's retreat which brought me peace. We know that the Holy See has not been strict in imposing the apparent discipline of this decree. Cardinal Vaughan had thought it necessary to point out the unfortunate impression it produced in England. There was an attempt to explain that the decision should be understood as referring to the "juridical authenticity, not to the strictly literary authenticity,"[2] which was the same as saying that the verse was part of the Vulgate, from which nobody had the right to delete it; but was it necessary to conduct "the most diligent examination" before they issued a statement to this simple effect? This later interpretation was viewed in the end as disciplinary, relevant to a given period and as having ceased to be binding. There was some talk under Pius X of having the decree expressly rescinded; it never was, but it seems indeed to have fallen into abeyance.[c] The whole question will necessarily be settled once and for all when the Benedictines publish their version of the Vulgate. Many people thought at the time that the Holy Office had wanted to fire a warning shot across the bows of the Catholic exegetes who were about to meet at the Fribourg Congress in Switzerland.[3]

The Fribourg Congress

I was at the Congress on August 16. The section dealing with exegetical matters had been separated from the religious sciences section, and I was made chairman of it. Vice-chairmen

---

a vote of the consultors having been taken, the eminent cardinals have ordered that the answer be: No."

c. On June 2, 1927, the Holy Office gave (the decree of 1897) its official interpretation according to which the Church did not wish to block the paths of scientific investigation carried out prudently and in submission to the magisterium, but only to affirm its right to intervene as a last resort in matters relating to the authenticity of the sacred texts.

were R. P. Brucker[d] and the illustrious Bardenhewer.[e] Secretaries were P. Rose and M. Minocchi, whose names I cannot write down without bitter sadness.[f] At the time all hearts were full of hope. I gave a short paper on the sources of the Pentateuch, passed by P. Berthier and P. Coconnier who were the examiners appointed by P. Frühwirth, and who were, as is well known, eminent and very safe theologians. P. Brucker listened to me attentively through his ear trumpet and seemed outwardly not at all scandalized.[4] My sketch was judged to be less trenchant than that of Baron von Hügel.[g] Nevertheless, outside the Congress, the rumor spread that the Mosaic authenticity of the Pentateuch had been called in question; there was a great stir. The following month I went to the congress of Orientalists in Paris.[5] I was bold enough to invite the Semitic studies section to a Congress in Jerusalem. This was obviously premature, and my proposal, received with much enthusiasm, did not even begin to be carried out. It is only this year (1926) that it has been possible to hold a congress of Orientalists in Syria and in Palestine.

The Exploration in Petra

While I was away in Europe, hard work had continued back at the School. P. Séjourné and P. Vincent had inspected the Cufic inscription in the Holy Sepulchre, which they had reproduced and deciphered admirably; they had also taken themselves

---

d. Joseph Brucker (1845–1926), French Jesuit, editor of the *Etudes*, author of numerous works on the Holy Scriptures, in particular *Questions actuelles d'Ecriture sainte* and *L'Eglise et la critique biblique*, in which he roundly attacks the progressive exegetes.

e. Otto Bardenhewer (1851–1924), patristic scholar, professor at Münster (1884–86), then at Munich. His main work: *Geschichte der altkirchlichen Literatur*, I-V (1913–32).

f. P. Rose, Dominican, professor at the University of Fribourg, and Salvatore Minocchi were both to leave the Church.—The biography of Minocchi has recently been written by A. Agnoletto, *Salvatore Minocchi. Vita e opere, (1869–1943)*, Brescia, 1964.

g. Baron von Hügel was not present at the Fribourg Congress, but there was read a long paper of his on *La méthode historique et son application a l'Etude des documents de l'Hexateuque* defending the documentary theory, and which was to provoke lively controversy. This particular Fribourg Congress was the *Quatrième congrès scientifique international des catholiques*. All such congresses were a French initiative. The first had taken place in Paris in 1888. There were three thousand participants at the Fribourg one. The next one was held in Munich in 1900, but it had no section on exegesis, so that discussion such as had arisen in Fribourg could be avoided. It was the last.

off to Madaba at the end of August to survey the monument of Elianeus, and to decipher its inscriptions.[6]

The Académie des Inscriptions had asked me to do a new exploration of Petra, and so, hardly having returned to Jerusalem, I left again with P. Vincent immediately after the feast of the Holy Rosary. This journey was extremely fruitful. It was a mistake on my part not to have described the journey itself along with the account of our halting places. Our no doubt excessive horror of anything which smacks of melodrama lay behind our giving only epigraphical and topographical findings.[7]

It was on the return journey that we visited Khirbet Fenan, being the first Europeans[8] to have trod that soil made sacred through the hard labor of the confessors under Diocletian, and a site of greatest importance in tracing the journey of the Israelites. We approached it coming down from Dhana, and never did an experience of such deep solitude impress us so much as at our evening halt in that shady valley. After Fenan, we went on down and, crossing the Araba, reached Jebel Usdum. I merely alluded[9] to the attack of a raiding party intent on killing us. Some tribes of southern Palestine, under a leader whose name P. Jaussen later got to know, had organized a pillaging excursion, and were lying in ambush to the southwest of the lowest slopes of the salt mountain. We pushed on escorted by two Circassians who had been with us for the whole journey, and followed at some distance by our muleteers, driving the mules which were loaded with the camping equipment.

On Wednesday, October 27, we said Mass at Ghor Safiyeh, and had passed along the southern edge of the Dead Sea on a track that was fairly firm before the rainy season. P. Vincent was starting to say in a cheerful manner: "And to think there was a time when we were afraid of this place!" when there was a burst of rifle fire to our left. "That will be some people settling accounts between themselves," he added. But soon we heard bullets whistling, and saw them embedding themselves in the ground. I said to P. Vincent: "Let us give each other absolution." And as he looked for his breviary, I yelled at him, "The shortest you can find!" At that moment our Circassian escort, whom I had entreated to shoot in order to defend us, were off like the wind, even though one of their horses had received a bullet in the neck; we followed them, scrambling up over rocks which had suddenly become quite accessible to our panic-stricken mounts; I lost my spectacles and my head-dress, but we finally made it to Zoara and safety. Our baggage went as plunder to the Bedouins, and the muleteers could retrieve only a few broken pieces of impressions. Fortunately the excellent copies made by P. Vincent provided evidence.[10]

During the scare, P. Vincent and I had faced the danger together. But in Petra itself, he had gone off on his own one afternoon, and by evening I had still not seen him return. Night fell quickly, and it was impossible to mount a search in that chaotic wilderness of mountains, steeply-sloping valleys and precipices. That night was the longest I have ever spent. In the morning, I roused up the people of Elji to seek out Mansour, as we used to call him in Arabic. We shouted, we beat around in the caves and the bushes, but it was useless. Then I noticed that a Bedouin who had come with me was following the flight of some vultures in an attempt to find at least his corpse.[h]

As we were returning sadly along the sik toward our camp which stood at the water's edge near the theater, the shouts of some galloping horsemen greeted us: "Mansour, Mansour!" I do indeed believe that the name Mamât Mansour, which features on M. Musil's map, came into being at that moment, and is meant to indicate the place where we thought that Mansour had met his death.

The Sources of the Pentateuch

How sentimental the emotions of that journey all seem, now after the war! No sooner had they passed than I fell prey once more to the perpetually harassing anxiety of theological questions. Should I publish the article "Les Sources de la Pentateque"? There was no lack of ominous warning signals. P. Faucher, always so alive to our interests, had been taking counsel. He sent me a letter from M. Vigoureux (December 5, 1897):

---

h. P. Lagrange refers to this incident in his commentary on Luke 17:37 and Matthew 24:28; cf. his *Commentaire de Luc*, 4th edition, 1927, p. 467; *L'Evangile de Jésus-Christ*, 1928, p. 387, note 2.

"I have read 'Les Sources de la Pentateuque' and would never have believed that P. Lagrange could write such an article. Moreover, I cannot understand how it came to be approved. If you publish it, there will be the most unfortunate consequences." There was another correspondent, whose name I have never known, and whose letter seems to have been copied so that I could not recognize the writing, who wrote: "P. Lagrange is a few years ahead of his time. You may be sure that before long we shall think as he does, but by trying to go too quickly on his own, he risks being dashed to pieces. . . . In any case, do not publish the article before you have informed P. Lagrange in full of the difficulty. I believe in fact that too much haste could jeopardize the *Revue* and even the School." Somewhat daunted, M. Batiffol suggested that I should send him a telegram if I agreed to a postponement. The telegram was not sent; the article appeared.

Dear God, enlighten me on the reasons for my decision, for which I shall have to account before you! I can still see myself at my cell window looking distractedly at the Muslim cemetery, with P. Vincent to whom I confided my anxiety. After the excitement of those days at Petra, and the proofs he had given of his masterliness, he was no longer my pupil, but my most faithful collaborator. The future of the *Revue* and of the School interested him as much as me. With the impetuosity of youth—he is seventeen years younger than I—he was all for pressing on. But I believe I took my decision conscientiously. It certainly was not to cause a stir, nor to win the favor of critics or learned men. Our latest work had placed us on a very good footing at the Académie des Inscriptions and with the enlightened public. We had only to continue. This was the path to honor, even more so in the Church, which had shown a certain satisfaction at the encouragement given us by the Académie des Inscriptions. Our ecclesiastical superiors would not have worried too much over this or that opinion about the East. Why should we be so set on encroaching upon theological terrain? Things would have sorted themselves out in the course of time without anyone's suspicions being aroused. One incautious step could provoke a decision which would close that path. All things considered, I was not obliged to sacrifice myself to what I thought was the honor of the Church. Was it not better to say with that witty prelate (Mgr.

Duchesne), "you look after your own interests and leave God to look after his."

Truth and Obedience

But it was precisely these considerations which I denounced within myself as opportunist and a breach of faith. The person who had written to P. Faucher, so cautious where timing was concerned, nonetheless promised acceptance in the future for the opinions he was asking to be kept quiet. Is this really how truth is served, and how we should serve these souls who risk conflict and ruin? Is it not the task of the present to prepare for the future? Can we ever move forward without taking steps?[i] And in another connection, do we have the right to move forward without it being proved that the move is permissible? On the whole the article was only an exposition of one way to approach the question of the sources of the Pentateuch, and did not clash with Catholic principles. It proposed no definitive solution. It had been extremely well received at Fribourg by the vast majority of the exegetes present. P. Berthier himself had written "Approved" in large letters. Finally I told myself that it was better to risk my own peace of mind and even my reputation than to keep silent out of worldly prudence, the more so since I was resolved to submit myself entirely to the decisions of the Holy See. In terms of human wisdom, as St. Paul says, I still cannot see that my decision—imprudent needless to say—was dictated by any unworthy sentiment. But religious perfection demanded more than this. I did not hide from myself the fact that I was, by some kind of ceaselessly active obstinacy, dragging along with me the assent of the governing Council of our Order, which so manifestly desired to avoid the fuss and the polemics which had come from the Catholics. Each one of the forward-looking articles had been judged sufficiently correct, but taken as a whole they were characterized too much as an innovation in the direction of higher criticism. As a religious, I had to tell myself that, if my superiors

---

i. In his lecture at Fribourg, P. Lagrange had declared: "It appears that the moment has come when we can no longer remain inactive without endangering the salvation of souls, and without banishing the intellectual strength which is bound up with it; it appears that by moving forward we can win many more souls."

leaned too far toward expediency, it was not my place to sit in judgment on their reasons, nor seek to make them aware of what had been done, albeit with their permission, but nevertheless a little regardless of their wishes. Therefore I did fail at least in the spirit of obedience; for this I ask pardon of them and of God.

THE ORDEAL (1898)

The First Attack

The attacks started in *L'Univers*, in a fairly violent article signed H.B., which initials some believed they recognized as those of the Abbé Babin, a Parisian priest. But M. Eugene Veuillot realized that the daily press is not qualified to deal with these questions, and that particular campaign was dropped. The real danger came from Loisy's numerous partisans who were to be found almost everywhere, and who affected to consider us as allies, if not consciously allies, at least fitted to promote their own business. Baron von Hügel had spoken of this assumption in Rome, and M. Margival[j] in Paris. M. Batiffol warned me in a letter (May 5, 1898): "It is in our interest most urgently to show that we are not towing them along behind us. I have stressed this as best I could in an article in *La Quinzaine*"—directed against M. Margival. I endorsed his reservations in the July Bulletin (pp. 465f). As for M. Vigouroux, it had been as our friend that he had forewarned us, but as the good friend that he always remained, he did not want to do anything against us. M. Le Camus, his loyal friend and traveling companion, whose attention I had drawn to a widespread rumor, wrote to me (June 10, 1898): "Your Franciscan does not have his facts right about what M. Vigouroux has been doing. Not once has he dreamed of writing anything against you. He had shown himself anxious after reading your article, but all the while admitting that in twenty-five years time, your theory would express pretty well exactly the

---

j. Henri Margival (1854–1914), curate at Saint-Honore-d'Eylau and senior lecturer at the Institut Catholique de Paris. He wrote for the *Revue d'Histoire et de Littérature religieuses* a series of articles which he gathered into one volume under the title *Essai sur Richard Simon et la critique biblique au XVII siècle*. Using Simon as a cover he adopted a defensive and critical attitude hostile to theology and theologians. He left the Church in 1901.

opinion commonly held by Catholics. . . . In Rome, last year's
three witnesses are making each one of us more circumspect. . . .
P. Brandi of *Civiltà* having spoken to the Pope of delating certain
learned men—you perhaps—to the Holy See, Leo XIII replied
that he had had enough of these strange executions of the great
workers of the Church," and so on. On the other hand,
M.Eschbach, superior of the French seminary, spoke to one of
our friends about the "vengeful article" in *L'Univers* and added
prophetically: "And it will not be confined to criticism in a newspaper."[11]

Denounced in Rome

That very April, a blow was struck in secret which could
have had the direst consequences for our School. On April 17
His Beatitude, the Latin patriarch of Jerusalem, Mgr. Piavi, of
the Order of St. Francis, had come to Saint-Etienne to bless the
basilica which was all but completed. Amiable as he was, whenever he wanted to be, and with the caustic but not charmless hu-
mor of a Romagnese which so delighted Cardinal Langenieux at
the Eucharistic Congress, he had been assiduously benevolent to
everyone. Well, two days previously, on April 15, 1898, he had
written to the Cardinal Prefect of the Propaganda a letter, the
translation of which I now venture to set down:[12] "Most eminent
Prince, the Sacred Congregation of the Propaganda is not unaware that the Dominican Fathers, established now for about fifteen years in Jerusalem, have founded here a school of Holy
Scripture not only for the young men of their Order, but open
also to clerical students of all countries and nations who gather
there, drawn by the easiness and opportunity they find of visiting
these lands in which unfolded the events and where were taught
the doctrines contained in the holy books. There is no doubt that
such a foundation has merited and merits the greatest praise and
encouragement, on condition, however, that it contributes to the
consolidation of sacred knowledge and the edification of the students. It is a fact that, from its very beginning, we have seen arise
against this school severe criticisms which have grown worse
with time, to such an extent that I can no longer allow myself, in
all conscience, to keep silent, as I would indeed wish, and refrain
from relating the matter to the Congregation so that it may take

those measures which in its wisdom it will judge expedient. The aforesaid criticisms, which have been made for several years against the teaching given by the Fathers, are all united in drawing attention to a marked tendency toward German rationalism, and particular facts have been made known to me in various and numerous circumstances. But what has provoked a veritable explosion of complaints and accusations is a lecture of P. M.-J. Lagrange having as its title 'Les Sources de la Pentateuque' and published in the *Revue Biblique Internationale*, in the January 1 number of this year. This lecture not only has given rise to controversy in the newspapers, but has invited letters from many churchmen of diverse nations to a priest of the patriarchate, expressing their amazement at the tendencies of this school, which they say are rationalist, and even Protestant. It may therefore be foreseen that the praiseworthy foundation of these fathers will come to lose all its good reputation and that the bishops of Europe will be very careful not to send their young priests to receive instruction which is already proving dangerous. And what has given the final blow to the reputation of the School is that we have seen a certain disciple go to even greater extremes than his masters, in proof of which I was shown this year's number, the February 5 edition, of *Echos d'Orient* in which there appears an article by a certain priest, Simeon Vailhé, who was formerly at the School.

"During the course of the last years, I was often tempted to make one or two observations to the superiors of these fathers, either in relation to certain ideas which I intended to criticize, or to the intemperate opinions which they were spreading concerning the authenticity of certain holy places, which has also scandalized the faithful from time to time and given rise to extremely unedifying controversy. But I have kept within the bounds of the strictest self-restraint. Now, however, no longer able to keep silent, and with the intention of safeguarding the rights of religion as well as the reputation of the School in question, which, once guided back into a better direction, can do much good, and bring honor to the Catholic Church, I have therefore thought fit to submit to Your Most Reverend Eminence the salient points relating to the direction things have taken, so that you may judge in your wisdom if there are grounds for working some reform that might save everything. I believe this would be a simple matter for Your Eminence by means of a few words to the Master General of the Dominicans. In order that Your Eminence may see for yourself the state of things, I am enclosing: (1) the number of the *Revue*[13] (2) an edition of the Paris *L'Univers* of January 20, and (3) this year's number of *Echos d'Orient*.[14]

"I am sending these three documents by registered post. I enclose also with this letter a written document which contains a sort of review of P. Lagrange's lecture which was compiled exclusively for my personal instruction. Your Eminence may do what you want with it, for I have no other aim in view in informing you than to justify my fears, which have provoked this letter. Humbly kissing your sacred purple," etc.

I found out that Mgr. Aurelio Briante, who had become custodian of the Holy Land, had joined his denunciation to that of Mgr. the Patriarch, but I have never known what was contained in it. In accordance with the traditional rule of discretion in Rome, the Master General refrained from telling me anything about this delation. But on April 29, 1898, he asked me for some explanations, as he said, in order to reply to accusations both old and new and, as I learned later, to the precise grievances of Mgr. Piavi.

It must be added that the Master General did not seem at all agitated. He wrote to me on May 17: "You did not misjudge the feeling of good will which inspired me to ask you for information," etc. Thank God that the superiors of the Order and its foremost doctors never doubted my loyalty, which reassured them, nor my honesty, which frightened them a little.

Therefore, as that April drew to a close, the council of the Order did not appear very worried by the combined action of the patriarchate and the province. The matter of the Franciscan traditions in the Holy Land, which were called the Tradition, had no bearing on the faith; I was clearly not responsible for P. Vailhé's article, even supposing it was a bad one; the only thing left was the matter of the Fribourg lecture, which had been very badly received by the body of professors of Holy Scripture, but in which pure theologians continued to see nothing contrary to theology.

New Difficulties

Meanwhile other serious difficulties were threatening us. Discontent had grown within our Order at seeing Abbé Batiffol playing an important part in the *Revue Biblique*. Some blamed him, quite wrongly, for the difficulties which I had had to face. The Master General wrote to me, apparently determined not to tolerate him any longer as secretary. Being conscious of the very great service he had rendered us and of the injustice of these complaints, I had made up my mind to defend him at all costs.

Then the province of Lyons had been struck with a great misfortune. After so many painful sacrifices during the Great War, few people remember the sinking of "La Bourgogne." Three Dominicans from Lyons had met their death at sea after having displayed heroic courage, giving absolution to their companions in adversity, and singing the "Salve Regina" as they went down. Among them was P. Joseph Baumann, brother to M. Emile Baumann and friend of P. Vincent of the novitiate of Saint-Etienne. To the Master General it seemed impossible to stand in the way of P. Vincent's return to that stricken province, for which it was asking as consolation after such a trial. I did not know what to say, and can remember saying an ardent and woeful prayer in the chapel of the Ursulines at Viriville (Isère).

Both problems were solved in an unexpected way, whereby I recognized God's providence once again on our house.

In the spring of that year, Mgr. Batiffol, whose standing among the higher ranks of the clergy was much greater than our denouncers imagined, was invited by His Eminence Cardinal Mathieu, archbishop of Toulouse, to accept the post of rector at the Institut Catholique du Midi. Despite his regret at leaving Paris, he had consented, and the assembly of bishops had immediately ratified the cardinal's choice. Rome showed no opposition. M. Batiffol really did not see his newly-acquired high position as an obstacle to his collaboration with the *Revue Biblique*. Rather he had it in mind to bring me to Toulouse where he had a professorship ready for me and where we would have directed together an enlarged *Revue* which would appear more frequently. I too had plans for inaugurating a private course in Catholic exegesis at the Sorbonne to match what was being taught in the religious department. But the Master General had had no trouble making me realize that we had to concentrate our efforts, and that his resources were not more than sufficient to keep Fribourg and Jerusalem going. To go to Toulouse, which did not offer the advantages of Paris, would have been a desertion. It was easy for Mgr. Batiffol to set up the *Bulletin* at his Institute, which he did, as we have seen, brilliantly. I therefore put my problems to him in friendly fashion. His departure from Paris and his elevation to the position of rector, resulting naturally in the conferment of the rank of prelate, were enough to prevent any unkind comments on his renouncing the now too modest title of secretary to the *Revue Biblique*. I thanked him for what he had done for us with all the warmth of genuine friendship, which nevertheless did not quite succeed in concealing from him the unfavorable disposition of certain members of the Order. He was unfortunately exposed to this later on.

Reorganization of the *Revue Biblique*

How were we to find a secretary good enough to replace him? In June 1898, P. Le Vigoureux had come to the end of his three years as prior. Since he was not re-elected, he was appointed directly by the sovereign authority of the Master General. A certain incompatibility of temperament, nothing more, had revealed itself between him and P. Séjourné. It seemed desirable to effect a mutually agreed separation. The French provincial agreed to assign P. Séjourné to Paris, and the Master General appointed him as secretary. His absence, so cruel a blow for me, was compensated by the certain knowledge that he would render us good service, and we considered this as a temporary absence in any case. When times became difficult, we would have in Paris a faithful friend, whose devotedness was never-failing, one whose religious spirit, desire to serve people, and attachment to the Dominican observances placed him beyond all suspicion of a lukewarm faith. We were deprived of our firmest support in Palestinian studies and for journeys, but it was one decisive reason for the Master General to ask P. Laboré not to deprive us at the same time of P. Vincent, who alone was capable of replacing P. Séjourné in this field, not to mention archaeology in which he was already an expert.

With the new secretary approved, P. Frühwirth turned his
mind to the reorganization of the panel of examiners. He proposed at first (letter of June 9, 1898) that material should be
checked by P. Scheil[k] and P. Sertillanges[l] in Paris, by P. Berthier
in Fribourg, and by P. Walsh in Vienna. How could the *Revue*
have appeared on schedule? I was very grateful to him for accepting a much simpler regulation.[15] The leading articles and the
miscellanea had to be passed by the examiners, but all the lectors
at Saint-Etienne and all those designated censors in the provinces
were considered competent to do the work. The director and the
secretary were responsible for the rest. This very liberal and flex-
ible arrangement, which nonetheless met the requirements of the
Constitutions, is good proof that at the time nobody had any
grave apprehensions at the mother house.

Studies on Genesis

Further proof of this lay in the fact that they did not reject
my scheme to publish a *Commentaire de la Genèse* which would
have expanded in concrete terms on the problem of the sources.
The manuscript was submitted by the Father General to an un-
rivaled theologian, upon whom the Holy See later bestowed episcopal dignity. He wrote to me: "The following is more or less
what I should like to write to the Very Reverend Master General:
I have read P. Lagrange's manuscript containing an *exposition exégétique de la Genèse*. In my opinion it is a responsible and erudite
work, in which the author manifests great respect for the divinely
inspired Scriptures, and great attachment to the traditional interpretation of the Church. . . . I have seen nothing in this book
which could incur disapproval on theological grounds. But . . .
having said that, it is to be feared that the abandonment of certain
views which are still in favor might be denounced as recklessness.
Criticism, however sane, however wise, would not be able to
overcome these views overnight. . . . To sum up, it is all a ques-

---

k. Vincent Scheil (1859–1940), Dominican (1882), professor of Assyriology at the Ecole
　des Hautes Etudes (1895–1933), epigraphist to the archaeological mission in Persia
　from 1901, first editor of the *Code d'Hammourabi*, member of the Institut (1908).
l. Antonin-Dalmace Sertillanges (1863–1948), Dominican, professor of moral philosophy
　at the Institut Catholique de Paris from 1900 to 1922, member of the Académie des Sci-
　ences morales et Politiques in 1918.

tion of expedience. Would it not be better if P. Lagrange published his work first in the form of articles in his *Revue*? etc."[16]

The Dangerous Misunderstanding

The Master General was to go no further than this last suggestion. Menacing clouds had also been gathering on our horizon, and it was at this point that the dangerous misunderstanding
arose which confused us with what was called the broad school.
In the article complained of, I had made a distinction between
two types of mind, the first of those who "fear to lose the whole
by abandoning a part"—and I was evidently not one of this
type—and the second of those who "by making it their business
to pull down the defenses which have become a constraint, hope
not only to preserve but also to win new ground."[17] I was not
condemning their intentions and I was not referring to any one
person, but when I associated myself with their hope for scientific progress, I nevertheless asked where lay the middle course,
from which I intended not to stray, and I took as my boundary
line and safeguard "the principle of authority by which we live."
I was laying myself open to the charge of being trite and presumptuous. Trite because no moralist writes without promising
that he will hold the middle course between over-harsh principles
and over-liberal solutions. Presumptuous because who was I to
propose a new method of literary criticism and exegesis? But people should have taken account of my settled design, however rash
or credulous it might be thought, to follow the middle course,
keeping always within the limits of dogma. So, uncompromising
die-hards on one side and brazen innovators on the other seemed
to have conspired to abolish all distinction between our ideas and
others far more radical.

Attacks Against the *Revue Biblique*

The signal was given by P. Méchineau[m] in the *Etudes* of November 5, 1898:[18] "It has not been without some surprise that we

---

m. Lucien Méchineau (1849–1919), Jesuit, professor of Holy Scripture at the theological
   college of Jersey, then at the Gregorian University in Rome (1907). He contributed to
   Etudes and leaned toward conservatism.

have seen our brothers in the faith thus crossing over into the foreign camp, which had been called until then the enemy camp. Several people consoled themselves by claiming, rightly or wrongly, that the deserters were not theologians and that therefore their adherence to the documentary argument was no cause to stir up Catholic opinion. But today this answer is no longer valid, if indeed it ever had any validity, for it will not be said that the eminent director of the *Revue biblique*, P. Lagrange, does not wield with equal dexterity the swords of the theologian and of the critic. Therefore the loss of men of his calibre to the camp of our adversaries has perturbed excellent minds," etc. So for this conservative theologian, P. Lagrange was a "deserter" to the enemy side.

As for M. Loisy, the inflexible rectitude of his character and a legitimate pride would not allow him to profit from opinions which he knew did not agree with his own. Thus, with equal care he avoided throwing in his lot with me, which would have been a failure to recognize his own worth, and treating me as a shamefaced disciple, which would have been an injustice. It was moreover repugnant to him to set up categories, and he thought that each individual ought to follow his own path, totally independent, in the search for truth. I fully realize the nobility of his attitude, but it has to be said that this lack of a social sense has always made him a loner. He did know, however, how those who to some extent despite himself formed his party were going to argue, and he was to write:[19] "P. Lagrange, who mentions these two groups of exegetes only to separate himself from both of them, should have measured his language in regard to the second, which is the one with which people are linking him, whatever may be the facts of the case, along with all the rest who do not belong to the first." And indeed there were widespread insinuations in the "broad school" that I was working, wittingly or not, to help them achieve their ends, either by not wishing to reveal my thoughts, or by not understanding the full significance of my advances.

Letter from the Pope to the Friars Minor

Shortly after P. Méchineau's article, there appeared the letter from the Sovereign Pontiff to the Minister General of the Or-

der of Friars Minor (November 25, 1898). Referring to the study
of Holy Scripture, the Pope said:[20] "In a matter of this importance, one must . . . avoid sacrificing more than necessary to the
new ideas, and it is even better to fear them, not for their novelty,
but because they are for the most part fallacious, having only the
appearance and mask of truth. Those who should have been least
credulous have nevertheless, here and there, begun to indulge in
a method of interpretation which is too audacious and too free.
Sometimes alien interpreters have even found a favorable welcome in the name of Catholicism, although their eccentric minds
obscure the sacred writings far more than they illuminate them.
And if the situation is not remedied rapidly, such harm will very
quickly become more serious," etc. The first reaction of the Franciscan Fathers in Jerusalem was one of surprise; they thought
there had been some mistake. They were hardly ones to bother
themselves about the march of progress. How could they possibly be suspected of shaking the traditions of the Church when
they were such loyal guardians of the traditions of the Holy
Land. The letter had obviously been misdelivered and was meant
for their neighbors. Yet it was nevertheless addressed to the
Friars Minor without naming any one person; was there not some
hint of something going on in their house? It was known that P.
David Fleming, professor of Sant' Antonio, and much valued as
an advisor by the Holy Office, had seemed to some less safe in his
teaching of the Scriptures. He hastened to throw himself at the
feet of Leo XIII, who refused to let him divest himself of his office, treated him with kindness and no doubt advised him to be
more cautious.

A YEAR OF ANGUISH (1899)

Loisy's Return to the Limelight

The situation in France worsened because of the extraordinary actions of M. Loisy. M. Margival soon disappeared, but, to
make up for this, there appeared, apart from the articles signed
by Loisy, other studies signed A. Firmin, Isidore Desprès, Fran-

çois Jacobé, Jacques Simon, Jean Lataix, Jean Delarochelle, all flowing from his pen.[n]

There was thus a great bubbling of the spirit of criticism, a veritable swarming. My collaborators and I appeared to be caught in this massive upsurge. Even with the best intentions, I served no doubt only as a trace horse for this new team. How was one expected to realize this without following all these manifestations with closest attention and with a quite extraordinary gift of discernment? I can well understand how mistakes were made, and I never felt bitter toward those who, lacking the divine gift of probing loins and hearts, held me in suspicion. According to the *Bulletin de l'Institut catholique de Paris*, M. Loisy had submitted himself and declared his adherence to the encyclical *Providentissimus Deus*. If he could distance himself from it later, was my fidelity to it any more secure than his? There were, however, differences.

Loisy and Lagrange

First of all, it must have been obvious that I was seeking, in all good faith, solutions acceptable to the theologians. That is why my exegetical work has always been rejected by non-Catholics, less perhaps for its inferior quality than because it was tainted with an inevitable bias. M. Loisy appeared determined to carry his research through to the end, with no other regard than for truth. This attracted many minds to him. The accusation of illogicality or of deviating from a straight path was leveled against an attitude which is the only one possible for those of the Catholic faith: to have recourse to the Church in matters of revealed truth which is beyond the reach of logic. It was this difference between our ultimate criteria which prompted Canon Ulysse Chevalier to remark amusingly: "You ask what it is that distinguishes these two critics. One smacks of heresy, the other does not."

---

n. Between 1896 and 1900, Loisy was to publish under eight pseudonyms, which he himself listed: François Jacobé, Jean Delarochelle, Jean Lataix, and Jacques Simons in the *Revue d'Histoire et de Littérature religieuses;* Pierre Molandre in the *Revue des Religions;* A. Firmin, Isidore Desprès, Etienne Sharp in the *Revue de Clergé français.*

Our Respective Positions

But what if our positions were the same? This was not the case. M. Loisy obviously did not accept the inerrancy of the Scriptures. He employed freely the term "relative truth," which I have always avoided, and was not concerned with working out a theological explanation to justify his historical criticism. I have always remained loyal to the traditional belief, reaffirmed by Leo XIII—although not as revealed dogma—that the Scriptures assert nothing that is erroneous. But the Pope had accepted that, in scientific matters, the inspired writer is speaking according to appearances, so that what he writes must not be taken as a categorical statement of fact. I have never promoted the foolish theory that biblical history was merely an outward appearance of real history, nor have I been inept enough to confuse science and history. What I did say was that, while taking account of the individual character of the two disciplines, it was legitimate to put forward for those things normally falling under the heading of history something similar to what Leo XIII had said concerning science. By this I mean that one could distinguish in primitive history popular ways of expressing things, in some later texts the systematic use of amplifying expressions, and in the accounts of historical events themselves details of setting, popular or scholarly phrases, stylistic turns, in which the full logical value of a properly historical assertion or negation is lacking. Put another way, inspiration does not change the ways of writing connected with history; it does not increase the number of assertions; but when there is an historical assertion, it imparts divine authority to it. I had even believed I could detect in the encyclical *Providentissimus Deus* an invitation to make these distinctions. I was wrong, since His Holiness Benedict XV interpreted differently the words of his predecessor.[21] But this last point could be dealt with separately.[22] Thus, if my path converged with M. Loisy's in tending not to see historical facts everywhere in the Bible, nevertheless from several standpoints the principle was different, because I had been careful to let it be known in these cases that the facts were not shown or stated to be historical by the sacred author, so that there were no grounds for accusing him of error. This is what some people have called the distinction between formal and material error, but I have always refused to adopt these terms. When there is no assertion of a fact as real, one can mention it without committing any error, even material, as when I say hypothetically of two people in a parable that Peter killed Paul.

As for the Pentateuch, I did not admit any more than did M. Loisy that it issued entirely from Moses in its present form, although people were trying to delude us into believing that the linguistic forms themselves proved that it dated unaltered from the time of Moses. I was in favor of a certain authenticity of substance which I was never allowed to expound, and I have always fought strongly against the religious evolution imagined by Wellhausen, somewhat along the lines of my article of 1892 of Hosea. One cannot tell either where M. Loisy would have ended up in this matter.

The Break with Dogma

More seriously, he was moving imperceptibly toward the break with dogma which came into the open in 1902. On the point of the evolution of dogma he had at his side another team, Abbé Turmel[o] and the enigmatic Herzog and Dupin. We found ourselves therefore on the eve of a general attack against the teachings of the Church itself. But the spirited fight we put up against the earlier intrigues of its adversaries, and the vigorous polemics of the *Revue biblique* against Protestant exegesis, liberal or radical, were the best guarantees of our future conduct. I also make the point of saying that we have always enjoyed a great deal of sympathetic understanding, not only from lay people and clergy, but even more perhaps from the religious orders. It has often been claimed that the silence of the Dominicans, and of P. Weiss in particular in his overwhelmingly successful book on the dangers to the faith,[23] was the result of a decision inspired by a feeling of team spirit. But it is well known also that if such team spirit is upset, it can turn with increased violence against the

---

o. Joseph Turmel (1859–1943), professor at the seminary of Rennes from 1882 to 1892. Afterward he published, under fourteen pseudonyms, various articles and books on the history of dogma from a rationalist viewpoint. He was not unmasked definitively until 1930. His chief work is *Histoire des Dogmes* in six volumes, published between 1931 and 1936. The enigmatic Herzog and Dupin are pseudonyms of Turmel. Cf. E. Poulat, *Histoire, dogme et critique dans la crise moderniste*, Paris, 1962, pp. 648ff.

black sheep which it suspects of compromising the whole of the body corporate and its honor. The Benedictines wrote nothing against me, as far as I know. The Franciscans, so ardently opposed to our sanctuary of Saint-Etienne, did not enter the fight on biblical terrain. Only the Jesuit Fathers made any clear, I shall even say violent, declaration, as we have seen. And yet many of them wrote me letters whose cordial tones denoted more than just personal sympathy. They knew they could count on my discretion, and I have never invoked these silent expressions of favor against the clamor which was rising outside.

P. Méchineau returned to the fray on March 5, this time without naming me, but indicating clearly enough in *Etudes* that the letter of Leo XIII to the General of the Franciscans confirmed the public denunciation in which he had referred to me as a "deserter." His article was entitled "Un avertissement de Rome à quelques critiques et exégètes catholiques," and was followed by an embarrassed commentary by P. Brucher, trying to be courteous, while associating himself in part with the criticisms of his brother Jesuit.[24] But I shall not dwell on articles which anyone can consult.

Letter from P. Frühwirth

P. Frühwirth had naturally been struck by the letter addressed to the General of the Franciscans, and he did not wish to receive a similar one. Therefore he wrote to me at some length in Italian[25] to tell me to take a lesson from what was said to others lest we cause it to be said to us. There was no reproof for the past, but a very urgent warning for the future. The letter was dated January 28. On January 29 the Master General added a postscript, again in Italian: "I had already finished when, thinking again and more clearly about the serious situation in which our college finds itself at present, it seems it would be a good thing both for you and the college itself if, at a convenient time, you were to give up the office of regent, and leave it in the interim to P. Azzopardi. You may, if you think it appropriate, come to Rome at some time which suits you. I believe it even more necessary, and this I impose under obedience, that the manuscript of every article which you intend to print in the *Revue biblique* should be sent to Rome before publication, and I reserve for my-self the choice of revisers and the final decision to publish."[26]

There was here a piece of advice and an order. Both were of equal value to me, especially since only I was involved. As soon as the letter arrived in Jerusalem, I handed over the regency to P. Azzopardi, and from that day all my articles have been sent to Rome for examination. I asked the new regent if I should not suspend my classes; he asked me to continue them. As for going to Rome, there was no urgency. I informed the Master General by telegram of the change of regent. What happened in Rome between January 28 and 29? I never did find out. I can surmise that it was at that moment that my writings were denounced either to the Index or more likely to the Holy Office, if it had not already been done.[p] It is also possible that the Master General made his decision as the final result of his own reflections, which is indeed what he seemed to be saying. In any case, on January 16 the situation was as yet still calm, for I received a letter of that date signed by Cardinal Satolli, who was then Prefect of the Sacred Congregation of Studies: "Thank you for your letter[27] and for having been kind enough to send me the *Revue biblique*, which I shall always read with interest. I know already how this *Revue* has won for itself a place of honor, even in the eyes of Protestant scholars. The teaching, which you and your worthy collaborators have drawn from the pure and abundant springs of St. Thomas, is the best guarantee of your sound Catholic sense and of the justifiable freedom which you need to bring to your critical problems without ever undermining dogma. I also congratulate you on the good you are doing through your School in Jerusalem. I shall not fail, for as long as I can, to support and encourage those institutions whose aim is to enhance the name of Catholic scholarship. Your School could not be more opportune."

---

p. It is doubtless at this point that the Prefect of Propaganda referred the matter to the Holy Office, following the denunciation by the patriarch of Jerusalem. On March 16 Mgr. Duchesne wrote to Loisy: "For the time being it is the *Revue biblique* and the Jerusalem School which are asking the questions. I hear that the Holy Office, warned by the patriarch of Jerusalem, has taken the affair to heart. If that is true, there is no doubt about the outcome. . . ." (Loisy, *Mémoires*, Vol. 1, p. 515).

The Storm Unleashed

But now the storm was unleashed. P. Le Vigoureux, the prior, in France at the time, echoed to me the Master General's anxiety, adding: "They are not happy with the article on Tobit" and "Some priests are forbidding their penitents to read the *Revue*."[28] However, the Master General answered my expression of obedience on February 16 with a most kind letter explaining that he had been led into taking these measures by reasons which came from outside, but which were of sovereign importance. My two examiners were to be P. Thomas Esser in Rome and P. Reginald Walsh of Maynooth (Ireland). In accordance with the plan of preparing for the publication of my Genesis in the form of articles, I had sent in one article on the flood, but the Master General wrote to say that it was not the time to publish articles of that type. However, with an eye to the future, he asked me to send the Genesis manuscript to P. Walsh, which I did, although I did not hold out much hope. I admit to being less submissive, at least within myself, to one step which the Master General took without warning me in any way. He asked P. Séjourné to continue the organization of the *Revue* under my direction, but went on to appoint P. Sertillanges, then secretary of the *Revue Thomiste*, to be the official secretary of the *Revue biblique* as well. Five examiners were appointed for all articles (apart from mine, for which an arrangement had already been made): P. Sertillanges with P. Mousabré, P. Villard, P. Gardeil and P. Schwalm. P. Sertillanges was to "oversee the editing," "under the direction" of the French provincial.

I learned all this in a letter from P. Sertillanges of March 7, 1899. I did not think I could accept this situation, because it was an unreal one, and because the rights of the priory at Jerusalem ran the risk, albeit imperceptible, of being disregarded. I therefore wrote to P. Monpeurt, the French provincial, a closely reasoned letter about how I felt, but I did not send it. I know him well and I knew his benevolence toward us. It occurred to me that he had accepted the arrangement only to be of service to us, without any design or the least thought of standing in our way or of hindering the *Revue*. Already P. Séjourné was writing to me with the news that P. Sertillanges was functioning as secretary as little as possible. I let events take their course. The great tact of P. Monpeurt and the understanding between P. Sertillanges and P. Séjourné settled everything.

But what dark forebodings I had! From the Master General (in French) on April 23: "Keep calm, do your work, pray, resign yourself to everything that the Lord means to send you." On July 16 (from the hand of P. Beaudouin): "In spite of the painful situation your Mother is in, neither the journey to France nor the one to Rome is opportune at this time."

The Encyclical of Leo XIII

On September 8 appeared an encyclical letter from Leo XIII to the archbishops, bishops and clergy of France. In it he dealt with the various topics of instruction to be given to clergy. Among other things he wrote: "On the subject of the study of the Holy Scriptures, We once again call your attention, Venerable Brothers, to the teachings We gave in Our Encyclical *Providentissimus Deus*. . . . Under the specious pretext of depriving the opponents of the revealed word of the use of arguments which seemed irrefutable against the authenticity and truth of the Holy Books, some Catholic writers have thought it very clever to adopt these same arguments themselves. Pursuing these strange and perilous tactics, they have worked with their own hands to breach the walls of the city which it was their mission to defend, etc."[29]

There was a certain similarity between these expressions and those I had used to describe the liberal school[30] in the article so fiercely criticized, a school from which I had been very careful to separate myself by adopting a middle path which avoided extremes. If one asks whom the Pope had in view, the answer is assuredly primarily Loisy with his associates Firmin, Desprès, Simon, Jacobé, Lataix, Delarochelle,[31] not to mention M. Margival, nor the students whom so many teachers could not fail to corrupt and lure away. I have no evidence to suppose that the Master General was given any indication, even indirectly, that we were one of the targets. However, he now insisted that I submit to him "absolutely everything" which I meant to have printed—articles, reports, reviews and so on. But he added, shortly after the papal letter: "Things are becoming a little calmer now, and we must not jeopardize the results we have already obtained." He feared that I might let myself be enticed into personal disputes. But I was, above all, anxious to preserve the scientific nature of the *Revue* without engaging in idle gossip. Moreover I did not attach great importance to the campaign led by M. Mémain, M. Maignen and M. Dessailly, and I have forgotten exactly when they wrote.

The Storm Abates

Good P. Cormier[q] wrote to me at the end of the year (December 8, 1899): "I am confident that your humble and obedient disposition toward the zealous work for the defense of the Holy Scriptures and the plan of redemption with which they are so profoundly linked is blessed by God. I have heard little talk about these matters lately. Yet there are certain deviations which I have heard attributed to others less well advised than you," etc. These introductory remarks were surely meant as a subtle exordium to an indirect monition, but it remained a fact that I had not lost my superior's confidence and, more than that, they were busily defending not a set of reasonably clear-cut propositions, but at least the legitimacy of the method used till now, with more or less success.

Before I leave the year 1899, I have one or two things to say about the article on Tobit which caused such a rumpus.[32] The previous year I met, at the house which served as friary in the rue du Bac, M. Vigoureux and the Abbé Le Camus. After exchanging a few words, M. Vigoureux mentioned an article on Tobit by his friend M. Cosquin. He sketched the broad outlines of the

---

q. Henri-Hyachinthe-M. Cormier (1832–1916) was then procurator general of the Order of Preachers. A man of great quality and supernatural prudence, he spent his long life in administrative positions of increasing prestige: secretary of Rev. P. Jandel, frequently prior and provincial, Assistant to Rev. P. Frühwirth in 1891, then Procurator General in 1896, he was to become in 1904 the seventy-sixth Master General of the Order, which he governed until the year of his death. It was in this last function that he had an important role to play in the life of P. Lagrange. The numerous allusions which P. Lagrange will make to the fact in the following pages are sufficient testimony to the filial confidence and veneration he felt for this wise, understanding and energetic Father, whose memory is preserved in an odor of sanctity by his religious family.

work for me. As I wished to rely on his authority, I asked him, since he was putting M. Cosquin forward, to use his authority also with the public. To this effect, a note from the editorial office was drawn up by M. Vigoureux and M. Cosquin, approved also by M. Captier, Superior General of Saint-Sulpice. The article itself was accepted without difficulty by P. Sertillanges. Therefore, in all this, I bore only a minimum of the responsibility.

The study of Ecclesiasticus by P. Condamin[33] was also fairly severely criticized. But he had the approval of the Jesuit censors. During this year, the only article I published was *Le Sinaï biblique*, approved in person by the Master General, and *Deux chants de guerre* taken from the Pentateuch.[34] The exploration of Gezer had greatly interested us and we recorded the moment when Mr. Macalister began his excavation with the discovery of the avenue of stelai.[35]

POSITIONS (1900)

Archaeological Congress in Rome

I was surprised and delighted by a letter I received at the beginning of April, dated March 29, from the Master General. He said: "The committee of the Archaeological Congress in Rome invites you to take part in its work. I am sending you the invitation which reached me only yesterday evening, and I authorize you to accept it." Thus the reasons which had led the Master General to prevent my going to Rome and to France no longer existed. He had not wasted a single day in sending me the "very late" invitation from the Congress Committee. Now I had no time to lose either, and I left on April 7, that is, as soon as I received the letter. In Rome it was not difficult to understand why this sudden change had come about. Cardinal Mazzella had died on March 26. Rightly or wrongly, it was widely assumed that it was he who pushed Leo XIII into taking severe measures. Even in 1895, Mgr. d'Hulst had heard that this was so.[36] Did he have predominating influence over the great Pope, who was such a master of his own mind? I would never dare to say so, but it is a fact that in Rome all those who were not extreme reactionaries were breathing more freely.

What was the point of this Congress? The Congress of Orientalists had been held in Rome the year before, without the Holy See's approval having been sought. The Master General had forbidden me not only to attend, but even to mention it in the *Revue biblique*. Perhaps Leo XIII wanted to show in principle that he was not at all an enemy of these scholarly assemblies. But what attracted me most to Rome was not the Congress at all, since my presence was of no special use to them; it was my project for a complete commentary on Holy Scripture, comprising various biblical studies, a project of which I had in fact just completed the basic copy (March 25, 1900). As always, I was going about things too openly, but my trusting simplicity also proved that I was not aware of any strong disapproval of our methods by the Pope.

The Project for Bible Studies

Nevertheless I realized that this enterprise was not the sort of thing to win us back the favor of the Society of Jesus, especially of the German Jesuits. In fact, either because they could not hope in Germany for a ready sale, owing to the abundance of exegetical literature, even Catholic, or because they yielded to the instinct which was then allowing Germans to gain ground in France. P. Cornely, P. Knabenbauer, P. de Hummelauer and "other priests of the Society" had founded a "Cursus" in Latin which was greeted with much success. I thought therefore that I had a duty to pay a tribute to the "monumental Cursus" and express the hope that our work would not duplicate theirs. Moreover, instead of being strictly exclusive, ours was open to "all people of good will." The first to give it a warm welcome was P. Albert Condamin, S.J., who, as is known, played a most distinguished part in it.

The program, as may well be imagined, was carefully studied by all Council of the Order. The Master General thought that he ought to consult the Prefect of the Sacred Congregation of the Index, who was then Cardinal Steinhüber, S.J. He was able to write to me on May 24: "Your program, or project as you call it, is approved by His Eminence the Cardinal Prefect and by the

Rev. Father Secretary of the Index[37] and may in consequence be printed as it stands." It appeared in the *Revue* in July.[r]

For a while, the Master General thought we would be obliged to publish the Vulgate text in the commentary. It was in Germany that the custom of omitting it had taken hold, and since the text to be translated was to be the original, the only role for the Vulgate would have been as a cross-reference. One more column would have further complicated an already loaded typography quite unnecessarily, since the Latin version is readily to hand. But if the project did not raise too much difficulty, its execution was to be surrounded by every precaution. I had abandoned the idea of starting with Genesis. Many Catholics, despite the much respected authority of P. Brucker, could not conceive of a book of the Bible being composed of pre-existing documents. But the difficulty was particularly great, if not for Genesis, at least for the Pentateuch as a whole, because of the Mosaic authenticity, and Genesis seemed to be the cause of the whole problem, despite what P. Brucker thought. I had therefore chosen the Book of Judges, for which the admission of sources seemed less pregnant with consequences, and the Master General appointed a first examiner for me. The examination was prolonged, but the work was finally able to appear in 1902.

Attitudes Toward Loisy

While I was thus pressing on, prejudice was still very strong and on June 16, 1900, the Father General wrote: "Since you left Rome, I have had new light thrown on the risk you were running; the difficulties have not gone away." On July 18: "While not serious, the situation still demands a certain prudence. I have taken my precautions; you must now have a better understanding of the usefulness of the measures which I took against constantly renewed attacks." I even had to refrain from replying. It was as though the Master General feared my fighting temper; in fact, all

---

r. P. Lagrange said among other things: "We need a Catholic commentary, which is based on a good translation of the *originals*, following a *critical* text carefully established, and with the special application of *literary criticism* . . . with which the Protestants are most occupied and which is at the bottom of almost all the problems discussed in our time" (*R.B.*, 1900, pp. 422 and 419; the italics are ours).

things considered, I do not think I sent more than a total of ten lines, in answer to a hundred pages which provoked me.

Mgr. Batiffol moreover was experiencing the same anxiety (June 2, 1900): "We must keep a weather eye open for squalls. People here are much exercised by Loisy's articles on revelation, and the Jesuits are joining the fray.[s] On this point I agree with them, for all this philosophy of religion will end up only by negating what little progress our realism could achieve. You are suspected of being in the same brotherhood as Loisy; take good care!" I cannot count the people who spoke to me in similar terms. I surely did yield too much to a certain sentiment of justice and honor. I shrank from making a fuss, of accentuating the differences between Loisy and myself, which were clear enough for those who could read, and from denouncing him as a "deserter," as long as he had not taken the one step to which his whole conduct was leading him. From Jerusalem it was not possible to follow closely the movement. Rather than embark upon a controversial dispute in which honesty would have obliged us to disengage ourselves also from certain too routine opinions, once having laid down the principles, we preferred to keep to the study of positive findings. Having stopped teaching the New Testament, from that time on I devoted myself entirely to the Old.[38] The main reason for this was, above all, its usefulness for the *Revue*. P. Rose had taken on the study of the Gospels, and his attachment to our work was the guarantee of a distinguished collaboration. He never became a professor at Saint-Étienne. He had been sent to us as a student by Rev. P. Nespoulous, French provincial, and had left us in 1895. But on being made professor at Fribourg, he had remained one of our family. His studies of the Gospels, which attracted considerable attention, culminated in a book with which he hoped to combat in an effective way liberal Protestant exegesis. His talent was fully revealed in 1899 and 1900.

---

s. The reference is to a series of six articles published by Loisy under the pseudonym of "Firmin" in the *Revue du Clergé Français* from December 1898 to October 1900. The series was interrupted by a condemnation from Cardinal Richard on October 23, 1900, according to a report by P. Brucker (cf. Loisy, *Mémoires*, Vol I, pp. 563 ff). There is an analysis of the articles of Firmin-Loisy by E. Poulat, *op. cit.*, pp. 74 to 88.

Consecration of St. Etienne

I come back to our chronicle. I was unable to return to Jerusalem for the consecration of the basilica (May 15). P. le Vigoureux turned the celebration into a splendid occasion. Mgr. Duval, for a long time apostolic prefect to our Dominican mission in Mosul, and the then delegate of the Holy See to Syria, graciously agreed to preside over the ceremony. Great joy filled the heart of one who had accomplished the restoration of a sanctuary raised in a previous age by an empress. He had not only built the walls of the basilica; he had furnished it with everything necessary to the right ordering of the liturgy: stalls, an organ installed by its Salzburg makers, altars supplied with candelabra, and an admirably equipped sacristy. His zeal did not stop there. He built the wing of the priory adjoining the church, and took such care as to provide spacious cells for the professors of the School so that they should have their special libraries, drawing tables, studios for photographic and epigraphical work. Each cell had its prie-dieu with a bronze crucifix, all in simple conformity with monastic poverty. Those who will live in the priory and pray in the basilica would indeed be ungrateful if they did not reverently preserve the memory of the second founder of the priory.

A LULL (1901)

A fairly calm year. While the Book of Judges was being examined, I was busy with semitic religions—faithfully keeping to the comparative method—for a knowledge of these seemed to me necessary to the understanding of the Old Testament. It was P. Hummelauer who resolutely took on the question of the Pentateuch. His ideas had changed completely since, in the Genesis commentary, he had singled out an Adamic document, another from the time of Noah and so on. Now, he made no bones about stating that the corpus of laws in Deuteronomy (XII, 1—XXVI, 15) came not from Moses, but from Samuel; the Pentateuch was the work of several centuries. I felt able to say: "The proposition is a new one; it will astonish the superficial observer who insists on the one sacrosanct unit; it will make the critics smile."[39]

Das Wesen des Christenthums

The whole burning controversy between Catholics and liberal Protestants was shifted to the field of Christian origins by M. von Harnack's celebrated book, *Das Wesen des Christenthums*. I reported on it at some length,[40] and was taken to task for this by *Civiltà cattolica*.[41] The article was not signed which was the custom in that periodical, but I knew who was behind it.[42] P. Léopold Fonck now came on to the stage. He adopted as his own[t] the polemic against P. Rose conducted by P. Fontaine, S.J.[u] in his book *Les infiltrations protestantes et la démonstration évangélique de la divinité de N.S.J.C.* M. Salvatore Minocchi's[v] new periodical, founded in Rome with the title *Studi Religiosi*, was very badly received by *Civiltà*.[43] It was not his intentions which were being called in doubt, nor his Catholic spirit. It was suggested that he and his group were associated with the new *Società cattolica per gli studi scientifici*, presided over by Father, now Cardinal Ehrle, S.J.: "Il presidente etc etc."[w] Was it not enough then simply to fly the Catholic flag? It was certainly a great misfortune that P. Rose and M. Minocchi should have left the Church. Their defection was exploited and used against us. But could we Christians allow ourselves to cast doubts upon intentions which *Civiltà* itself held as beyond reproach, and was there no other way of holding on to these distinguished scholars than to offer them the choice between resignation or submission to individual guidance? We wish it to be said of P. Rose that, although he did resign, without any fuss, he never wrote to my knowledge one single line against the Church his mother, nor Jesus Christ whom he desired to serve with all the strength of his mind and will.

Such was not at that time the attitude of M. Loisy. Thus,

---

t. Léopold Fonck (1865–1930), an Austrian Jesuit, professor of Holy Scripture at the University of Innsbruck in 1901, then at the Gregorian University in Rome. In 1909 he founded the Pontifical Biblical Institute. He was one of P. Lagrange's principal adversaries, as will later be seen.

u. Julien Fontaine (1839–1917), a French Jesuit, fought by means of several writings against modernist "infiltrations."

v. Salvatore Minocchi (1869–1943), an Italian priest, director of *Studi religiosi* (1901–1907); an exegete of modernist leanings, he returned to the lay state in 1908 and married in 1911.

w. Translation of the text quoted: "The president, P. Ehrle, might also have some wise advice and practical information to convey to the new group."

when he allowed himself a few insinuating remarks about a kind of temporary dissimulation on the part of the *Revue biblique*,[44] I felt I ought to state that it was "in no way our intention to follow in his footsteps later on, even if circumstances were to allow it." We have often been accused by the Loisystes of separating ourselves from him as a precaution. There was much more substance to the accusation of those who complained that we had waited so long in order to underline "the reckless and over-assertive attitude which sometimes marked M. Loisy's conjectures."[45] On this occasion we had actually said it even though with much consideration and discretion.

Master of Theology

At the end of his second three years, P. Vigoureux had accepted the office of prior in Lille. P. Séjourné was elected on July 2 and the election confirmed. After a fortnight's work in Madaba (July 15 to August 2), I left with P. Vincent for France on August 6. I was in Rome long enough only to receive from P. Frühwirth the ring of master of theology (September 29), after which the Master General instructed me to take over as regent again. I saw my mother for the last time in September at Roybon. On Christmas Day, P. Meunier, that excellent man, died suddenly at the convent of the Order of St. Clare, where he had been preaching.[x]

Loyson's Visit

I suppose I should add that in May, M. Hyacinthe Loyson[y] came to the priory to see me. I did not think I had to repay his visit, a thing moreover which we rarely do for the numerous people who come to us from all over the world. Yet in order not to offend his soul, for whom we have prayed so much, I sent him my card. His insistence forced me to write to him that I could see no opportunity for us to meet. I was only too convinced of my

---

x. One of the Dominican fathers who helped in founding the monastery of Saint-Etienne.

y. Hyacinthe Loyson (1827–1912), a priest in 1851, St. Sulpice (1851), novice of the Dominicans for five months (1859), Carmelite friar (1859), preacher for Advent at Notre Dame (1864), who broke with the Church in 1869; from 1873 to 1874 the curate of an "Old Catholic" parish in Geneva, in 1879 he founded the "Gallican Catholic Church" which was later to attach itself to the Old Catholic Archbishopric of Utrecht. He followed the modernist movement very closely, but took no part in it at all.

powerlessness to bring round this warped mind which was always ready to give plain answers. He replied: "Would it be true to say, as has indeed often been said, that the spirit of intolerance is, in Jerusalem at least, almost exclusively the prerogative of the Latin Church?" And therewith he assured me of his "sense of esteem and participation in liberal science, in religious faith and in fraternal charity."[46] Alas!

FAMILY PICTURES (1902)

A year of difficulties, of painful disturbances. *Foris pugnae, intus timores.*

P. Vincent Is Moved to Rome

On March 20 I received in Jerusalem a letter from the Master General, by kindness of P. Desqueyrous, asking me to make the necessary arrangements for P. Vincent to go to Rome, and to prepare himself on the assumption that he was not to return to Jerusalem. This blow, far more formidable for us than the attacks from outside, sorely distressed me. Once again I made a retreat. It was quite obvious that our chief support, the reason why we drew so many students, was our closeness to the very soil and associations of the Holy Land. P. Vincent's talent for picking out the smallest architectural details, his scrupulous insistence on sketching them exactly as they were—which was such a rare scruple among draughtsmen who were perhaps more easy to please—this gift allied to his ability to interpret documents, to a sure sense of history and philology, all these qualities made him the lynchpin to the future of the School, much more indispensable than myself. P. Séjourné had been given back to us, but as prior, and in Paris had reimmersed himself in the practice of ministry, and was booked to preach for several Lents to come. He was in fact in France now, and it fell to me to carry out an order which broke my heart. Bent on total obedience, my only thought was to send P. Vincent off to his unknown destination, which I suspected might be Fribourg. P. Azzopardi, who as former regent of the college had a contribution to make, interpreted the situation as I did. But being more used to administrative practice, better versed in canon law and casuistry, he pointed out to me that nobody had spoken in terms of catching the first available boat, merely of making necessary arrangements. The most necessary arrangement was to submit our difficulties to the Master General himself. It was easy for me to yield to this advice. The Master General was kind enough to reply that he understood our distress. But the Sacred Congregation of Propaganda was offering P. Vincent the job of reorganizing and directing its museum. This was both an advantage and an honor for the Order. "As for the special skills involved in cartography and in textual commentary, would it be impossible to find another member of the Order who, if he devoted himself to this study, could soon fill the gap left by P. Vincent?" While upholding his decision, the Master General in fact authorized P. Vincent to remain in Jerusalem until the end of the academic year.

What happened? It seems that the Propaganda itself cancelled its plan. It was anxious to hold on to the Borgia manuscripts which had been made over to it. But the Pope preferred, quite naturally, that they should be added to the Vatican Library. P. Esser, who had generously sided with us in this affair, wrote to me on May 4: "*Victoria! Victoria!* Rejoice and be glad, Reverend and dear Father. Our case is won! All talk of that arrangement has ceased." This was also what the Master General wrote to tell me on May 3, in veiled terms. His letter reached me on May 9, unusually quickly. That evening I did indeed rejoice: but the next day, May 10, I lost my mother. The tender compassion which the Master General showed toward me at that time was consolation in my immense grief.

Study and Work

When I had completed *Etudes sur les religions sémitiques*, I would have happily dedicated them to P. Le Vigoureux, but with his customary modesty he was grateful enough for the intention alone. It had been my intention that the semitic religions should serve only as a contrast to the development of the worship of God in Israel. But I had become totally absorbed in the work and gave myself up to it wholeheartedly. P. Scheil, whose attitude toward us was always very brotherly, and whose collaboration was such a privilege for the *Revue*, suggested to Macridy Bey[z] that he offer his fine discoveries at Bostan'es Sheik, near ancient Sidon, to us for publication.

We set off, P. Vincent and I, to talk to Macridy Bey in Baalbek. Afterward we split up at Rayak, he going back to Jerusalem and I to Damascus, then on to France. Hardly had I arrived in Paris than I was called to my sister who was dying. I had the profound consolation but also the pain of ministering to her spiritually on her deathbed.

Lectures in Toulouse

It was after this double bereavement in a single year that I had to give the lectures in Toulouse which I had undertaken with the express permission of the Master General. They were written in October at the priory in Toulouse. I can never prepare myself enough for speaking. I intended to keep to the oral exposition which I had prepared, although it was actually a reading. Mgr. Batiffol was keen for my lectures to be a success, but did not want there to be any trouble. He had chosen a room which could not hold any more than two hundred people; ladies were excluded except with special authorization, which was not given to more than a dozen, a limit fixed in advance in order to avoid ruffling people's susceptibilities. However, there was quite a fuss. Complaints were made to the archbishop about the novelty of the doctrine. Mgr. Germain came to shield me by showing himself sympathetic. Present at the fifth lecture, he took it on himself to quiet the grumblers, whose identity I can leave to the vindictive imagination of the reader.

On the very evening of the sixth lecture, November 11, I took the train to Marseilles where I took ship immediately. Cholera was rife in Palestine, especially in Jaffa, and I was in a hurry to return to my desk. Jerusalem was still untouched, and one could not travel there from Jaffa without spending ten days in quarantine at Bittir, a doubly lamentable stipulation.

---

z. Archaeologist to the Ottoman government.

The Letter *Vigilantiae*

Therefore I left the ship at Beirut, but I did not know how to get to Jerusalem. What passes today for child's play was then well nigh impossible in the rainy season. Mgr. Duval most kindly offered me hospitality in Beirut. He showed me the letter *Vigilantiae* which I had not had time to read in Toulouse. I was struck by the new tone of the Pope's words. To say that his thinking had changed would be to fail to understand the strength of that thinking, revealed in its unwavering intensity by his long pontificate. But this is a different matter. In his letter to the French clergy, the Pope had pointed out the danger.[b] This danger had not evaporated. On the contrary, he made further mention of it, and uttered the same reproof against anyone who might infringe the rules set up by him. But now he put forward the cure for the disease. He was going to direct the defense of the Scriptures by setting up a commission for biblical studies, and he wanted this defense to be critical: "Their function will be to direct all their attention and their efforts in such a way that the divine writings everywhere receive from our exegetes even that more critical interpretation which our age demands, *ut divina eloquia et exquisitiorem illam, quam tempora postulant, tractationem passim apud nostros inveniant.* . . . First, having observed very attentively the direction which studies are taking, they will have to think that nothing of what the moderns have with their ingenuity discovered is outside the scope of their work. On the contrary, if one day they find something useful to biblical exegesis, they must take care to seize it without delay and pass it through their writings into common usage. They will thus have to cultivate actively the study of philology and its attendant sciences, and foster their continuous progress. Since, in fact, it is through these sciences that attacks against the Holy Scriptures are generally made, it is also in them that we must seek our weapons, so that there may be no inequality in the struggle between truth and falsehood," etc.

What a contrast with the attitude of the unyielding conservatives: "What is the good of reading the modern critics who can

---

b. Cf. *supra.*

only lead us into error? The Fathers have said all there is to say!"

Thus the Holy Father was opening up a royal road; he was forcing action, and consequently progress, without failing to point out what politicians call the peril from the left: "Let the science of criticism, assuredly useful for a perfect understanding of the sacred writers, become the object of study for Catholics; they have our fullest approval. Let them perfect themselves in this science, availing themselves if need be of the works of heterodox writers. We shall not stand in the way. But let them take care to recognize, as they come into frequent contact with such writers, the foolhardiness of their judgments,"[47] etc. The letter was dated October 30. There was not a moment to lose. In Beirut I rapidly drafted a word or two of thanksgiving which was to be printed in the *Revue* in January after the papal letter. Then, having at last found a small boat about to sail for Haifa, I set out for Jerusalem.

At the Biblical School
From Haifa I was able to reach Nazareth without too much trouble. An American with no experience of the area, and a young Frenchman who, I later discovered, was a deserter, asked me to take them along. In Nazareth we found horses with great difficulty, but only to take us as far as Nablus. From Nablus with fresh beasts we could be led only as far as the Lubban where the sanitary cordon passed. I telegraphed all this to Jerusalem from Jenin. At the Lubban our muleteers went off, leaving us to negotiate with the health officials. What a joy it was to see P. Savignac coming down the hill with some horses! "P. Vincent is a little run down," he said. It was not until I arrived in Jerusalem on December 6 that I learnt of P. Vincent's fall in the street on November 5 and of his being taken to Sainte-Anne. They had thought he was dying and given him conditional extreme unction. It was no more than a case of cerebral anemia brought on by overwork. But he needed a long period of rest.

Already the School was gaining new strength. In the spring of that year, P. Jaussen and P. Savignac had made a fine journey to Sinai, returning via Petra. Their publication of the new inscriptions at Petra was the start of a collaboration rich in hazardous explorations and in epigraphical discoveries; we began to call them in Arab fashion "the sons of the road." P. Abel[c] was beginning to learn about topography, geography and the literature of the Byzantine Empire. It was already possible to predict what the future held for P. Paul Dhorme,[d] who had come out in December 1900. The novices from the French province had arrived, and those from the province of Lyons had returned from America. In Paris, P. Raymond Louis took on the job of secretary of the *Revue*. As P. Genocchi wrote (October 14, 1902): "It is still possible to have storms, even on a fine day. That may well be so; but at this moment the sky is beautiful and cloudless."

THE BIBLICAL COMMISSION (1903)

After a long absence and such a difficult return journey, I desired to spend the winter in quiet study. On Sunday, February 1, as I came out of vespers, I received a telegram calling me to Rome. P. Séjourné had arranged his departure for the following day with a view of his Lenten sermons; my small bundle was ready in a moment, and we set off together. P. Vincent had

---

c. Felix M. Abel (December 29, 1878–March 24, 1953), a Dominican, had come in his youth to be a novice at Saint-Etienne and consecrated his life to the Biblical School first as student, then as professor. A man of vast erudition and very sure feelings for criticism, he acquired unsurpassed mastery of the Greek sources, texts and inscriptions about ancient Palestine, its history and topography. He worked with P. Vincent on the historical part of his books on Christian Jerusalem, Bethlehem, Hebron, and Emmaus, and he published other works also, notably *Grammaire du Grec biblique* (1927), a commentary on the Book of Maccabees (1949), *Géographie de la Palestine* in two volumes (1933 and 1938), and *Histoire de la Palestine depuis la conquête d'Alexandre*, in two volumes (1952).

d. Edouard Paul Shorme (1881–1966), student then professor at the Biblical School from 1900 to 1931, was a specialist in Oriental languages and Old Testament exegesis. He published in that period, apart from numerous articles in the *Revue biblique*, a *Choix de textes religieux assyro-babyloniens* (1907) *La Religion assyro-babylonienne* (1910), a commentary on the Books of Samuel (1910) and a commentary on the Book of Job (1926). He left the Church in 1931, and taught at the Hautes Etudes, then at the Sorbonne, and finally at the Collège de France. His main publications in this second period were *La Poésie biblique* (1931), *La Religion des Hébreux nomades* (1937), *La Littérature babylonienne et assyrienne* (1937), *Les Religions de Babylonie et d'Assyrie* (1945), and *Présentation de Saint Paul* (1965). From 1956 to 1959 he was editor-in-chief of an annotated translation of the Bible for *La Pleiade*, in two volumes. He was reconciled to the Church before his death.

shown himself so averse to coming with us that Fr. Prior did not want to compel him. But as we were held up for a day in Jaffa by the boat's delay, he sent word for him to join us, and we took him away with us.

L'Evangile et l'Eglise

Just a few days before this sudden departure, we had received *L'Evangile et l'Eglise*, the first of M. Loisy's little red books. After the condemnation by the cardinal of Paris of an article by Firmin,[48] he had abandoned his interest in apologetics. He wrote of himself:[49] "Compelled, as it were, to take refuge in the field of scholarship, he intends to stay there, not out of indifference to theological questions and the interests of the Church of which he is proud to be a member, but because the situation in which certain persons have tried to place him in the eyes of the Catholic public opinion demands such reserve of him." Unfortunately, after Harnack's book *Das Wesen des Christenthums*, he abandoned his reserve and this time presented himself in his true colors, without his cohort of pseudonyms, and with his visor raised. M. Houtin has expressed it well: "He felt even more in a hurry to intervene because he was keeping his own synthesis of Christianity in readiness and, as it were, in his top drawer. To the essays he had prepared on Jesus and the Kingdom of heaven, the Church, Christian dogma, and Catholic worship, he added introductory statements setting them up in opposition to Harnack's system."[50] It was therefore at the same time the refutation of Harnack's system and the exposition of a new system. I took the little book from my pocket and had plenty of time to read it during the five days of quarantine which we spent at anchor off Alexandria. There could be no mistake. M. Loisy did indeed refuse, for excellent reasons, to recognize the Christ of the Gospels in the watered-down Christ of the Protestants, dressed as he was in the garb of liberal Protestantism. He also upheld the notion of "Church" against corrosive individualism. But in his view the Church had not been founded by Jesus, and Jesus had become God only by a transformation of the primitive faith. This faith had hailed Jesus at first only as the Christ, a quality which derived from the belief in his resurrection, and in its turn this belief was founded upon the apparitions of a ghost. With this, everything was clear, and I promised myself to tell the readers of the *Revue Biblique* just as soon as I had the opportunity. This was my first concern. Since in Rome I was less far away from Paris, there was time for a twenty-page review to appear in the April edition.[51]

Cardinal Rampolla

We came therefore to Rome, and it was not without anxiety that I asked the Master General the reason for this pressing and formal summons. He looked contented and said with a smile: "Go and see His Eminence Cardinal Rampolla; it is he who asked you to come."

I had never been presented to the illustrious cardinal secretary of state, Leo XIII's right-hand man. I thought his time too precious for me to rob him of even a couple of minutes of it. I had seen only the cardinal vicar, His Eminence Cardinal Parocchi, with a few attendants, and had admired the simplicity of his audiences. Without seeking permission in advance, one presented oneself in the evening at the vicariate, just when he was coming back from his walk. One had one's card presented, and one was received in one's turn. The cardinal took great interest in our studies. He had even said, at the installation of Mgr. Duval, that the Dominicans had neglected Holy Scripture for a long while, but that they had regained their position through the foundation of the Jerusalem Biblical School. This ease of approach and indulgent manner which is found in Rome with prelates in the most elevated positions has always touched me greatly. It is a tangible mark of the maternal feeling of our Mistress and Mother, the Church. But the cardinal secretary of state, at the very summit of the Vatican, seemed to inhabit an inaccessible world.

The *Revue Biblique* and the Biblical Commission

He nonetheless received me just as graciously, and told me straight out that the Holy Father, having announced in *Vigilantiae* that the Commission would have a periodical as its mouthpiece, was turning his eyes now to the *Revue Biblique*. There followed yet another mark of kindness which touched me even more deeply, as I never expected so much gracious condescension: the Pope, who could as a matter of course have issued a command, was not even expressing his firm desire. He was deigning to treat with us on equal terms, lest he should encroach, be it ever so little, upon what could have been taken as a privilege vested in the Order of Saint Dominic or in the priory of Saint-Etienne. He was certainly offering us a great honor, but we were at full liberty to reply as we wished.

Despite these flattering overtures, which are still today the object of so many attacks and even accusations, I did not dare at first to believe in such honor, nor secretly taste such joy. I asked the cardinal if I might speak to him with filial openness, and when he smiled, I was bold enough to suggest that people were perhaps not too happy with us and wanted us in Rome the better to supervise and keep a tight reign on us. "You do indeed mis-apprehend the mind of Leo XIII," said His Eminence, equally astonished now by my fears. "His intention is, on the contrary, to show that it is possible to write in Rome, under his gaze, in full scholarly freedom, without, of course, interfering with dogma."

At that point my heart overflowed with joy and tears came to my eyes.

But that was not all. The Pope had resolved to found in Rome a Biblical Institute, whose doors would be wide open to the skills of every Order, calling upon seculars and regulars alike, and I was to have my place there, while remaining the director of the *Revue*.

When I returned to the mother house, I was able to gauge the joy caused by my nomination as consultor to the Biblical Commission. On November 30 of the previous year, there had appeared a first list of consultors in which my name did not ap-pear. Fr. David Fleming, appointed secretary with P. Vigo-ureux, recounted how the Pope had wanted to extend the list, and there had been a skirmish—he called it a battle—over my name. With this name accepted, it was a victory for moderate progressive exegesis, or as Dom Amelli put it so well: "del pro-gresso senza rottura."ᵉ On January 26 my nomination was com-municated to the Master General. The letter he sent me immediately, and which came back later from Jerusalem, gives some idea of his satisfaction:⁵² "I am not able to express in words

e. Translation: "for uninterrupted progress."

the joy that filled my heart from the moment that I received the folded page from His Eminence, the Cardinal Secretary of State, in which it was announced to us your nomination as a member of the cardinals' Commission for Biblical Studies. The contentment that I feel about it is so much the greater since the result was thought so much the less possible after the crisis suffered by you and by me some years ago. . . ."[53]

What had happened? I never discovered; with the Roman congregations, discretion is absolute. I have always imagined that Mgr. Piavi's letter had been forwarded by Propaganda to the Holy Office. Surely not all of my writings, already numerous, were examined. But the criticized article on the *Sources du Pentateuque* must have been subjected to a severe examination. Of this I can be certain—that Mgr. Piavi was encouraged not to worry about it. Would Propaganda have taken this decision on its own? If, therefore, the Holy Office decided that there were no grounds for condemnation, I had come unscathed through a dreadful test and the Holy Father's choice could indeed fall upon the *Revue Biblique*.

On learning that the disease was spreading, Leo XIII was convinced that it could not be stopped by adhering to the usual range of solutions offered by Catholic exegesis. There had to be movement forward; we had to make use of weapons more effective in defending the walls of the city, even though they might have been torn from the hands of the enemy. The choice of the *Revue Biblique* as the official organ of the Commission was sufficient evidence that its methods could at least be put to useful purpose, apart from proceeding with greater caution. What is more, I received not a single reproach for the past. Cardinal Sartolli only asked, with regard to the dignity of the Holy See, for *"qualche cosa di più nobile."*[f]

Hesitation and Perplexity

I admit this was what frightened me. To be noble would surely demand a diplomatic courtesy toward contributors who were more illustrious than competent. What would be the position of the *Revue Biblique* relative to the Commission? What

---

f. Translation: "something more noble."

would be the complexion of the Commission itself? This second point was beyond my competence to answer, but it dominated the first point, and it was not long before I realized that there was still much that was uncertain about the whole arrangement.

It will be asked how it was that my opinion counted for anything in a matter which should have been settled between the Holy See and the Master General of the Dominicans. This was yet another mark of the very moving regard which those who could give orders had for a situation and the people involved in it. I had never allowed my name to appear as director of the *Revue*. But it was known that I had founded it; I was to carry on as its director. Above all, I represented the interests of Saint-Etienne which nobody wanted to sacrifice to a new arrangement. But how were these interests to be safeguarded?

It was nevertheless impossible to refuse what the Pope was offering. I considered refusing it only hypothetically in order to convince myself that to do so would be disastrous to our work. I wrote down some rough notes which chance has preserved: "If we refuse everything a periodical will be founded with other personnel and, if it does not succeed, at least the *Revue Biblique* will fall out of favor. If a School is started without us, we shall become competitors, the shop opposite, the grit in their eye. The standing of Saint-Etienne as a house may seem less at risk; in fact, it would be compromised. It would be tantamount to turning our back on the appeal and the confidence of the Holy See, on a real duty, for the sake of a narrow, perhaps blind, attachment, to the original nature of our work."

Passing to the other extreme, I did wonder if we should not resign ourselves to a total transformation. Would we still have students when the Pope had established a biblical school in Rome? They would surely come no more except to see the country, which can be done in a year, and with a reduced staff. The most qualified of our teaching body would be moved to Rome, and Jerusalem would be no more than the "permanent mission" desired by Abbé Thomas. But the Holy Father had not made this point clear. It would hardly be discreet, even less would it fit in with the traditions of our Order, to offer him services in a way which would be tantamount to soliciting jobs. Otherwise it would have been tempting to try out that new combination. I shall copy word for word what I wrote in February 1903, because it is precisely what the Jesuit Fathers carried out: *"Pro domo.* If the spirit of the *Revue Biblique* and the method of the Jerusalem School appear to the Holy See capable of rendering service, it would be an easy matter to move the theoretical section of the Biblical School to Rome with the *Revue.* Three or four professorships would be established at Easter. The School at Jerusalem would be retained chiefly as a School for practical studies. Having completed his course in Rome, the student would go to spend a year in Jerusalem to do geography, topography and archaeology *in situ,* and acquaint himself with the customs and languages of the country. The Order, having exhausted its own resources, would have recourse to the generosity of the Holy Father for the endowment of an establishment in Rome."

Some people of greater sense thought that it would be wrong to solicit favors and a grant of money at the same time. Later, when Pope Pius X declared that he could not set up the Biblical Institute because of lack of funds, P. Fonck offered to cover all the costs. Then he asked the faithful to make contributions toward the Institute which the Holy Father wanted. It was no more difficult than that, but it had to be thought of first.

At first, we did not believe that the Holy See could be stopped by a question of money, and in fact we did nothing about soliciting any privilege. His intention was to call upon various Orders, and we would have regarded it as a little indelicate to claim a leading role. As I could not work out how the *Revue* would function in Rome, I left it to the two secretaries to organize it in accordance with the wishes of the Holy Father. P. Fleming informed me that *Civiltà,* already established in Rome, had certainly not hesitated as I was doing, and, anxious to be chosen as the organ of the Commission, it had enthusiastically entered into the views of the letter *Vigilantiae.* P. de Hummelauer, completely won over to the critical study of the Bible, was setting a brisk pace, to the great astonishment of the readers of this dowager of Italian periodicals, and especially of Neapolitan ones. I have supplied a few examples of this new approach in the *Revue Biblique.*

The Organ of the Biblical Commission

But it was us the Pope wanted, and P. David Fleming,[g] who was his confidant in all this affair, knew it better than anyone. As for M. Vigouroux who was not in Rome, he kindly wrote to me from Paris (March 20, 1903): "I can well understand your bewilderment. When I arrived in Rome, everybody started speaking to me about the *Revue*. I emphasized as best I could all the reasons against the creation of this periodical, but they were not accepted. I cannot now make a fresh attempt, especially as, since then, the creation of the *Revue* has been announced publicly, and one cannot ask the Pope to reverse his decision. In these new conditions, would it not be best if you undertook to publish in your periodical the official·communications of the Biblical Commission, while otherwise retaining, so far as possible, your own autonomy? I can see that there would be many good reasons for doing this. It must not be possible to say that a periodical cannot be scientific nor adequately independent if it has a particular attachment to the Church. . . . The interests of your own Order would point in the same direction. The *Revue*, by this new arrangement, could become a very powerful instrument under your direction. If you do not take it on, it will be entrusted to others because of the decisions which have been taken; for financial and other reasons it is likely to be handed over to a different religious Order which may well follow a narrower path. This will not benefit your Order, nor the Church, for priests and lay people alike will thereby be exposed to much disquiet, and the work of the Biblical Commission will be impeded."

I have spoken earlier of the conservative misgivings of M. Vigouroux; they matched his personal feelings. If he was now envisaging the work of the Biblical Commission as relatively wide-ranging, it was because he too had fallen in line, like *Civiltà*, with what were regarded as the views of the Pope. A few days after I had received this letter, on March 28, Leo XIII approved for the

g. David Fleming (1851–1915), an Irish Franciscan, who restored his Order in Great Britain. Provincial in 1891 and Vicar General from 1901 to 1903, he was appointed consultor to the Holy Office in 1897, consultor to the Biblical Commission in 1901 and secretary of the Commission in 1903, in which position he showed himself "liberal, skillful but opportunist," according to E. Poulat in *Alfred Loisy, sa vie, son oeuvre*, Paris 1960, p. 351.

Revue a statute drawn up by Fr. Fleming, under the title of *Basi generali*. It will be found among the documents in a copy made by P. Vincent. It stated: "The writers of the *Revue* will enjoy full freedom in their scientific work, provided that they keep within the limits of Catholic doctrine as laid down in the encyclical *Providentissimus Deus* and in the Apostolic letter *Vigilantiae*. The direction of the *Revue* will be the same as it is now, and if some change is judged necessary or expedient, nothing new will be introduced without the prior consent of the Commission."[54] The *Revue* was to be the organ of the Commission for the acts promulgated in its name; the Commission would have no responsibility for anything else.

The matter of the *Revue Biblique* was thus settled. Everything was carried out in accordance with the wishes of the Pope. In 1904 there appeared a *Nouvelle Série*, which was honored with communications of the Biblical Commission. Nothing else changed. I do not believe that one can find the slightest difference between the new series and the old, except in the matter of scientific progress. *Dies diem docet*, and our young teachers were reaching maturity. As there had been no change in our material organization, there was no reason to claim from the Holy See the compensation which was mentioned in the *Basi generali*. This meant that the priory of Saint-Etienne retained ownership.

A Division with the Commission

The Commission began its meetings, with rules which practice would clarify and perhaps modify. It opened with all the outward appearance of an academy freely discussing scientific questions. Thus Cardinal Rampolla declared that he saw no reason why the sittings of the consultors should not be public. It was the consultors themselves who rather feared the publicity. The Commission has been much blamed for having changed its character and become just one more Roman tribunal, a sort of annex of the Holy Office for the definition of propositions of a biblical nature. It could not be anything else, and from the start I jotted down for my own sake the ambiguous and impracticable nature of a body which was supposed to be simultaneously a tribunal assessing matters which bore upon dogma, and an executive committee for the active promotion of scientific studies. I had no hesitation in writing in my notes: "A tribunal of simple scholars which assumes the right to settle out-of-hand any scientific questions which are still being discussed would cover itself with ridicule and would founder under the weight of its own helplessness and universal derision." And if the advisors were acting simply as scholars, why should their opinions have to be submitted to a committee of cardinals, who alone were able to pass judgments as a last resort?

I admit to sharing M. Loisy's aversion for administrative science. I wrote: "Administrative approval is a burden which must not be added to the doctrinal burden, which we accept willingly as a religious duty of a supernatural kind." Ever since I was a child, I have been impressed by the maxim which Montalembert borrowed from St. Colomba[55] (or from St. Columban): *Si tollis libertatem, tollis dignitatem.* In fact, the consultors must have been telling themselves from the outset that they were being asked only to proclaim, in the name of revealed principles and of theology, to what extent exegetes were free to raise problems and to solve them. For in the Bible perfectly open questions always border on points of faith because of the authority of the dogma of inspiration, to which the Catholic exegete must always bow. But as a guide, his experience of the Bible cannot fail to be of great use. Leo XIII's stroke of genius seemed to me to be that he laid down the principle of competence: that biblical questions must be settled only by people who have devoted their lives to this chasm of light, and of obscurity too, since the Bible is obscure, as we have always maintained in the face of the Protestants.

Dogma and Biblical Scholarship

Thus I wrote: "It is of sovereign importance that articles of faith should not be brought more or less consciously into a scientific study. It is for the Holy See to be watchful, and the creation of a Commission is very timely indeed, an act worthy of fullest admiration. Objections were raised that specialist knowledge, which was not always possessed by other consultors, was needed to settle certain cases. This objection no longer holds. The wide variety of opinion represented within the Commission proves the breadth of view of the Holy See and is one guarantee of its impartiality. This is an immense advantage for a tribunal of the faith; for if so many men of such diverse opinions declare that the faith is at risk, nobody can reasonably challenge their verdict. And unanimity on such a point is possible because, within the diversity of their scientific opinions, they all follow the same rule of faith."

With my basic optimism, I simply forgot that it was precisely on the point of judging what belongs to the faith, what limits the dogma of inspiration imposes on criticism, that the Commission was divided into two roughly equal groups. I also overlooked the fact that the Commission proper, that is, the cardinals, could take a decision opposed to the view of the majority of consultors. I am not saying that this has happened; I am only saying what could happen. This was possible because I had recently renewed my confidence in pure theologians. Having learned from their setback over the question of the three witnesses, they should no longer, I told myself, be so anxious to encroach upon the domain of biblical questions under discussion. With regard to professional exegetes, they are referees, as it were. If the faith is really in peril, one can count on their zeal. But if exegetes cannot agree on questions of textual or literary criticism, long may they continue to argue. In formulating this line of argument, I did not think, either, that the Holy Office would, by suppressing the Congregation of the Index, be led to deal directly with biblical matters. Therefore the decisions of the Holy See are not to be evaluated, but rather simply to be accepted, no matter which tribunal is charged with making them.

A Pronouncement on Loisy

By March 1903, one thing seemed to me obvious and urgent, leaving aside all conjectures about the future of the Biblical Commission. As our first move, we had to show quickly our disapproval of M. Loisy's outburst. I had been waiting too long to demonstrate the differences between the *Revue biblique* and him, out of a false sense of honor, because it was repugnant to me to confer a seal of orthodoxy upon myself by treating him as a deserter. But now that he was battering away, more or less openly but very definitely, at the Catholic Church and at the foundations of Christianity, it was even more essential to act. I straightway conveyed my feelings to Fr. Fleming and P. Gismondi,

whom I found not only cold and reserved, but resolutely hostile.
Yet on Fr. Fleming's side at least it was certainly not because he
had the least doubt about M. Loisy's position. I pressed the matter several times, without success. But if the Commission wished
to mark out the path it proposed to take, there was no better way
of opening the proceedings. It was not until later that I understood. At that time, Loisy's little book, which had been denounced, was being studied by the Holy Office. Fr. Fleming and
P. Gismondi,[56] both of them consultors, knew this, but could not
tell me. Now, the matter having been laid before the Congregation of the Holy Office, the Supreme, as they say in Rome, it
would have been extremely tactless of the Commission to compete with it. The Commission, which was supposed to meet only
twice a month, was not able to get through a lot of work, and we
confined ourselves to conversations about the situation.

Progress

Without waiting for my decisions, progress was being made
on all fronts. The case of *Civiltà* was the most obvious and most
typical. The *Biblische Zeitschrift*, founded in 1903 with M. Sick-
enberger and M. Gottesberger as directors, had the same leanings as *Revue Biblique*; P. Fonck's dire warnings made this quite
clear. *Studi Religiosi* had even set too quick a pace. Within our order, the accession of P. Zanecchia, former regent of the Minerva,
a pure Thomist, could not pass unnoticed. The first edition
(1902) of *Die Hohere Bibelkritik*[57] (by P. Hoepfl) was noted. But I
cannot now begin to go into the detail of these manifestations.
The best sign for me was the extremely flattering welcome which
I received everywhere. My vanity was thus satisfied. Fancy that!
I would say to myself that even the most sympathetic minds were
guessing that it would need twenty or thirty years of hard work
before the critics were allowed to restate commonly received
ideas, and now here was the Holy See asking me to work at this
very task.

Discordant Notes

However, there were many things which moderated this
joy. Opposition was even more passionate, as was proved by the
work of M. Ceresete, director of the *Scuola cattolica*.[58] Attitudes

were being changed in order to fall into step with the Holy
Father, but were feelings changing as well? P. Gismondi, professor at the Gregorian University,[h] saw everything in a very
gloomy light. "Father," he said, "do you know what the physi-
cists mean by endosmosis?" I still had some idea. "Well," he continued with a wry smile, "it is the same for criticism. It will only
be when the whole world is saturated with it that it will begin to
penetrate through to Rome." "Nonsense," I replied, "we kept
going in spite of your Society, and now that we are walking hand
in hand, it will be plain sailing." But in disquiet of P. Prat,[i] in
touch constantly with his brethren, and his allusions to my short-
sighted optimism, did not cease to worry me. "There will be
much opposition," I said one day to Cardinal Rampolla. "We do
not fear opposition," was his reply. Indeed in the reign of Leo
XIII there was nothing to fear. Yet while those piercing eyes still
shone with brilliant sparkle, the whole appearance of his body
was practically transparent: could he withstand even a breath of
wind? Cardinal Rampolla would have continued his work, but
would he be his successor? I had been struck by the words of
Mgr. Sogaro, the successor of Mgr. Comboni as head of the mission in the Sudan. "I do not know who will be elected Pope. But
I am certain it will be a bishop, a pastor. We have had enough of
diplomacy."

The thought of being installed in Rome merely to be sent
away again or pushed to one side, as happened to P. Prat and P.
Gismondi, was not a pleasant one. But I have already shown that
even favor, involvement in the administrative machine, the necessity of accepting gracefully for the *Revue* mediocre articles
from on high, the time wasted in antichambers, the whole process of adapting to the way of life of polite society, did not hold
for me the attraction of our Bedouin existence. My only thought
was to return to Jerusalem; we would see what happened after-

---

h. Enrico Gismondi (1850–1912), an Italian Jesuit, professor at the University of Beirut,
   then at the Gregorian University in Rome (1888), where he taught Oriental languages
   and exegesis until his fall from grace in 1904 (cf. below). He was consultor to the Congregation of the Index and to the Biblical Commission.
i. Ferdinand Prat (1875–1933), a French Jesuit, professor of Holy Scripture and consultor to the Biblical Commission in 1903. Subsequently he became well known through
   his work on St. Paul and the life of Jesus.

ward. Leo XIII agreed to my leaving. "Yes," he said with kindness, "go to Jerusalem for Easter. Then you shall come back. I shall put you to work for us."

Return to Jerusalem

I was held back by a very painful attack of erysipelas followed by a tertian ague which did not respond to treatment. One day I took advantage of the fine weather to leave for Brindisi with P. Vincent, who had stayed at my side during my illness, and we arrived in Jerusalem on May 2. There I felt myself overcome once more by the sweetness of living among those whom I regarded as my children, so enthusiastic for our work, especially since it had received such valuable encouragement. To work in peace, in solitude, with the memory stimulated by all the places where Our Lord and his most holy Mother had lived, with the patriarchs standing on the first horizon of history—how could I tear myself away from this dream which had become such a fascinating reality? And simply to make myself a prey to a life of restless ferment and struggles! Obedience did not forbid me to make clear my difficulties, but I blush to think how I blamed the Roman climate as being too severe for me. This was true, but it would have needed a far greater danger to keep me from serving the Pope.

Would this service be accepted for long? I admit to some treacherous speculation about the great indulgence shown to me when I excused myself on health grounds. In answer to my tale of woe, Cardinal Rampolla wrote on June 22, not without a slight touch of displeasure, concerning my determination to steal away: "Your letter of May 13 duly arrived, and I hastened to submit it to the Commission of Cardinals. My most eminent colleagues and I have judged that there are no grounds for changing or even modifying what was decided regarding *Revue biblique*. All the observations made in your letter have already been taken into consideration, and there is not one new point of such serious nature as might warrant a departure from the written agreement between the Holy See and the Order of Preachers, to which you have yourself given approval. The Commission of Cardinals therefore asks me to inform you, Most Reverend Father, that in regard to *Revue biblique*, we must simply remain *in decisis*. For the rest, you have no disastrous consequences to fear, either for the *Revue* or for the School in Jerusalem or for your Order. The intention of the Holy See throughout has been only to give you and your Order a pledge of its benevolence and its esteem. As for the *Institut de Hautes Etudes bibliques*, it is evident, Father, that you are not in possession of the detailed facts. I can assure you, Father, in advance that you will be fully satisfied as soon as you know of the measures taken in its regard by the Holy Father. It is perhaps superfluous to add that the Holy Father will ask nothing of you which does not accord with your strength and your health. It only remains for me to encourage you to continue your work for the good cause, and to assure you, Father, of the particular benevolence with which I am," etc.

Pope Leo XIII died on July 20, 1903, at the age of ninety-three years. *Lumen in coelo.*

Cardinal Mercier

At that moment when that other great light had just been extinguished, or rather, Leo XIII, started to shine more brilliantly in heaven, I cannot resist a desire to quote a few lines from Cardinal Mercier, dated June 27, 1903. This is the only indiscretion I shall commit, because it cannot harm such a great reputation, and will cover me with his protecting shade: "I consider it a duty to thank you. I was and still am little versed in biblical criticism, but I know enough about it to be tormented by certain doubts which I could not manage to resolve. Your works, which I had not had time to read earlier, have clarified many things for me, and given me general guidance where before I had none. Moreover I know of more than one person, Reverend Father, for whom you have done a great deal of good. I thank you for this very sincerely. In addition, I congratulate you on your courage, which is necessary in order to speak plainly on these delicate questions."[59]

Leo XIII, Cardinal Rampolla, Cardinal Mercier—I have always drawn such comfort from the benevolent support of these. I well know that obedience is owed to the present Superior, and that it would be a dangerous illusion to rely upon past favor as an excuse for being less submissive in the present. But I could tell myself: The Holy See had duly examined my teachings, and, far from rejecting them, has judged them capable of being of service. Whatever clamors arise, I shall await a pronouncement from the Holy See itself before I make any changes, since I am always ready to keep silence and draw back if it wishes, well aware that I have done nothing to seek favor.

The Historical Method

It was at the beginning of 1903 that the little volume *La Méthode historique* appeared, containing the Toulouse lectures.[60] One of the two designated examiners was in doubt over a point in the last lecture. P. Frühwirth therefore kindly read it himself, after which he gave the *imprimatur*. What attracted even more attention to this little book was that it was short and easy to read, and also that it contained concrete examples. Yet it confined itself very carefully to the principles laid down by *Revue biblique*. While I was in Rome, a copy had been sent to the cardinals on the Commission, who courteously acknowledged receipt of it. I cannot claim that this showed approval, but the welcome given to it by the Catholic press was generally sympathetic, and Mgr., now Cardinal, Bourne, had it translated into English. I think I can say that since 1903 I have written nothing which gives a greater impression of independence in the face of dogma and theology, nor any propositions more liable to censure. Thus, it is *Méthode historique* above all which has been singled out, and which is still invoked, in order to overwhelm me, as if it were some vexatious memory. It was no more than a clarification for the public at large of a method which had been judged at the very least useful in the search for a more scientific criticism.

Pope Pius X was elected on August 4. We did not know what his intentions would be regarding *Revue biblique* and the new Institute. As early as August 27 the Master General wrote to tell me to "wait in silence." This I was quite prepared to do. I learned in a letter from a consultor to the Commission, dated December 7, that the Holy Father had agreed that *Revue Biblique* should become the organ of the Commission, and should begin a new series. The consultors agreed that its former situation should be maintained, but that the decisions made should not be cancelled. As for the Institute, they let it be known that the Pope was very

short of money, and that they would do no more than improve
the courses in Holy Scripture in Rome, without further expense.

Loisy Condemned

On December 23 the Index published a decree condemning
several of M. Loisy's books in accordance with a decree from the
Holy Office of December 16. In a letter dated December 19, Cardinal Merry del Val wrote on this matter to Cardinal Richard,[61]
noting that this decree had been issued "after close consideration
and prolonged study." The examination had therefore begun under Leo XIII. There were whispers among informed people that
the condemnation had been delayed because the report of the
counsultor charged with the examination did not arrive at that
conclusion, and that the consultor was P. Gismondi, S.J. The fall
from grace of P. Gismondi, who was relieved of the course in exegesis which he had been giving for fifteen years without arous-
ing any dangerous question whatever, confirmed this rumor
which I personally believe to be true.

M. Loisy sent letters to the archbishop of Paris, to Cardinal
Merry del Val, and then to the Pope, none of which was considered as containing sufficient submission or retraction. The polemic against him even worked its way into the newspapers. Most
often people made do with demonstrating that he was no longer a
Catholic, which was not difficult. It was unusual to find any
careful discussion.

The alarm sounded against him had not died down before
many controversialists turned upon the School of Jerusalem. A
Jesuit priest, and sincere friend, wrote to me as early as September 30: "It has been said . . . that the Biblical School in Jerusalem
should be suppressed, or rather should cease to function." M.
Dessailly wrote in *La Vérité française* on December 3, 1903: "From
now on, whenever thoughts turn to exegesis, they will no longer
turn to M. Loisy. . . . M. Loisy is therefore no longer the leader
in France of the new school of exegesis, and it seems that his place
is to be taken by P. Lagrange. . . ."[62] In the camp of those who
upheld M. Loisy as a critic, for it was only too obvious that his
apologetics were unsound, P. Lagrange was held to be somewhat
of a tightrope walker, because he considered—and still does—

that the best way to uphold the essential marks of Catholic Christianity is to practice conscientious exegesis and a complete and loyal criticism.[63] Blows rained down from both sides. From both sides we were called upon to renounce criticism, by some because they thought it dangerous, by others because it could not be employed by a believer.

Mourning in Jerusalem

Let me return to our priory. The summer was made sad for us through bereavement. When the spring caravan came back, P. Jerome Brookes had a bad attack of fever, and he died on June 9. I exhorted him to offer his life for the conversion of England. "It is only a little life," he answered with a smile. But his love was great! After this death, it was the turn of Brother Antoine, the valiant lay-brother who had supervised the construction work on the church and priory. Then while I was giving the conventional retreat, P. Blais fell victim to a disease of the liver. P. Jaussen succeeded him as novice-master. On the feast of Saint Stephen, December 26, I received notice of my nomination as correspondent to the Académie des Inscriptions et Belles Lettres.[j] This demonstration of high esteem for our School was totally spontaneous. It was our first link with that illustrious body.

DISQUIET ABOUT *LA MÉTHODE HISTORIQUE* (1904)

A New Edition of *La Méthode Historique*

The first edition of *La Méthode Historique* (2,200 copies) had rapidly sold out. I asked the Master General's permission to prepare a new edition, adding a letter to Mgr. Batiffol on *Jésus et la critique des Evangiles*, which had appeared in the Bulletin of the Institut de Toulouse. Upset by M. Dessailly's attacks in *La Vérité Française*, P. Frühwirth hesitated, and he submitted the book to a new examination. He wrote to me on February 26, 1904: "The attacks of M. Dessailly have had no other effect than to rekindle my vigilance. Your *Méthode historique* and your latest articles and note have been examined carefully and have all been sent to M.

---

j. P. Lagrange had been elected on December 18, 1903.

Lecoffre for printing. . . . You can rest in peace on this point."
In fact, at the highest levels in Rome there was still no change of
course from the direction given by Leo XIII. They knew how to
differentiate between the teachings of M. Loisy and the attempts
of loyal Catholics to make a place for criticism.

The New Series of the *Revue Biblique*

The first number of the new series of the *Revue Biblique* came
out in January, and Fr. Molini, O.F.M. under-secretary of the
Commission, wrote on behalf of Fr. Fleming: "His Eminence,[64]
and all the members of the Commission, are happy with this first
number," etc.[65] As I had written to point out the reasons for not
abandoning the critical approach, the Rev. Father added: "I am
asked to assure you that the entire Commission is immensely concerned about people's peace of mind, including the peace of mind
of those who study. It hopes that this peace may flow from the
fair and reasonable freedom granted to studies to enable them to
satisfy the just demands of biblico-historical criticism, which are
necessary for the progress of biblical studies at the present time.
It is to this end that the work of the Commission is principally directed, and this is the spirit which inspires all its efforts." Since I
had expressed the wish that either the Holy See or the Commission should express its acknowledgement that these balanced demands were legitimate, I had grounds to hope that a document
along these lines would be sent to the *Revue Biblique* after the imminent publication of the decree instituting degrees in Holy
Scripture, and after further numbers of the *Revue* had appeared.[66]

The letter of Pius X on the degrees was featured in the April
Revue. It was a move which gave an appreciable boost to biblical
studies; we could not but rejoice. As soon as the degrees in Holy
Scripture were instituted, and as we were then the only Biblical
School, I had quickly asked if we might have the favor of confer-
ring them. This privilege was subsequently accorded to the Pontifical Institute of the Jesuits.[k] The Commission, to whom I had
addressed my request, did not show itself eager to grant the right:
"The consultors and the cardinals have decided: *Recurrant in sin-*

---

k. The Biblical Institute acquired the right to confer degrees in 1916. (Apostolic letter
Cum Biblia Sacra of August 15, 1916.)

gulis casibus. The Holy Father has confirmed this. Apart from that, they all praised the zeal and talent which the Dominican Fathers have shown in such positive ways through the Biblical School and the *Revue Biblique.*"[67]

Within our Order, P. Frühwirth had retired after twelve years of being Master General, and his office had been taken over by P. Cormier, who had followed our studies for such a long time with great paternal benevolence. He wrote to me on October 8: "I have traveled much, and hear nothing but good of the *Revue.*" Nevertheless he refused me leave to give lectures in Brussels (October 8, 1904).

The Momentum Continues

The advent of Pius X had therefore in no way stopped the momentum begun under his predecessor and, it seemed, encouraged by him. We shall give here only two pointers to this. It was in 1904 that Mgr. Horazio Mazzela, S.J. published his *Praelectiones scholasticae dogmaticae breviori cursui accommodatae* which were honored with a letter from His Holiness Pius X. To what extent he coincided with the theories of P. Lagrange can be seen from a few extracts printed in the *Revue Biblique*, 1906, pp. 490f. Even P. Lagrange has always refrained from distinguishing absolute truth and relative truth, whereas Mgr. Mazzela wrote (p. 355): "*Veritas Scripturarum non sensu absoluto, sed sensu relativo ad intentionem Sacri Scriptoris intelligenda est.*" The second sign is the publication in Mgr. Bardenhewer's *Biblische Studien*, much more conservative than the *Biblische Zeitschrift*, of the famous section by P. von Hummelauer entitled *Exegetisches zur Inspirationsfrage*. According to a writer in the Cologne *Pastoralblatt*, approved by P. Fonck,[68] "the theory of von Hummelauer accords exactly with that of the Dominican, P. Lagrange." Not quite, however. It is true that P. von Hummelauer, till lately a supporter of the *stratum adamicum*, *stratum noachicum*, accepted all my theses, even giving them a greater semblance of system, but for all that he attached an exaggerated importance to the word *Toledoth* as being an indication, in the Bible itself, of a particular literary genre.[69]

Of course we did not think that a change of Pope implied that all biblical problems were solved. Those exegetes convinced of the usefulness of criticism continued to use it in the absence of any other direction.

The movement continued, as we shall see, but in the middle of 1904 something happened which started a relentless struggle by several Jesuits in every country against the historical method and the director of the *Revue Biblique*.

Attacks of P. Delattre

Nobody could have accused me of forging ahead along new paths of criticism. I was at the time absorbed by the study of the Semitic religions[70] and of that of the Persians, as the *Revue* of 1904 shows. During the vacation I had gone with P. Vincent to Hama, Homs, Palmyra and Aleppo. When I came back on August 31, it was not long before I received the book by P. Delattre, S.J., entitled *Autuor de la question biblique. Une nouvelle école d'exégèse et les autorités qu'elle invoque*. Liège, given its *imprimateur* on May 2, 1904. The book was entirely directed against my historical method, with a short excursion against two Flemish writers, P. Sanders and M. Poels. This was a very serious attack by a well-known Orientalist whose collaboration I had myself been eager to obtain. I sensed still greater danger when I learned that the Holy Father had read the work, and had then called P. Delattre to be professor at the Gregorian University, replacing P. Gismondi. I did not know this yet when the book fell into my hands. If I had, good taste would have barred me from taking up the fight. I scribbled a riposte and sent it to Rome: *"Eclaircissement sur la méthode historique à propos d'un livre du P. Delattre, S.J."* The Master General did not wish to deprive me totally of the right to reply; but he insisted that only two hundred copies of the pamphlet should be printed, and that they should not be commercially available, but should be treated as a manuscript which he reserved to send to the Holy Father,[71] to all the members of the Commission, to those cardinals present in Rome and to a few other people.[72] Their reaction would enable a judgment to be made about the advisability of a wider circulation, and the *Revue Biblique* would not be caught up in an argument with a consultor to the Commission. Therefore it carried no reference to P. Delattre's[73] pamphlet, except on the cover! For the administra-

tion greeted without suspicion an advertisement bearing the enthusiastic approval of *Civiltà cattolica:* "P. Delattre, a
distinguished orientalist, demonstrates convincingly how weak
and insubstantial are the structures upon which is based the new
school, which deals with biblical exegesis along the lines of the
so-called 'historical methods,' etc."

The Campaign Against the Historical Method

It is worth pausing for a moment in regard to this absurd
misunderstanding. And here is the reason. *Civiltà* had once again
altered its opinions! It was without doubt following the instructions of P. Martin, Superior General of the Society of Jesus,
who, on November 4, 1904, wrote to his provincials, rectors, lectors, writers and all members of the Society to put them on guard
against the perils of the new fashion in exegesis. Was he aiming at
M. Loisy and his supporters? Judgment had already been pro-
nounced upon him. No, he was putting the Society on guard
against an exegesis which some claimed to have the support of the
Holy See: *qui Sedem Apostolicam talibus commentis astipulari credide-
runt.* Now, only a madman could have dreamed up such a claim
for Loisy's exegesis, even before his condemnation, and there
was no need whatever to send such a letter in order to reinforce
the effects of the condemnations. The slightly equivocal idea of
the Superior General was obviously to include a different
method in his condemnation or at least to draw attention to it as
a grave and damnable peril. He names this method the "historical
method" just as *Civiltà* does, referring to P. Delattre's book
which was entirely directed against the "historical method" of P.
Lagrange: "*non enim,* etc."[1]

I cannot think that any provincial, rector, lector, writer or
simple member of the Society was dim-witted enough not to realize that the Superior General was referring to the *Méthode historique* of P. Lagrange as that work of ungodliness which was
pursuing the same goal as Strauss, the overturning of revealed religion. It was thus under the impetus of the central power of the

---

1. Translation: "The inventions used by Strauss to undermine the whole of revealed religion now being obsolete, Your Reverence is not unaware that a different ungodliness,
namely the method called historical, has set out to achieve the same goal."

Society that so many works appeared, directed above all against the man whom they called the leader of the broad school.

P. Schiffini, who sent us the fine document from his superior,[74] is only providing a commentary of it when he declares that all Loisy did was to extend this senseless method to the whole of Scripture. To the possible objection that I wrote only in order to refute Loisy, the good father replied: "Readers may judge whether this is merely dust in the eyes. In any case, God is not mocked."[75]

The word having gone out from on high, it was promptly obeyed. To finish with this campaign, let us quote only two works: *Critica y exegesis. Observaciones sobre un nuevo sistema exegético de la Biblia*, by P. Lino Murillo, S.J., Madrid, directed almost exclusively against P. von Hummelauer, and *Der Kampf um die Wahrheit der h. Schrift seit 25 Jahren*, of P. Leopold Fonck, S.J., Innsbruck, 1905. In this last work, one can at least find some information. It is well known that the author excels in bibliographical information. I am grateful to him for having explicitly mentioned that I had expressed in the *Méthode historique* those views on the biblical question which I had been putting forward for years in the *Revue biblique* and elsewhere.[76] The little book of lectures was therefore not the unveiling of a new system, but a simple popularization of theories which had already been stated, denounced, examined, without being condemned, and even allowed a free rein in Rome. P. von Hummelauer, of course, abandoned biblical studies in order to devote himself to a very fruitful ministry. We shall return to P. Delattre later.

Disappointment

The same year 1904 caused me some disappointment. Our collection, *Etudes Bibliques* was barely advertised at all, because the only parts which were available were *Judges* and the *Etudes sur les religions sémitiques*. I was counting on the collaborators of the *Revue* to prepare other parts. They did not decline, but some of them, starting with P. Rose, undertook to write short books of commentary for the publisher Bloud. That was certainly a quicker way of achieving some results. The success of P. Rose's books on the Gospels[77] caused M. Bloud to found the *Bibliothèque de l'enseignement scripturaire*, a collection directed by Mgr. Batiffol,

P. Rose and M. Touzard. Mgr. Batiffol even invited me very cordially to contribute to it. He said pleasantly that this little flotilla could not possibly overshadow our fleet of battleships. I was all for completing our collection of large works in this way, in the interests of the public at large, but I remained firmly convinced that we must first lay down a solid base and inspire confidence with careful study. Then if we felt that innovations were necessary, they would be less suspect, and would be more easily accepted if backed up by a large body of proof. Yet in fact all the important members of our team were deserting us, since, for this new collection, M. Cersoy was to do a commentary on Wisdom, and M. Hackspill on the Books of Samuel. I had simply to let things go ahead, without abandoning my original design. Again for the new collection, Mgr. Batiffol wrote *L'Enseignement de Jésus*, and M. Touzard *Le Livre d'Amos*. A short commentary on St. John, drawn up by P. Calmes and based on his large volume, was won by M. Lecoffre for our own *Etudes bibliques*, and that was where it rested. Some Jesuit fathers have quite recently inaugurated for M. Beauchesne, publisher, another series which will doubtless enjoy a more brilliant future.

Under this year I must also mention the brilliant debut of P. Dhorme in the *Revue: Un papyrus hébreu prémassorétique*,[78] signed X because this father was still a student. P. Jaussen, P. Savignac and P. Vincent made a fine exploration of the Negev, represented only in part by the study on Abdeh.[79] P. Abel established his mastery of Greek epigraphy.[80] The present professorial body, already so competent, gave promise of even better things for the future. But there were threats hanging over our work.

THE FATE OF THE *REVUE BIBLIQUE* (1905)

During the month of February, we noticed that P. Vincent, still very thin, seemed to be wasting away even more. We were worried about his frequent dry cough. A sounding of his lungs indicated tuberculosis. Dr. Mazaraki spoke cheerfully to him but, as he leaned over his back, he gave me a more than telling look. Until winter was over, it was impossible to think of traveling. I was soon convinced that it was urgent for me to go to Rome, whatever it cost me to leave P. Vincent in that condition.

The Reorganization of the *Revue*

The Master General did not seem worried, but I knew that the fate of the *Revue Biblique* was at stake, at least as property of the Priory of Saint-Etienne and even of the Order. The great majority of consultors had always been hostile to the arrangement announced by Cardinal Rampolla on behalf of Leo XIII, and which he had in theory supported, whereby a periodical should be entirely the organ of the Commission. In fact, there had been absolutely no change in the way the review was directed: the communications from the Commission had the place of honor. No consultor had pleaded his title in order to have an article accepted. But it was inevitable that certain consultors should wish to take advantage of the situation of privilege to bring pressure on the *Revue* to follow their ideas, or at least to exclude those which displeased them. Thus the Commission resolved to replace our Master General with examiners appointed by itself. Any consultor could claim this title, and I could envisage the possibility of having P. Delattre in person as examiner, or P. Méchineau who replaced him as professor at the Gregorian, where his success had been more than mediocre. However, that respect for established rights, which brings so much honor to the Roman Church, made its influence felt over the first selection. The Commission appointed P. Lepidi,[m] Master of the Sacred Palace, as examiner *de jure et officio*. Two further consultors were attached to him, P. Kaiser, O.P., and another member of the same Order agreed by the Master General. This decision was approved by His Holiness on February 13, but was not communicated to the Master General until March 2. We had no cause to complain of these first appointments, but from then on the consultors were answerable to

---

m. A. Lepidi (1838–1925), a Dominican, professor of philosophy at Louvain and at Saint-Maximin, regent of studies of the Dominican provinces of France (1868) and of Belgium (1872), professor at the College of the Minerva in Rome, consultor to the Congregations of the Holy Office and of the Index, Master of the Sacred Palace from 1897 until his death. He "exercised a moderating influence in the doctrinal matters under his jurisdiction" (E. Poulat, *Alfred Loisy*, p. 375).

the Commission, and we could not change them. In Jerusalem, certain pieces of information made me fear a much more troublesome intrusion. I asked permission to come to Rome; it was granted by telegram. I left, I think, on March 9.

Audience with Pius X

P. Cormier was very keen for the *Revue* to remain ours as far as possible, and he asked for an audience with the Holy Father for me. Under Pius X our situation was basically more favorable because he was not anxious to stir the Commission into much activity. He showed himself benevolent toward it, and gave it a new function by creating the degrees. He thought of it more as an instrument of control than as an assembly of scholars whose positive aim was to promote study through their individaul or collective work. He deigned to receive me with kindness, and as to the object of my request, of which he had been informed, he declared that he would follow whatever Cardinal Rampolla, president of the Commission, might decide. He was then pleased to question me on the vacancy of the Latin patriarchal see of Jerusalem. The Franciscans, he said, wanted to have a Franciscan; the canons were asking for a secular priest. I took the liberty of replying that the Holy See, when it created the Latin patriarchate, had intended to give a father to all the priests in the Holy Land, regular and secular, and that, for my part, I found it difficult to understand that anybody who entered a religious Order should have done so with a view to wearing a mitre. I had heard talk of the prediction made by a Carmelite sister who had died in Bethlehem with the odor of sanctity; she had announced that the next patriarch would be a saint! "I shall have to look for him then," said the Pope. And he appointed Mgr. Camassei, who was for all of us a true father and a model of piety and virtue.

Freedom of the *Revue Biblique*

It was not without some apprehension that I awaited Cardinal Rampolla's decision. Would he insist that the Commission should continue to watch over it so that the aims of Leo XIII would be more fully realized? But the situation had certainly changed! The *Revue Biblique*, organ of the Commission, might be led into following a direction opposed to its first intentions. He

quickly gave as his opinion that we should regain our full freedom, except for the offical communications and the usual rules of
doctrinal revision. This is what was decided, and approved by
the Holy Father on May 6. The editorial note featured in the July
Revue[81] is but the copy of a text composed by M. Vigouroux,
adopted by the Commission and approved by the Pope.[82] The
second secretary, Fr. Fleming, wrote a letter which was entirely
unofficial: "Your visit to Rome has done good. *All* the cardinals
spoke highly of you in the last session. We voted unanimously to
suppress censorship here. . . . The idea of a periodical for the
Commission was absurd. . . . With a little patience we will be
able to achieve good results and avert the danger of the disastrous
suppression of a balanced and sound line of criticism."[83]

P. Delattre Returns to the Attack

I was less fortunate with my riposte to P. Delattre. I had
asked permission of the Commission to publish it. Once again, I
had to admire the respect in which the rights of the individual are
held in Rome. The cardinals, all except Cardinal Segna, who did
not want publication at any price, decided that to fail to allow
publication or to forbid it might appear too distressing or too
harsh: it was thus not prevented on condition that it was made
quite clear that the Commission had nothing to do with it and
that the author undertook to submit to the Holy See.[84] These two
conditions were, of course, totally reasonable. But the note
added that the riposte contained several elements which needed
correction (*plura in dicto responso reprehendenda contineri*) and that it
was passed *ad duritiam cordis*. Thus P. Cormier refused absolutely
to give his approval to the pamphlet, which remained unpublished.

This did not stop P. Delattre from giving his reply to it in a
pamphlet called *Le Criterium à l'usage de la nouvelle exégèse biblique,
Réponse au P. M.-J. Lagrange, O.P.*, in 1907 with a preface: "We
believe we can say that this small work is a partial commentary
on the encyclical of Pius X about modernism. It is an anticipated
commentary. . . ." The Rev. Father knew very well that I had
not hidden from him. Having received a first copy of my *Eclaircissement*, he asked for two more which were immediately granted
to him. He also knew why my reply had not appeared, and was

thus aware that he was attacking an adversary who was bound
hand and foot. Did anyone point out to him that this conduct
lacked nobility? The most he could claim was that several people
had read my pamphlet. But he really overstepped all limits when
he published a third pamphlet entitled *Une lumière sous le bosseau*[85]
which begins thus: "The light under the bushel is the pamphelt
entitled *L'Eclaircissement*. Under the bushel because P. Lagrange
was keeping it hidden in order to attack P. Delattre in the dark
and with impunity. *L'Eclaircissement* keeps itself hidden as much
as it can." And again this sentence: "M. Minocchi, who is *the* authority on the interpretation of P. Lagrange's intentions, contra-
dicts   our   information[86]   and   states   that   the   author   of
L'Eclaircissement did, when all is said and done, himself sentence
his work to obscurity. We should have preferred not to believe
this, but we have had to recognize on this point the overwhelming worth of M. Minocchi's words. He has enlightened us and, at
the same time, given us the right to speak of the secret pamphlet"
(p. 6).

Thus, far from admitting that he was attacking a disarmed
adversary, P. Delattre claimed that he had discovered an adversary in ambush! And there was more: "In reality, M. Minocchi is
claiming for P. Lagrange the right to fight an enemy condemned
to silence, with only his friends looking on" (p. 5)—condemned
no doubt by his nobility of soul! But had he not replied in his *Criterium?* Apart from the fact that M. Minocchi, quoted by P. Delattre, said absolutely nothing of the kind, by what authority did
M. Minocchi speak in my name? The perfectly correct information of the Rev. Father is passed over in favor of the testimony of
M. Minocchi, simply in order to link me to a scholar who was already in the process of very seriously compromising himself. He
accused me of a cowardly move in order to justify his own. We
shall let it go at that. I speak of these things without acrimony and
even without bitterness. It should, however, be known how a
section of Catholic opinion was stirred up against what some
were affecting to call the broad school.

Since I had been forbidden to make any proper answer to P.
Delattre, it was not for me either to throw any pointed comments
his way *en passant*. I kept silent.[87] I did not go into hiding. But silence is a tactical move. A reply is a declaration of war and a lack

of charity. I remained in Rome only a few days, and did not wait to hear the decision about the *Revue*, which I felt would be favorable.

I was anxious to fetch P. Vincent from Marseilles, where he arrived ill, from Jerusalem, and take him to Lyons where we would have a serious consultation. As a result of this, we installed ourselves at Saint-Bernard, on the Petites-Roches plateau, perfectly sheltered from the north by the Massif de la Chartreuse and overlooking the valley of the Isère. An immense sanatorium has since been built there. We were then by ourselves in a modest inn, where Mgr. Batiffol and Abbé Bouvier and Abbé de Vienne came to join us.

We returned via Greece, traveling straight from Marseilles to Kalamata at the south of the Peloponnese, which we crossed by train as far as Argos. But we at least made an excursion to Messene—a childhood dream—with that enchanting descent into the valley of Pamissos. Then we saw Tiryns, Mycenae, Eleusis and Athens.

On the Nature of Dogma

Some have been surprised to read in the *Revue*[88] an article on the nature of dogma, which seemed outside our customary preoccupations. Let it not be forgotten that I was ceaselessly being urged, by very well-meaning friends, not to appear to be in sympathy with a growing anti-theological movement, which was already what we now call modernism. This was not easy, owing to the ill-defined character of that movement. But M. Le Roy's article *"Qu'est-ce qu'un dogme?"*[89]—the work of a distinguished and serious-minded person[n]—bore upon the Scriptures through the person of Jesus Christ. It seemed that our intervention was consistent with our work in apologetics and within our domain. As M. Le Roy was highly esteemed at the University I approached Abbé Wehrlé,[o] former pupil at the Ecole Normale, who could be

---

n. Edouard Le Roy (1870–1954), mathematician and philosopher, successor to H. Bergson at the Collège de France in 1921, member of the Académie Française in 1945. During the modernist crisis, his three books, *Dogme et critique* (1906) *Le Problème de Dieu* (1907), and *Le problème du miracle* (1912), aroused lively controversy.

o. Johannes Wehrlé (1865–1938), friend and correspondent of Maurice Blondel. On P. Lagrange's contact with Abbé Wehrlé, see Maurice Blondel and August Valensin, *Correspondence*, Vol. I, Paris, 1957, p. 225.

called his equal. We thus showed we were sincere in our constant
assertion to surrender nothing when dogma is at risk. M. Le Roy
felt this criticism very much and gave a reply. He had every
right. But the rank prejudice to which I had just fallen victim
made me fear that we should be thought to have accepted an attack in order to provoke the response, or, at the very least, to
stand indifferent between the warring parties. I therefore insisted
that M. Le Roy should lodge an official complaint. Actually he
was good enough to scale down the fairly lengthy article which
he had at first sent in. This abridged version appeared in January
1906.

It was during the month of August that Fr. Fleming was
moved from Rome. Following the Roman custom toward persons of honorable reputation, a means of escape was arranged for
him by appointing him provincial of his Order, though he had
been Vicar General and was on the point of being elected General. He was replaced as secretary of the Biblical Commission by
Dom. L. Jaussens, of the Order of Saint Benedict. In the sixth
volume of his *Summa theologica* in 1905, he had adopted P. Lagrange's exegetical stance on the Hexameron.[90] But on the Scriptures he had neither knowledge nor opinions of his own. We
could not but miss Fr. Fleming very much, an honest and
friendly person.[91]

The Commentary on Genesis

In 1905, I was still so little aware of the real situation that,
keeping to my plan of preparing people for the publication of the
commentary on Genesis, I pressed to put into the *Revue biblique*
an article on the patriarchs, discussing: "How do they fit in with
history?" I claimed to prove, against the mythical school, that
they existed and had had a function as religious leaders. I did
concede, however, that the course of their lives had been outlined
in Genesis in a way more popular than scientifically historical.
The narrators had been simple enough to draw hardly any distinction between the court of the pharaoh, lord of Upper and
Lower Egypt, and that of a Bedouin sheik such as Abimelek.
This essay, with which I was very pleased, was not passed "because of the circumstances" and remained unpublished. Nevertheless the Master General did not refuse to submit my

commentary on Genesis to examination. I had taught this book five times over, each time with enthusiasm, for its charm is even greater when read in Palestine, at Bethel or Mambre, or upon the heights overlooking the Jordan, the territory chosen by Lot. But it was no easy matter to find examiners who would take responsibility for its publication. P. de Groot, whose authority was considerable, turned my pleas down. He was determined to support me if ever the work had been approved, but did not feel sufficiently sure of himself to take a direct path in that struggle. It was therefore decided to consult the Commission itself. I do not think that it was at my request. My memory is not too precise here, but it would have been contrary to my whole way of going about things, which was never to claim any absolute guarantee; I was rather often overconfident in not hesitating to let the public be judge of discussions. If the Master General wished to take this precautionary step, it was rather at the suggestion of the good P. Kaiser.

Thus the commentary was printed, without an introduction, and up to Chapter VI, 4, in the hope that we could print a longer run later. Meanwhile, it was limited to very few copies, sixty or so, if I remember rightly, with the note *pro manuscripto*, and sent to the cardinals and consultors of the Commission. They were in possession of this document at the beginning of January 1906, when P. Séjourné came to Rome.

3. The Unrest of the Modernist Crisis

FOREBODINGS (1906)

Minds in Confusion

P. Séjourné'could not have failed to recognize the very conservative mood then prevalent in Rome, though he was more of an optimist than I, even sometimes to the point of illusion. In truth, this conservatism was no more than the response of authority to a most disturbing movement within the seminaries. It was after M. Loisy had been condemned that his ideas spread most in Italy. His adherents made no bones about telling everyone that, while his works had indeed been put on the Index, efforts at extracting from them any propositions truly subversive of Christianity were meeting with failure. When young men of little experience, and society women, began to claim expertise in biblical criticism, discipline in the seminaries was jeopardized: bishops complained![1] As for resolutely distinguishing Loisy's approach to criticism from the legitimate methods, the Commission had no encouragement, and would not have been able to arrive at any positive conclusion, even after many long years. While minds were so confused, the most incompetent innovators were speaking loudest.

The Attitudes of the Pope

It was inevitable that suspicion should spread, and that, at the very least, a sort of status quo should be imposed. P. Séjourné saw fit to speak to the Holy Father about the projected commentary on Genesis. "We are at a difficult moment," was his reply: "it would be better to await the decisions and the docu-

ments which are being prepared." Mgr. le Camus, then bishop of
La Rochelle, had been even bolder. The letter he had solicited
from Pius X upon offering his *L'Oeuvre des Apôtres* to His Holiness
had indeed come, but written in the usual diplomatic terms,
nothing more precise than vague flattery. "But this was not," he
told the Pope, "what Your Holiness had promised. Your intentions have surely been misunderstood!" And he got what he
wanted: the Pope indicated a middle course between those who
resort to excessively critical methods and those who do not want
to break in any way with the traditional exegesis hitherto in
force, "even at a time when, provided that the faith is safeguarded, wise progress in scholarship is beckoning them imperi-
ously to do so. Most fortunately, it is between these two extremes
that you are marking out your course," etc.[2] Mgr. Le Camus was
surely not alone in following the path of progress. We too liked to
think that we were part of his group—as indeed he himself
thought. The important thing was that the Pope had asserted the
need for progress.

He proclaimed this need again, in more solemn form, with
an apostolic letter on the teaching of Holy Scripture: "The
teacher of Holy Scripture will consider it his sacred duty never to
depart in the smallest matter from accepted doctrine or from the
tradition of the Church; he will assimilate all true progress in this
field of knowledge, and all the discoveries of modern scholarship,
but he will turn his back on the unfounded theories of innovators."[3] Mgr. Le Camus had been working not only on his own behalf. He wrote to me on February 19: "I spoke at length (to the
Pope) of you and of the unwarranted suspicions cast by some
upon the absolute correctness of your ideas. Pius X had been
charitably given to understand that you were in no way a theologian and that that was why your teachings were becoming dangerous. I remarked to His Holiness that theology rested upon
exegesis, and that it was first of all necessary to reach a profound
understanding of the texts before using them to construct theological theses, something which the old champions of the Roman
tradition seem to forget. Moreover, the Pope did realize that
nothing would stop the new exegetical surge which was gathering force in Catholic circles everywhere, even in Italy, and that it
needed to be channeled in the right direction. Hence his letter on

my latest works, which, he tells me, serve as his spiritual reading matter, just as my life of Our Lord had served as a basis for his meditations. . . . Truth to tell, Nancy (Mgr. Turinaz), Fontaine and Co. are not pleased."

On June 27, the Holy Father gave approval to the decision of the Commission on the Pentateuch, by which it considered that it was opening the door a certain distance to literary criticism, either on the theory of Moses' secretaries, as they have been called, or by the admission of additions, notes and explanations. In order to appreciate the full significance of these concessions, we must remember that scholarly champions of the authenticity of the Pentateuch had been accustomed up to then to base their arguments on the antiquity of its linguistic forms.

Père Cormier

Following this decision, P. Cormier wrote to me (August 24, 1906): "As for your work on Genesis, I very much doubt that it is entirely in line with the views and the spirit of the latest decree of the Commission. . . . I shall have the matter examined, and I shall hold consultations, if I can do so discreetly. I shall then be all right with God."

I shall pause at this comment, which reveals so well the steadfast disposition of this saintly man. I knew him very well indeed, and I was constantly requesting him to settle matters in which anyone else might have been guided by human motives. It never entered my mind that he might act in any way for any motive other than that of pleasing God. I have never thought to appeal to the deep affection which he surely had for me, nor have I ever had cause to fear that he aimed to please others or to curry favor. His prudence was the result not of selfish optimism, but only of his willingness to conform to the directives of the Holy Father. What is more, he did not hesitate to bare his thoughts to the Pope. Pius X esteemed him highly. I repeat that it was providential for me to be under obedience to him.

He himself was a man with remarkable gifts of composition and of style, and he spared me no criticisms. Because he had long since come to know the innermost workings of my heart, he at one time reproved me severely, at another encouraged me to continue with my work, even when I was begging him to let me relax. He always regretted that he had neither the competence nor the intention to make judgments, and therefore he felt at greater liberty to show forbearance than some particular examiner; yet, as a last resort, he occasionally intervened in order to settle a matter, as he did for the article on "Pascal et les prophéties messianiques."[4] Evidently I had complained to him about a kind of régime of terror that was being practiced against scholarship, for he sent me this marvelous letter[5] so characteristic of the way he thought, and of the way the Sovereign Pontiff's mind worked also, for no doubt it was he to whom the letter alludes: "This terrorist regime, I neither know of it, nor am I subjected to it, nor do I practice it. In my cell (which I rarely leave, as I am not in too good a state of health), I do my best to think about what should be done, bearing in mind not only the intrinsic significance of the matters involved, but also people's states of mind and the consideration necessary for dealing with them. If I cannot tell whether I am being too free or too strict, I take advice from above, ready to change tack at the slightest indication and to act more intensively, less intensively or merely differently. I have never received anything from that quarter but advice full of fatherly love for us all, and shrewdness, too, about the dangers which beset the man of God in this field.[6] This amounts to saying that, if one does not exercise a regime of terrorism, one is bound to be fearful, fearful for those young clerics weak in scholarship and in holiness who cry 'exegesis' to bolster independence and to mock tradition, just as they cry 'democracy' in the secret desire of seeing it contribute to the overthrow of Church discipline. Fearful even for those possessed of more talent and priestly holiness, but inclined, involuntarily and without doubting themselves, even perhaps in good faith, to lose or lessen the true sense of things divine and see in authority only a coercive power, whose prohibitions and censures must be avoided at all costs, rather than seeing it as a power capable of increasing a man's stature and making his works fruitful."

Work at the Biblical School

I intended to spend the summer at Jerusalem. As I suffered from erysipelas, P. Séjourné asked permisson for me to go to the waters at Uriage, which had done me a great deal of good ever

since my young days. However, this was judged to be unneces-
sary, and I merely rejoined P. Vincent at Saint-Bernard, and we
traveled back via Athens and Crete. A visit to Cnossos and a few
days in the museum at Candia opened out to us a new world,
Greece before the Greeks. I was sorely tempted to return to the
history of religions! But people like Mgr. Ireland reminded me
that there were questions more urgent for Christian thinkers:
"Do not stay too long in Crete; there are more important excavations waiting for you."[7]

At the Biblical School, P. Jaussen was beginning his study
of Arab customs after a new and fruitful exploration of Retra. P.
Dhorme was settling into the field of Assyriology in which he
was to become a master. His *Choix de textes assyro-babyloniens*,
ready since the beginning of 1906, could not be published without long and prickly negotiations. In spite of his precarious
health, P. Vincent had completed *Canaan d'aprés l'exploration récente*, an admirable work which formed the basis of Palestinian archaeology and still serves as bedside reading for specialists. The
authority of the School was clearly increasing in scholarly circles,
just at the moment when it was becoming suspect to certain persons in the ecclesiastical sphere. In founding it I had had no
doubt that it would be very well received in the Church, but I
certainly had never hoped that it would have such a fine reputation for scholarship.

THE REPRESSION OF THE MODERNISTS (1907)

The winter of 1907 took me to Rome to put the final touches
to a new plan for studies. I had intended to use the opportunity
to make a long-awaited journey to Upper Egypt on the way. But
I was obliged to pause in Cairo, and, after a few days in the Ab-
bassyeh Hospital under the care of the Sisters of Saint Vincent,
had time only to go straight to Italy. Not all the members of the
Committee had yet arrived. There were those who had worked
out a second scheme at Louvain the previous May under the
chairmanship of the Master General, PP. Dummermuth, de
Groot, Weiss, Gardeil, Belon, and de Loë. They were to be
joined by P. Buonpensieri, regent of the Minerva. I was sur-

prised that the flourishing Spanish provinces were not represented. I mentioned this to P. Cormier, with the frankness which
I always showed toward him, at the risk of receiving a scolding.
After a few objections he replied, "Anyway it is too late to send
for someone who has not studied the matter. You shall have, my
dear Father, P. Coderch as your ally." P. Coderch was appointed. I had brought the matter up only out of gratitude to
Spain, where I had studied for six years at Salamanca. Without
realizing it I had gained a very precious support.

Studies in the Dominican Order

If I devote some time to the ordering of studies, this is because the change brought about by the new program would not
have been possible without the existence of the School at Jerusalem, whose progress the Order was beginning to follow sympa-
thetically, and because reciprocally our house gained a great deal
from the new arrangement. The plan which had been proposed
at Louvain prescribed eight years of study, though without totally excluding—with a dispensation from the Master General—
a reduction to seven. It laid down for the two first years seventeen lectures a week entirely on philosophy, since the four lectures on science were to be understood as "science related to a
philosophical physics and psychology," in addition to the three
lectures on the history of philosophy and ten on pure philosophy.

If this regime were imposed on young men still under the
charm of literary studies, it would be enough, as I had written to
the Master General, to "send them off their heads." But it would
also have involved a failure to recognize both the needs of the
present time and the tradition of our Order, since Oriental languages (including Greek), so strongly recommended by our chapters, were not even mentioned. We were shutting ourselves up in
a magnificent and sublime metaphysical ghetto which few students could reach and to which few would be attracted. I wrote
at that time "The principal purpose of the proposed schema, to
which everything else is, if not sacrificed, at least subordinated,
is to instruct lectors of Thomist theology. Only they will receive
the full fruit of their studies, and it is to this that everything con-
verges, in such a way that all others drop off the tree like dry
fruit, either after three or four years, or after five or six. What is

more, those who are sacrificed or rebuffed in this way are not only people of normal intelligence but very penetrating minds, who would render admirable service to the Church and bring great honor to the Order, but are not specially gifted for dialectical reasoning and metaphysics. It might be said that we are intending, as certain trainers do, to form only one type of racehorse."

I considered, therefore, as my printed statement of opinion had made clear, that "in Church doctrine there are two roads, one philosophico-scientifico-speculative, the other historico-philologico-positive." Consequently, these disciplines should not be imposed on everyone—for gone are the times when we thought them necessary for the understanding of the Mosaic account of the origins of the world—but only on those who were to follow the former of the two ways; for those who were to follow the latter of the two, they should be replaced by languages. Furthermore, I asked, at the very least, basing myself on the opinion of Fr. Kennedy, who unfortunately was absent, that there should never be more than fifteen compulsory lectures a week.

The Duration of the Studies

As for the duration of the studies, eight years did not seem to me excessive, provided that they were quite differently arranged: six years to the lectorate and two years of special complementary studies afterward.[8] At Jerusalem we had always been satisfied with these six years of what I called passive study, which the students were always keen to finish. But when they were encouraged to win distinction by a special subject, their appetite revived, and they willingly underwent a course tailored to their particular interests. P. Dummermuth, who in fact was very sympathetic to the idea, smilingly objected to me that all I wanted was to attract to Jerusalem young lectors of Holy Scripture.[9] But with absolute sincerity I answered that it would be no bad thing to found at Rome, for example, a faculty of canon law, at Fribourg to specialize in history, at Louvain in positive theology or the social sciences, at the Saulchoir in philosophy. In this I was trying only to give my thoughts concrete form without having the least intention of getting mixed up in these colleges. In the end the idea was adopted. But a decision to reduce the basic course to six years proved to be impossible; seven was the limit, and this altered the whole nature of my project. In addition, as I had spoken very strongly against the privileged position of science, in the end nothing at all was laid down about it. Refusing to admit its exclusive privilege, but far from blind to the need for some science, I had said, "We are convinced that our Order will lose its authority in philosophy if it does not have philosophers fully conversant with modern science." Subsequent events have amply demonstrated the truth of this.

In any case, although according to the previous schema Holy Scripture figured during the first four years only in the third year, under the heading *Tractatus de auctoritate historica librorum Novi Testamenti per tres horas*, the distribution finally adopted was: 1st year: Hebrew—two hours; 2nd and 3rd year: Special introduction to Old and New Testament—two hours. For the four years of theology there was general agreement.[10] In the face of the overwhelming demand of the chapters for a course on public speaking I make bold to repeat my written statement of opinion: "The course in public speaking should be abolished. Read the works of Cicero on this subject and you will understand that it is pointless." This great orator, the first of rhetoricans, teaches very aptly that an orator is formed above all by listening to great masters. And, in fact, the *ratio studiorum* of 1907 did not include a course on sacred eloquence.

Our meetings took place from April 2 to April 6, and the *ratio studiorum* was promulgated by the Master General on April 6. I had been alone in requesting that it should be submitted to the chapter which was to take place at Viterbo. The Holy Father approved everything. On April 4 he was good enough to receive the commission, presented by the Master General. When my name was called out he asked: "*Come stanno a Gerusalemme?*"[a] And that was all.

Suspicion
I am writing these memoirs on Easter Sunday, April 4, 1926, and I can still feel, dominated though it is by gratitude to God, the piercing sadness of Easter Sunday, March 31, 1907.

---

a. How are things at Jerusalem?

What a welcome in 1903 and what a welcome in 1907! Confidence had given way to suspicion. Even sympathy increased the sadness of the occasion. Hardly had I been ushered into the presence of Cardinal Rampolla, in his little palace of Saint Martha, when he cried out "Go gently, Père Lagrange, go gently." And then more quietly, "The Holy Father is uneasy; bishops have written. . . ." For my part, I had written nothing new, and the cardinal's good will toward me remained unchanged; but he was also upset, as I have just said, by disobedient tendencies which once in a while appealed to the *Revue Biblique* as their justification. After that, what ought I to expect from Cardinal Merry del Val, the secretary of state? He appeared to me in all the splendor of a prince of the Church, heightened by the marvelous background of the Borgia apartments where he was then living. He even had a few gracious words for me when I asked after Mme. Merry del Val, his mother, to whom I had been introduced in Vienna, where her husbannd had been Spanish ambassador. Then came regrets for the deplorable situation of souls, particularly of the young clergy. I knew it well enough but, as no one could dispute this deplorable situation and the regrets were only too justified, I dared to put to His Eminence the decisive question: Was the remedy to turn the clock back, to hold on for grim death to positions—not those of Catholic tradition, but the stock-in-trade of seminary professors—or would it not be better to advance as the Holy Father had recommended in his letter to Mgr. le Camus? "Aha!" replied the cardinal sharply. "That letter has been much misused." There followed other visits of which I have only a confused memory; I was sinking deeper and deeper into a sea of bitterness.

Prohibition of Publishing

In this situation how could I think of publishing the commentary on Genesis? I still flattered myself that the publication itself would dispel a number of prejudices. The cardinals and consultors of the Biblical Commission, who held my proofs, had not been willing to pronounce upon, or even officially to examine this essay.[11] I was therefore referred back to the Master General. He for his part objected that he could not move forward because the Commission had taken the matter in hand. Nevertheless, after a year of silence, it was clear that it would not depart from its stance of silence, and if this silence did not constitute approbation, it did not constitute disapproval either. A theologian as conservative and thoroughly Thomistic as P. Dummermuth unhesitatingly supported the project of publishing.[12] The Master General gave his consent, and work was about to begin when I received the following letter from P. Cormier, dated May 29, 1907: "It is our duty to inform you of the instructions we have just received through the agency of His Eminence the Cardinal Secretary of State relating to the proposed publication of your work on Genesis. It is the wish of the Holy Father that the work be published neither in book form nor in the *Revue*, nor as proofs, nor in any other form at all. Consequently we are informing the *Revue Biblique* that it is not to start printing your articles. We fully sympathize, my dear father, with the sorrow which this news will bring you, and we pray our father Saint Dominic that he will gain for you the grace to accept this trial in a religious spirit. We beg our Lord graciously to grant you, your work and your beloved School his most generous blessings."[13]

This evidence of paternal sympathy toward me was not enough for the Master General, who had originally authorized the printing and did not wish our poor, very poor, house to shoulder the expenses. He reimbursed M. Lecoffre for the expenses which he had incurred for the proofs—if I remember rightly, the sum of six thousand francs.

Steps Taken Against P. Condamin

I was not the only one to incur such a prohibition of publishing. P. Condamin had submitted for examination a long literary and historical introduction which was to complement his translation of Isaiah. Of the four examiners designated, two had expressed some doubts about whether its publication would be opportune. The General of the Society of Jesus entrusted a new examination to P. Murillo. In spite of his extremely unfavorable judgment, the General finally gave permission to print, and fairly rapid progress was being made when, on the same day, toward the end of May, again by the agency of Cardinal Merry del Val, the Pope asked the General that "immediate and precise orders" should be given to halt the printing of this work because "the Pope has good reason to believe that this work does not deserve his approval." The General of the Jesuits did not see fit to remain silent, and sent back to the cardinal a detailed message which led him to grant that "it is clear from these explanations that the information previously given about the book was inaccurate." But the order remained in force and has so continued to the present time.[14]

What was the source of the information? We never discovered—at any rate I did not. And I add that I have no reproach to make to the Holy Father. He had his reasons, more imperious than those produced by a denounciation. P. Yves de la Brière, S.J. seems to me to have put it correctly, without intending any offense to Pius X. This great Pope acted in certain cases like heads of state who proclaim a state of siege or martial law, in circumstances where pressing danger demands exceptional steps. There was danger, the Pope well knew. It was for him to re-establish the general safety whatever the cost to certain individuals. At this very moment he was proposing to publish a list of condemned propositions. Doubtless he did not wish to be said that he was severe toward some and too indulgent toward others. Silence seemed to him the most appropriate attitude, to allow meditation on and profit from the information given by the decree *Lamentabili*.

The Decree *Lamentabili*

In fact the measure which the Holy Office adopted was the condemnation of sixty-five propositions without any author's name. The thought of M. Loisy especially at that time could not be expressed in short, sharp propositions. Perhaps also there was a determination to avoid the sort of controversy about rights and facts which had so disastrously prolonged Jansenism. Teachings themselves were condemned and, though it was obvious enough that most of the propositions reproduce the physionomy of M. Loisy's teaching at that time, some among them would have been repudiated by that author. But what is wholly clear is that not a single one of those propositions had been directly or indirectly stated with approbation in the *Revue Biblique*. A good number of them had been attacked; others had not been mentioned. The Holy Office had, therefore, accurately discerned what in the critical movement deserved condemnation, and had delineated it clearly. We should, then, have benefited from this clarification. Once the thunderbolt has fallen those who have escaped it think themselves safe. And in fact I am confident that none of our most implacable adversaries applied any single one of the propositions to us. But the accusation continued to be leveled at us that we did not reverence tradition sufficiently, that we did not have the *sense* of the Church, that P. Lagrange in particular was too assertive in his new opinions, too enthusiastic about modern critical scholarship, not respectful enough of the direction of Church authorities.

We would have had to repeat again and again our protestations of docility and obedience, yield to those incessant demands to define the exact nature of our submission—demands made by people who had no right to do so, and no respect for the susceptibilities of an honest person.[15] Once an honest man has given his word, it is useless for him to repeat it for the benefit of one who will not believe it. On the contrary, he would merely be making himself suspect in the eyes of those who know how honorable people behave. Nevertheless I did my best to demonstrate the solid foundations and the solid benefit of the decree of the Holy Office.[16] But suspicions did not go away. In order to render them ineffective, I entirely abandoned the study of the Old Testament except in function of the New, and since my superiors would not allow me to say goodbye to biblical studies, I devoted myself to the study of the Gospel. This left no gap. P. Dhorme, with his masterly command of the subject, kept a link with the Bible through the ancient East. In June of that year, the School for the first time presented candidates for the examinations of the Biblical Commission. PP. Abel, Colunga and Mainage received their licentiates.

P. Lagrange, Prior

P. Séjourné having completed his second triennium, P. Lagrange was elected prior. Then several of the brethren went with him to Hebron where he had a pleasant stay. Our tents were among the vines near the Russian tower, in which we had set up a portable altar. We had the unpleasant experience, however, of hearing for the first time a gramophone in the land of Abraham.

We were wondering whether the Master General would confirm the election; then on August 12 we saw P. Savignac riding down the road from Hebron, bearing the letters patent. I signed them *apud quercum Mambre*, a childishness excused by the charm of such a memory. On my return to Jerusalem, I buried myself in rabbinic messianism. It was the only period of my life when I have found work wearisome. What chaos! What lack of a sense of reality! What lack of any real human feelings in the absence of real religious feeling hidden by the turgid style. P. Abel was perfectly correct—though he might have hesitated to say it in front of a distinguished Jew—that there is more wisdom in the *Antigone* of Sophocles than there is in the whole of the Talmud. One might even say that the Talmud contains no trace of wisdom at all.

As soon as I had been appointed prior, I gave up the post of rector, which was entrusted to P. Jaussen. But at his request I continued to teach. Such was the advice of P. Walsh, the canonical visitor.[17] It was the first official visitation of the priory.

Work at the Biblical School.

That year there appeared *Les Coutumes arabes au pays de Moab* of P. Jaussen, and *Le Messianisme chez les Juifs*. Hardly had he mastered the subject of Tranjordanian Arabs than P. Jaussen pushed his explorations still further. Taking as his companion P. Savignac, whose sure touch in both philology and archaeology were great assets, quite apart from his gift for photography, he undertook from March to May 1907 an archaeological mission in Arabia, that is, the Hejaz, and more specifically Medain-Saleh, the second necropolis of the Nabateans, far more fertile in inscriptions than Petra. The results were presented in a magnificent book published in 1909 by Leroux.

In Beirut the Jesuits, who, it may be said, had been spurred on by the results of our School at Jerusalem, had opened an Oriental Faculty, whose organ was the *Mélanges*, so much appreciated by the learned world. In 1907 a course of exegesis was added, making the similarity to our School even closer. P. Durand, S.J., unburdened himself to me on the subject, with some embarrassment. "Do I need to tell you that in all this no thought of rivalry ever entered our heads, and still less any implied criticism of your work at Jerusalem?"[18] Were there then people in-

clined to think that the Jesuits were critical of our teaching? What
an extraordinary notion—though such a notion might well be
supported by the pamphlets occasioned by P. Martin's letter. As
for rivalry, Beirut was far enough distant from Jerusalem to save
us raising any difficulties. Nor in fact did we. If only things had
gone no further! It was at least some consolation that I heard it
said of me by one of the most distinguished minds in the Society:[19] "To put the matter fairly, progress since the *Revue Biblique*
began to be published has already been notable and full of promise. There are, and will be more and more, men well trained in
method and sufficiently masters of their subject to borrow from
our adversaries the weapons which constituted their strength,
without simultaneously adopting their errors. It is a consolation
to your friends to realize that you, perhaps more than anyone else
alive, have contributed to this great movement. This will come to
be recognized more and more with the passage of time."

Batiffol Leaves Toulouse

Also this year, Mgr. Batiffol left Toulouse. I need not go
into the details of this sad affair. Rome refused to make a decision; the bishops held back. The archbishop of Toulouse, Mgr.
Germain, insisted on the removal of his rector. Mgr. Batiffol refused to resign, but allowed Cardinal Richard to recall him to
Paris. Truth compels me to say that during the fifteen years of
our partnership, he had always come down on the side of what
we considered the right way, critical scholarship which did not
lose contact with theology. He was one of the first to combat
Loisy, the first to attack Fr. Tyrrell, S.J., whom his confrères
treated with a curious indulgence, though certainly their attitude
changed when he was no longer one of their number. Batiffol
was, incidentally, much more optimistic than myself about the
dangers to which a violent reaction would make us liable. On August 10, 1907, he wrote to me of his profound satisfaction with
the decree *Lamentabili*, in his familiar style, more respectful deep
down than superficially: "The sixty-five *theologoumena* are only
hitting at the errors which we are fighting; we've got nothing to
complain of and the mark is hit with well-calculated accuracy,
and hit hard. For once the Holy Office has had some good marks-
men who have not hit our own lines. What we are defending is

the journey toward more moderate ideas. One more reason to rely on Rome and to make an effort in Rome." Back at his post as chaplain of Sainte-Barbe, Mgr. Batiffol was, of course, all the more free to continue his work, which was consecrated to the defense of our Mother the Church, *Matri Ecclesiae*.

A TIME FOR PATIENCE (1908)

Minocchi in Revolt

In February I at last had the leisure to tour Upper Egypt with P. Savignac. With us was M. Reilly, an American Sulpician. At Aswan we found M. Clermont-Ganneau, and joined in on his excavations for a few days. The outcome was less brilliant than he had hoped. The Germans had already put their finger on the right place. But that was no reason against publishing the documents he had. Only the Khnum-animals in the Cairo Museum testify to his activity. We returned on March 8, and what sad news from Rome greeted me! M. Minocchi, already in open revolt, was claiming the protection of my name. So I was considered responsible for his defection. A little Italian paper, *Riscossa*, had written on February 15:[20] "The Florentine professor has already shown his intention beforehand with this declaration which is the product of a pride which goes beyond all bounds: 'I shall never act against my formed conscience as a Catholic and a scholar, for which I shall have to answer to God on my deathbed.' It is a conscience formed on an authority which is suspect, extremely suspect—that of P. Lagrange, which he prefers to that of the Church." Luckily the Master General, relying on his personal knowledge and the evidence of his theologians, was not the person to be intimidated. He wrote to me on February 18: "The excerpts which I enclose show that the enemies of the Church and of the faith are trying, as I said to you in my last letter, to link themselves to the faithful servants, in order to bring into disrepute the measures which the Holy See considers that it must take. But these efforts, even if they have some temporary success, will in the end make all the clearer what these enemies are really scheming, and this will strengthen the truth. Prudence, patience and confidence." Nevertheless the amazing effect of M. Minocchi's maneuver reached as far as the Pope. On February 23 I received a letter saying that a French lady, whose husband was ambassador of the royalists, had asked him to condemn me.[21] I cannot believe that Pius X gave the least credit to this feminine theology, but when receiving the bishop of Grenoble who was presenting to him one of his priests, a former pupil of ours, M. Dumaine, he had said sadly: "*Jerusalem! Pater Lagrange . . . aliquando claudicat.*"[22] In a letter of February 1, 1911, P. Cormier light-heartedly comments on that saying: "The leg which represents learning and criticism is alert, indefatigable, precious. The other, dedicated simultaneously to the defense of tradition and to the spreading of rules or advice emanating from the teaching authority to suit the needs and dangers of the present time, does not refuse to cooperate, but follows the other with an air of inferiority—at least one often has that impression."

An Ominous Crack

Soon afterward, an ominous crack caused me to be very sharply apprehensive. I had asked for a review of *The Theology of St. Paul* by P. Prat, S.J., from one of his confrères, thus sure that I would be able to please them both. The sincerely cordial answer was nevertheless a refusal, solely on the grounds of a wish expressed by their superiors "to suspend for the moment, in order to avoid false interpretations and possible complications, our collaboration with *Revue Biblique*. . . . At present the treachery of certain people and their hypocritical rationalism has brought suspicion upon scientific exegesis."[23] The hopes, contained in this letter and in a note from P. Condamin, for a better future after a temporary prohibition were, unfortunately, never realized. The ban on *Revue Biblique* was not everywhere understood so rigorously, but I was never again so keen on occasional collaborators. Now we would have to expect other withdrawals. A Roman professor was kind enough to write to me that *Le Messianisme chez les Juifs* had been for him a "veritable banquet." But how could he write a review of it? "It would be repugnant for me to speak of you without saying what I think, and a frankly favorable review would be misinterpreted by those who wield great influence at this moment. In short I would compromise myself without doing you any good."[24] I had to content myself with this explanation which claimed to be loyal and which was only too well-founded.

Cardinal Sevin and Loisy

This makes me all the more grateful to Mgr. Sevin, at that time bishop of Châlons and later cardinal of Lyons, already well-known as an opponent of *Le Sillon* and a very reliable theologian. He remembered our discussions at the seminary of Bourg, our common homeland, when one day, having embraced each other in an attempt to consult a large book, we continued to argue about efficacious grace without noticing that we were squatting on the ground. He wrote to me on August 20, 1908: "You never believed that I could ever doubt you, or number myself among your adversaries or those who unjustly censured you. Whenever I have had the chance I have affectionately and warmly spoken in your defense. . . . Why do our exegetes lack your theology?" The same letter contains a sort of prophecy of Pius X which has not yet been fulfilled. The bishop of Châlons was asking him how he should behave toward M. Loisy who belonged to the diocese of which he had charge. "Believe me," said the Pope, "you will have to act when he is converted." "He, converted? He, return after having gone astray out of spiritual pride?" "Yes, my son, he will return." "May God fulfill Your Holiness' prediction!" "He will return, and you will give him good advice." Unfortunately Cardinal Sevin is no more.[25]

SILENCE AND REFLECTION (1909)

Pius X and P. Lagrange

The attitude at Rome remained very severe, even with a tendency to exaggerate the gravity of the Holy Father's criticism. Here is an example. The Master General was told that the Pope, in discussing the biblical question with the archbishop of New Orleans, had said[26] of P. Lagrange: "There are grounds for fearing that he will not change unless he feels the iron hand of the Holy See." In an audience of Monday, June 21, P. Cormier was quite open about it with Pius X, fearing that, at the instigation of various adversaries, he could be meditating some act of sternness.

So he begged him, if he had particular charges to make, to inform him of them, so that he could alert P. Lagrange and avoid a public reproach, or even a formal censure. "He said to me," wrote the Master General to a provincial of the Order,[27] " 'Now there is nothing, but it is the past.' He gave me further to understand that no disciplinary measure was in preparation and that he had no doubts about the good qualities of that father. 'But,' he added, "he does not pay enough attention to theology.' " P. Cormier was careful to relay to me only the reassuring elements in this conversation. He passed on to me only the first part, "Now there is nothing, but it is the past," commenting, "I think he meant Genesis and the ideas expressed on historical appearances and on the mixed, composite, semi-legendary character of the patriarchs."[28] Then he chided me vigorously for keeping silence, that is, for making no retraction on these points. Circumstances seemed to him favorable.

Bible and History

La Méthode Historique, of which 4,400 copies had been printed, was now completely out-of-print and much in demand. I would have liked another thousand or two thousand copies to be printed. The Master General would not give his consent and invited me to use the opportunity to rework the book completely in view of the new light given by the Holy See and its comments. He urged me in terms which I still find moving so many years later, "Personally, I am waiting eagerly for something of this kind, realizing how much esteem and confidence this would add, not only to the Biblical School at Jerusalem but also to the whole Order. This would be an act of charity on your part and, at the same time, one of clear-sightedness and humility which would affect your whole future—a holy death included."[29] Now that death is at the gates I wonder how I can have refused such a gracious and respectful request, in spite of all my liberty of conscience. But truly I was in a difficult position! The lectures for *La Méthode Historique* having once been given could be re-edited only from start to finish. The Master General was not content that changes should be indicated only in the form of footnotes. The whole book would therefore have to be reworked, or rather a new book written. I had just abandoned this whole field on the grounds that it was too dangerous. And when I asked to be shown the passages that needed correction, I was told to find them myself by referring to papal documents. The Pope had never made any specific charges to the Master General, and the papal decrees on modernism did not refer to such questions specifically; we were certainly not in the sights of *Lamentabili*. The Master General was thinking of Genesis, of the patriarchs. But the Genesis commentary had not been published, and the patriarchs were still in my boxes, where they remain to this day.[30] There remained the question of historical appearances, an important and recurrent complaint. But had I ever claimed that the Bible contained no more history than natural history? This mistake had always been far from my thoughts, and I had never suggested anything like it. I granted only that certain stories which had been believed to be genuinely historical only seemed to be so, and this hypothesis had been accepted for certain cases by the decree of the Biblical Commission on June 23, 1905. I will even reproduce the text. The question ran: "Is the principle of exegesis acceptable which holds that the books of Holy Scripture which are accepted as either partially or wholly historical sometimes recount what is not properly speaking and truly objectively history, but that they render only what seems to be history in order to indicate something which is not contained in the literal and historical meaning of the words?"

Has anyone ever supported this thesis exactly in this form? No matter. It is well known that the Congregations habitually express questions in the way best suited for resolving questions. But well-informed people would not hesitate to answer. "This is just P. Lagrange's viewpoint." And they would add, "This viewpoint has been condemned, since the answer was *negative*." In fact, however, the negative answer, since it is in opposition to an unqualified thesis, which was not mine, would allow a discreet use of the criterion proposed. "The answer is negative except in a case, which must not be easily or casually accepted, and only if the feeling of the Church is not opposed to it, and when it is the judgment of the Church, where it could be proved by solid arguments, that the sacred writer had no intention of writing history truly and properly so-called, but intended to put forward under the appearance and form of history a parable, an allegory or some meaning other than the literal and historical sense of the word."[31]

Suspicion and Self-Justification

Was it really the moment, in 1909, to go back over such delicate matters? Basically, the danger of our position was that we had seemed to be on the same side as those scholars whose abandonment of the faith had saddened the Church. This abandonment was attributed to their critical scholarship and the conclusion was hastily drawn that there was a premeditated and treacherous plan afoot to drag down the Church to the lowest depths. There was no more solid proof that such a Macchiavellian plan existed than there had been for the beginning of Jansenism. It was only gradually that certain souls had departed from the true way and had fallen into error. It goes without saying that at a certain moment their inner convictions no longer made sense of their being in the Church. Even then they could delude themselves; hypocrisy began only with the clear realization that they were playing a double game. We were suspected of this hypocrisy, as a letter from the Master General shows clearly enough: "It was an exaggeration to say that there was a proposal to suppress our School officially, or to let it die of starvation. But no one could deny that there was a lack of enthusiasm to favor it, in the absence of some reassurance about the secret thoughts occurring there, however correct the exterior." Is it ever possible to defend oneself against accusations of hypocrisy?[32] God alone proves the mind and the heart. To right and to left there were exaggerations of propositions which the best theologians had not condemned. Placed and indeed cramped between those who desired my destruction in order to ruin the School and those who were all the more surely bringing it nearer by making me responsible for their defection, had I any refuge more sure than silence and recourse to God?

Among those who retained some confidence, for example the members of the Master General's council, our attachment to scientific exegesis at the risk of hurting some of the faithful was considered a mistake. I do not claim that this matter is easy to resolve. At a time when the principal intellectual forces are united against the Church and the Bible, can a Catholic have any other

thought than to defend that Church and Bible? Is it even opportune to let Catholics know specious objections? Since Scripture
has God as its author, it should be a continuous source of edification for believers. Why desert these dwellings which are solid
because they are heavenly, simply in order to undertake a combat
about philosophy and history, as if Scripture were not the mistress of them all? Let them offer their support when appropriate,
but let them never raise their heads against accepted positions.
Such was the conviction of P. Nardelli, the Master General's assistant for Italy, whom he happily entrusted with the examination of my articles and books. The only exegesis worthy of a
member of the Order of Preachers was one of pure apologetics
and edification. This way of thinking has a certain attraction; it is
tending to sweep the field. In the same way, people will say:
Why bring the faults of the Popes to light? Others will do quite
enough of that. Let us say about the Popes only what will lead the
faithful into the path of obedience and even of devotion to the
Pope. Fair enough! But there are grounds for fearing that this opportunism is somewhat short-sighted.

It seemed important to get rid of a number of heretics whose
preaching was endangering the salvation of the faithful. But if a
few condemnations, however justified, occasioned a general dis-
affection toward the Church, do they still seem apposite after this
passage of time? The same holds good in the search for truth. It
often clamors impatiently, and can bring great difficulties to certain souls. But if it is possible to assert that the Church, the pillar
of truth, leaves the search for truth to others, will not the harm be
greater still? We have been told often enough that we are not free,
that we are confirmed from beforehand in the truth. Surely we
need to show that we are not afraid of truth? And when it is a,
question of philological, literary or purely historical problems,
how is it possible constantly to use as a smokescreen the feeling of
the Church, that is, a middle road to which no one has ever kept?
Can independent thinkers not have hit the mark? Then why not
admit it loyally? Leo XIII and Pius X suggested that we should.
What reason have we for forgetting this part of their instructions?
But that is enough to excuse me, or rather to indicate the line of
excuse to which I was looking at that time.

More docility would have done me more good. When I think of the very generous welcome which Pius X gave to my submission in 1912, I tell myself that if at that time I had written him a filial letter, in order to open my heart to him more completely than I had done before, his suspicions would have been dissipated. I condemned myself too completely to doing nothing which could be construed as a *captatio benevolentiae*. And what could one letter do against the constantly renewed attacks which reached His Holiness?

In this year of 1909, the Holy Father founded the Pontifical Biblical Institute of Rome and entrusted it to the Jesuit Fathers.

Financial Difficulties

At about the same time, as I was still prior and was very unhappy about the feeding of the house, and feeling that I was not good at what the Master General pleasantly called "stretching out my hand," I decided that I should open a subscription with P. Cormier's agreement. Some kind persons did not fail to interpret this almost desperate measure as a plot to protest and to provoke protests against the new Biblical Institute.[33] But the decree is dated May 7, and I have no recollection when it reached us in Jerusalem. My supposed reply would have had to be pretty prompt, since the Master General, who saw in it no more malice than it in fact contained, wrote to me as early as June 18: "As for opening a subscription for the School, it seems to me best that this should not be included in the *Revue* because of the intellectual character of the periodical. But in itself it seems to me thoroughly proper, and I would never eye it askance." And he added delicately: "We are criticized on other points, but not for indiscretion in raising money, and we must keep up this reputation."

In any case the foundation of a new Institute entrusted to the Jesuit Fathers, no less than their enforced secession from the *Revue Biblique*, had done nothing to damage my excellent relations with the French Jesuits. It is undeniable that our labors were followed more closely by them than by the Dominicans. That very year P. d'Alès asked me for some articles for his *Dictionary of Apologetics* (I managed to accept only the word *Iran*) and I asked P. Lebreton to accept for his Library of Historical Theology the book of P. Petitot[b] on Pascal. P. Goupil, the biblical correspondent of *L'Univers*, assured me of his sympathy,[34] and P. Pinard de la Boulange, as soon as he became a master in the history of religions, made a point of telling me the care he had taken to refer to my works, and their importance.[35]

The Master General had not allowed me to deliver in Paris the conferences which Mgr. Baudrillart had asked for. But those of P. Dhorme on Assyro-Babylonian religion made known his mastery of that subject, constantly renewed as it was by excavations.

In 1909, the publication of the *Acta Apostolicae Sedis* began. The decisions of the Biblical Commission properly belonged there, and henceforth the *Revue Biblique* did not have the privilege of promulgating them. It is to reflect this new situation that we have stopped giving them prominence. This change was an obvious one to make, and was not imposed on us.

The year 1909 witnessed the resumption of the journeys of P. Jaussen and P. Savignac in Arabia, which contributed so powerfully to establishing the reputation of the School with the Académie des Inscriptions et Belles-Lettres. At the time of this major difficult and even dangerous undertaking, crowned as it was with complete success, I pause only for an amusing contrast at a little skirmish against the sanctuary of Saint-Etienne. On the evening of December 26, the feast of St. Stephen, there arrived in Jerusalem and Bethlehem an anonymous pamphlet, distributed pretty widely by the post: *Il luogo del martirio di S. Stefano e le sue chiese in Gerusalemme*. It was a charming way of wishing us a happy feast while unashamedly attacking the authenticity of our sanctuary. I immediately replied in a few pages, which provoked another retort. The Master General, informed by receiving my little note, blamed me quite severely for having it printed without his authorization. As for Mgr. Radini Tedeschi, bishop of Bergamo, who had been put forward as the author, he did me the honor of writing: "The *fragments* of letters published on the sub-

---

b. Hyacinthe Petitot (1880–1934), a Dominican, student and then professor of dogmatic theology at the Biblical School from 1900 to 1912, who was well known for his books on philosophy, hagiography and spirituality.

ject of the little building over the place of St. Stephen's stoning were not intended for publication, nor were the letters as a whole."[36] I let the matter rest, as the question was discussed in a workmanlike fashion by P. Vincent and P. Abel in their great work on Jerusalem. I mention the somewhat ill-considered attacks of the Assumptionist P. Vailhé only to record the help given us by the Bollandist P. Peeters. Cardinal Rampolla, in his life of St. Melanie, also came down on our side.

A YEAR OF CALM (1910)

The Commentary on St. Mark

A year of calm and of hard work.[37] Thus the commentary on St. Mark was completed and approved at Rome. That winter I left Jerusalem only to spend three days in Jericho during January. I was preaching the retreat for the Christian Brothers at Bethlehem when, on August 30, P. Crechet, the sub-prior, and P. Vincent brought me the Master General's confirmation of a second triennium. I was completely bowled over, but I did not dare to refuse, since it was a formal precept. The Master General was kind enough to thank me.

In 1910 P. Jaussen and P. Savignac made another journey into Arabia which covered the School with glory. I would have dwelt on it at length except that it provided the material for a splendid book which was published in 1914 by Geuthner. An interesting trip on the Dead Sea at the beginning of January provided P. Abel with the theme for a very pleasant volume which had a lively success. The School really was equipped with excellent professors, every one of them a master of his field of specialization. But the number of students did not increase. Neither among the secular clergy nor among the Orders, even our own, was there any increase in the realization of the usefulness of the biblical studies done at our School. Furthermore, zeal for biblical studies having grown cold, if the stream still existed, it ran toward Rome. P. Petitot lectured at the Institut Catholique in Paris. PP. Abel, Dhorme and Boulanger made a journey to Aleppo and Antioch.

Recherches de Sciences Religieuses

This year saw the foundation of an important *Bulletin d'an-cienne littérature chrétiènne*, founded by Mgr. Batiffol in partner-ship with M. de Labriolle. Its aim was too specialized to risk any rivalry with us. Such was not the case with *Recherches de sciences re-ligieuses* founded by the French Jesuits; thus P. de Grandmaison, the director, wrote to me: "This collection would certainly never have seen the light if *Revue Biblique* had still been open to us,"[38] that is to say, if the Jesuit Fathers had not been obliged by their superiors to withdraw. And the prohibition can hardly have been absolute, since at that time P. van Kasteren offered me an article which appeared in 1911 (pp. 96ff), as did also one of his con-freres, an article which I had to refuse. Nevertheless I gave the new periodical a warm welcome, for which I was thanked: "I have read with gratitude the very fraternal passage which you are kind enough to devote to *Recherches* at the end of the July number of *Revue Biblique*: *Bella gerant alii*! There can be no doubt that our program, if not in the way it works out, then at least in its spirit, coincides with yours."[39] We maintained the most courteous re-lations with the new periodical, as also with the excellent *Analecta Bollandiana*. The Bollandist P. Delahaye was no less well dis-posed to us than P. Peeters. He said to me one day that in their houses of study—he meant in Belgium, England and France— our word was law, an exaggeration excused by politeness. It was wrong of me to reply, airily enough: "Is it then in order to uphold the same beliefs, presented in better form, that the Society wishes to destroy our work?" I should have distinguished be-tween two kinds of people within the Society: those who, far from attacking us, showed an increasingly lively sympathy with us, even in public, and those who showed themselves so stern. Fr. Martindale was among the former. I had written a little pam-phlet against the *Orpheus* of Salomon Reinach. Fr. Martindale translated it into English and wrote to me: "If this has given you any pleasure, such was precisely my aim in doing it."[40]

The Biblical Institute at Rome

At the Pontifical Biblical Institute in Rome the attitude was rather different. We were not the only ones to be disquieted by this tendency to lord it over biblical studies throughout the world. The success of P. Fonck's lectures had been triumphant, in the presence of several cardinals, numerous prelates and an audience of more than five hundred. Mgr. Ladeuze, having been appointed rector of the University of Louvain, was immediately denounced to Cardinal Merry del Val, and could not appoint M. Coppieters to take his place because of "criticism by P. Fonck of the *Synopsis Evangeliorum* published" by him. A professor at Rome, a friend of the Institute, or at least an ally of it, whose loyalty had never seemed to waver, wrote to me: "The Society of Jesus wishes to be the uncontested mistress of teaching at Rome, and will soon achieve this position, unless there are unforeseen accidents. It must be admitted that the high standard of their ambitions is equalled by the low standard of their scholarship."[41]

Indeed our fathers in Rome, with their high ideal of learning, did not fear the comparison between the Jesuits and ourselves. At least one of them wrote to me: "Every serious thinker will recognize the advantages of your situation."[42] Unfortunately that was precisely where our greatest danger lay. It was the situation which had, if possible, to be taken away from us, or at least shared. There are indications to show that this was the motive behind a new and more decisive campaign against us. To settle down beside us to do the same job as ourselves would have been an odious move without the honorable pretext of doing it better than the men who were failing to satisfy the head of the Church.

BEFORE THE STORM (1911)

Reactions to the Commentary on St. Mark

Without the black mark of the foundation of another biblical institute at Jerusalem, the year would have been very calm as regards the biblical question. My commentary on St. Mark, which came out at the beginning of the year, made a very reassuring impression. A Roman professor wrote to me:[43] "You have done the task of a scholar—it was expected; you have done the task of a priest and a convinced apologist—in certain circles where you are known only by travesties of the truth it will be an agreeable surprise. I dare prophesy therefore that this work will be received with the highest favor by Catholics of every shade, even at Rome." Although he had become very prudent and was obliged to remain extremely reserved, Cardinal Rampolla wrote to me:[44] "At the same time as bringing very great honor to you and to the illustrious Order of Preachers, your book will bring light, I hope, to students of Sacred Scripture. May the Lord graciously bless your efforts for his glory and the good of souls, and reward you generously."[45]

Nevertheless there was the standard denunciation, with a charge of tendentiousness; this came from P. Ilario Rivieri, also S.J., in *Scuola Cattolica* of March and of May, of whom P. Cavallera, also S.J., was to say later[46] that he "had no weight in exegesis." But there was no need to be an expert to cast suspicion. That skirmisher did not win much credit.

Incident and Declaration

Thus the Master General did not seem to be disquieted in any way. There was only an unexpected incident which ended satisfactorily. In a letter of July 26, 1911 the Master General said to me: "An affair has occurred in which you have been caught up—in spite of yourself, certainly. A German priest was prepared to swear the oath prescribed by the Holy See only on condition that he could continue to understand the Scriptures in the sense of his masters, P. Lagrange and P.N.,[47] especially on Genesis, asking why he was being attacked when those fathers were not. . . . As far as you were concerned, the answer was given that you had taken the oath in question without any reservations, which guaranteed your obedience to the Holy See. Nevertheless, for your sake and for that of the School of Saint-Etienne, they want an explicit declaration from you, etc." In conformity with the suggestion of the Master General I made out a declaration in the following form: "I, the undersigned, make the following declaration:

I. I have taken at the appropriate time the oath prescribed by the *motu proprio Sacrorum antistitum*, by signing the official form which I have sent signed to P. Cormier, Master General of our Order.

II. I have accepted and do accept frankly and sincerely the decisions and responses of the Holy See, as every Catholic should do, according to the rules and distinctions taught by approved theologians.

III. I am prepared to reject opinions I have expressed if they are rejected or reproved by the Holy See, and I submit to it in the same way anything I write in the future."

The Master General was kind enough to reassure me that "all those who have read your declaration have formed a very favorable impression from it"[48] and that especially the cardinals of the Holy Office were very pleased with it.[49] The suspension of the German priest which had been threatened was not imposed, in the hope that he would voluntarily submit, thanks to the tactful handling of his bishop. I do not know what happened.

A Suspect

The Master General informed me of another wish of the cardinals: "To silence those who shelter under your name in order to stand up against authority, they ask that, whenever a response or declaration of the Biblical Commission is published, you should add some indication of acceptance, instead of merely giving a bare quotation as in the past." This was to ask once more that I should acknowledge that I was permanently suspect, for is it the practice of canonical periodicals to express acceptance of all the measures that they transcribe? Was it not evident that as religious we had the sentiment of Catholics? I expressed my distaste for these continual protestations.[50] Anyway the situation did not arise, for before the decision of the Commission on June 26, 1912 the blow had already fallen on me. From everything that went before, it is plain that there had been no previous hint of the blow which was about to strike me.

Journey to Cairo

I come now to the sequence of events. The perfect peace of the priory was a little disturbed at the beginning of winter. At Sexagesima I went down to Jericho with a few of the fathers. There we experienced a truly extraordinary cyclone, trees torn up, roofs ripped off, even the roof of a European-style hotel. At Jerusalem the snow lasted a long time. Then I was due to spend four or five days in Cairo (March 5–11). I hesitate to give the reasons for this, even in this intimate diary. In Vienna I had studied Egyptology for a year with great zest. I had tried to arouse among our students a vocation as an Egyptologist, but we were too few. However, there was good hope for the future. I was therefore much attracted when Baron Descamps, one-time minister in the Belgian government, then on pilgrimage to Jerusalem, gave me a message from Baron Empain, who was engaged in founding Heliopolis, that he would like to see me about the project of a foundation for our Order. To avoid acting behind the back of Mgr. Duret, vicar apostolic of that area, I went down to the White Fathers where he was living, and explained the matter to him. M. Empain offered us some land at Heliopolis, took upon himself to build a church and made over to us a considerable sum for building a religious house. I could not conceive that the French province would refuse us some pastors; we could then train up one or two Egyptologists affiliated to the Jerusalem School. This fine mirage vanished when Mgr. Duret, pressed hard by M. Empain, finally consented to establish his episcopal see at Heliopolis, a condition laid down by the Foundation Society for building him a church and a residence. Novice in diplomacy as I was, I could only withdraw, though glad to have made the acquaintance of the members of our Third Order at Cairo, who were so devoted to the Order.

Excavations at the Mosque of Omar

I forget why I left for France as early as April 18. Hardly had I left when the Master General, prevented by reasons of health from coming to Jerusalem personally, promulgated a visitation by correspondence. This rather defective way of conducting a visitation merely created an unhappy unrest in the priory. I was extremely upset when I visited the Master General at Fribourg to inform him of the situation. Thank heavens, everything went off all right. I got back to Jerusalem on July 24. An incident which had happened as I was leaving was still being talked about. A sudden rumor spread that the Mosque of Omar, the Sacred Rock, had been violated. We were linked with the business; so, although I never speak about excavations, I must say a word about this strange campaign.

The previous year an Englishman named Captain Montagu Parker, helped by Mr. Wilson and other friends, had come to do some research on the Tower of David. He had no connection with the English Society of the Palestine Exploration Fund, nor with the English consulate. The work began with the greatest mystery; everyone was kept away. There was a rumor that the leaders were following a cabalistic calculation about the position of the tomb, according to certain combinations of numbers which had been revealed to them: vast treasures were going to reimburse the hunters for the money which they were so freely spending. M. Dalman, the director of the German evangelical institute, had been asked to steer clear. Exasperated by this way of treating ancient monuments, P. Vincent dragged me along to Mr. Parker and told him roundly that this was not the way archaeology was done in Jerusalem, that a serious investigator could have no better guarantee than a discreet confidant; and finally, promising absolute secrecy, he asked to follow the excavation. This openness made a great impression on Mr. Parker, and he said that the site would always be open to us. P. Vincent was even authorized to make any plans he wanted, and no one would insist on authenticating them. It was in this way that the excavation, even if it did not yield up a farthing of treasure, brought some highly interesting results. P. Vincent imparted them to the public in a book *Jérusalem sous terre*, which was published both in English and in French. It was when everything was over and as a sort of remedy of despair, when his theory had been proved wrong, that Mr. Parker secretly and during the night undertook some soundings under the Sacred Rock. But this time P. Vincent had the good sense to keep out of it. Thus it was easy for me to exculpate him.[51] However, *Revue Biblique* had the benefit of this Palestinologist's reports.[52]

P. Dhorme's articles on *Les Pays bibliques et l'Assyrie* illustrated by the most recent discoveries the connection between biblical lands and Assyria, originally sketched by M. Vigouroux. If there was any reproach to make against *Revue Biblique* it was certainly not that it stuck to sterile controversies, supporting an opinion out of time with theology, but rather that it was absorbed in Oriental history, archaeology and epigraphy. In this last field,

the lihyanite inscriptions of P. Jaussen and P. Savignac opened
new avenues.

The Plans of P. Fonck

Nevertheless, as I have already hinted, we were under
threat. When P. Fonck decided to found an auxiliary to the Pontifical Biblical Institute of Rome in the East, he did not at first
dare to fix his choice on Jerusalem. It is an inviolable tradition in
the Church, reflected in law, that no religious Order should set
itself up in any town to do there a work being done already by another Order. Leo XIII had approved our Biblical School, and
Pius X had echoed this by granting the title of minor basilica to
our Church. Granted that we had not deserved to be replaced by
others, the Society of Jesus could not hope to dispute our position; and to install themselves beside us was certainly very prej-
udicial to our work. Could the ten or twelve pupils we had in the
best years conceivably be divided between two Institutes? On
the other hand, the Institute at Rome had realized the importance
of our journeys. It meant to keep the right of guiding its own students in Palestine. It must therefore have a pied-à-terre, but by
no means necessarily at Jerusalem. So first P. Fonck considered
Haifa, where the German element was fairly numerous and powerful, and he was welcomed with delight by the German consul.
He came to Saint-Etienne on September 14 and put me in the
picture about his projects. He added that he had only promised
our Master General not to go contrary to his wishes; and in this,
said he, he would have succeeded. That is precisely what I am
still not wholly convinced of. P. Cormier, thinking and acting
like the saint that he was, had certainly said that two institutes
could do more for the glory of God than one: *modo Christus prae-
dicetur*. But by then he was already fitting in with a *fait accompli*.

If the situation had been normal, he would not have hesitated, I imagine, to ask for our sake that the ordinary rules should
be observed. If it was a center for excursions that they wanted,
Beirut would suffice, with the link to the university and the Oriental Faculty. The truth is that P. Cormier did not want to be
told by the Pope—if he was not in fact told it—that the Dominicans inspired less confidence in him than the Jesuits. There is no
doubt that this reason was given.[53] This was the procedure al-

ready used to gain exclusive rights for the Institute in Rome. Proof: an article in *Corriere della Sera*, alluded to by *Bulletin de la Semaine*. I no longer have to hand the copy of *Corriere*, but this is how I analyzed it:[54] "*Corriere della Sera* imagines two schools of exegesis. The one marked by a spirit of breadth, too broad no doubt for its own taste, is the Dominican school; the other, safer and more moderate, is that of the Society of Jesus. And it is because the Jesuit school is safer and more moderate that the Holy Father has entrusted to these religious the Biblical Institute that he has just founded at Rome." I refused, first of all, to grant that I belonged to the broad school in this sense, and, second, to contrast the Jesuits and the Dominicans as to exegetical schools. Besides, the same talk was going on at Rome as at Milan. M. Maurice Pernot picked it up in *Débats*[55] as though it were a well-known fact: "And furthermore, the Vatican was giving indications of the reasons for this exclusion:[56] the ideas professed by the Dominicans were too liberal and too independent and were causing mistrust; even if the scholarly works of P. Lagrange were not yet condemned, this did not mean that their spirit was approved of. On the contrary, it was held that the Jesuits offered all the guarantees of moderation and obedience, and that the direction they would give to the Biblical Institute would be exactly that desired by the Holy See." Is this not simply a case of *hic fecit cui prodest*? Were the Jesuits alone in the Church orthodox? Would all the other Orders be keen to encourage the situation of exclusiveness which was being given to the Jesuits? But if that line of argument is plausible as regards the foundation in Rome, how much more so when the Pope's bad opinion of the Dominicans of Jerusalem seemed to be the vital condition for establishing the Jesuits there! In one place this is stated categorically enough.[57] *Unità Cattolica* of December 24, 1912 quotes *Verona Fedele* relating the vicissitudes of the Biblical Institute at Jerusalem. The correspondent of the paper had asked for an interview with a professor at the Roman Institute. He spoke to him of the difficulties the project had encountered. "But the Pope was not prepared to abandon his plan, which had been made all the more firm by the fact that in the teaching of the Biblical Institute he saw an absolute guarantee of orthodoxy, which is sometimes lacking in other Schools of the same type, and, as soon as circumstances would allow, he charged P. Fonck, rector of the Institute, to go to Palestine in order to open the auxiliary house in the name of, and at the expense of, the Holy See." Thus, according to P. Fonck's fellow professor, what had totally decided the Pope was the need to remedy the lack of orthodoxy found in other *institutes* of the same type. This plural is astonishing, because the Biblical School at Jerusalem was the first and only one of this type. Nor are the Dominicans mentioned by name. But who is being referred to, if not they? The School was to have been set up on Mount Carmel, continues the professor interviewed, but "reasons unconnected with the wishes of the Holy See were against this. After long investigations and on the advice of competent persons, it was resolved to make Jerusalem the place. The protection of the auxiliary house will be entrusted to the French colors, etc."

On September 14, 1911, P. Fonck said the same thing to me, omitting the assertion about my orthodoxy; but what he did not say to me, he said to anyone who wanted to listen, and this was the blow below the belt. Those hostile views were related to me by too many trustworthy people to leave me any room for doubt. He also said—and this to me—that he would not lack for money, having made sixteen novenas to the Sacred Heart. I objected that among these funds were a hundred thousand crowns which an Austrian committee had laid down to send a student either to Beirut or to Jerusalem. "Oh, a hundred thousand crowns!" he replied, smiling. "It is a lot for us," was my last word.

Captivated by the thought of a new institute, and a papal one, under the protection of the French colors, the Minister of External Affairs, or at least M. de Margerie who was then in charge of the East, gave P. Fonck the best possible welcome, and I was not able to make him understand that the Pope, being a sovereign, would not allow any other flag than his own to fly over his Pontifical Institute. Besides, it never entered my head to have recourse to the French government in order to stand in the way of a plan of the Holy Father. It is an old maxim, to which I stubbornly adhere, that God holds nothing more dear than the liberty of his Church. *Si tollis libertatem tollis dignitatem.* P. Fonck's visit left me quite overcome. The prospect which it laid open for us was that of a pottery vessel against an iron one. In spite of ourselves, we would inevitably be regarded as opposed to an Institute which was not only pontifical but was honored with the favor of the Holy Father—a favor denied to us. The least polemic, which would then have become unavoidable, would easily assume the air of rebellion, and that was the last thing we wanted.

Letter to the Pope

Thus as early as September 15, in agreement with the moderators of the School, I wrote to the Holy Father, asking him to relieve us of our post, willing as we were to give way to others where there was no room for two.[58] This letter went, of course, through the proper channels, but I do not know whether the Master General saw fit to pass it on to the Pope.[59] No doubt he thought that such an approach would be his business and he did not see it as his duty to make the approach. At least I never heard any more. So this year ended with dark forebodings. Nevertheless our activities kept going at full speed. On October 4, P. Carrière left with the Abbé Tisserant,[c] a former pupil of ours, for Mosul and Baghdad. He did not return until March 1912, after a serious attack of typhoid, of which he was cured in the French hospital of the Sisters of St. Vincent de Paul at Damascus.

THE TERRIBLE YEAR (1912)

The Part Played by P. Fonck

My terrible year. I shall be brief. It would be childish and indelicate to make a parade, or even to take too much notice, of

---

c. Eugene Tisserant, born at Nancy in 1884. After beginning the study of Oriental languages at the Biblical School (1904–1905) and being ordained a priest in 1907, he became scriptor and custodian of the Vatican library, where he distinguished himself by learned studies in the field of orientalism. Pro-prefect of the Vatican library in 1930, created bishop in 1936 and cardinal in 1937, he became Secretary of the Congregation for the Eastern Churches (1936–1959), and librarian and archivist of the Roman Church (1959). A member of the Académie des Incriptions et Belles-Lettres since 1938 and of the Académie française since 1961, he many times showed his esteem for and grateful memory of his former teachers at the Biblical School.

the letters of sympathy that I received, a good number of them emanating from the Society of Jesus, perfectly sincere and heartfelt. Nor will I dwell on the part, always in the shadows, played by P. Fonck in the build-up of suspicions against me. But as his plan of establishing at Jerusalem a house auxiliary to the Biblical Institute at Rome exactly coincided with the blow which fell on me, I will quote one fact, a single one but incontrovertible, which provides ample evidence of his attitude toward our School.[60]

Abbé Capelle de Faveau, a Belgian, wrote to me from Rome on February 7 to ask if he could come and stay with us during his journey in the East, and take part in our study journey after Easter. He wrote to me from Cairo on March 4 to say that circumstances over which he had absolutely no control had forced him to change his original plans. He would explain everything to me verbally. He later told me that P. Fonck had told him that his presence—even in passing—at the Biblical School would gravely compromise his future, and that he would certainly not be appointed professor at Namur. This provides an indication of what the hostility of the *praeses* of the Roman Institute portended for us and our students.

Resignation of the Office of Prior
Nevertheless everything seemed calm at Rome. Having been attacked by some periodical or other, I had asked to defend myself. The Master General refused permission, thinking that the fuss would subside on its own, and the advisor who had suggested putting my answer to one side later justified himself on the grounds that my position seemed at that time to be unassailable. I alone am in a position to assert that I was not deposed from the office of prior, as has been believed. I had accepted the second term only with repugnance, and I felt that, since the visitation by letter, the Master General no longer had the same confidence in my qualities as prior; he considered me too weak. One incident hurt me: the Master General had always reproached me for being too impressionable, too easily excited; nor was he wrong. Finally on July 7 I asked him to accept my resignation. He consented and I received his answer on July 26.

Decree of the Congregation of the Consistory

Perhaps he had already heard indirectly of what was afoot. A professor at Rome wrote to me on September 3 that at the beginning of July he alerted Cardinal Rampolla and P. Cormier, who knew nothing about it. If the Master General had given some credence to what he heard, he was perhaps all the more inclined to accept my resignation; but I am morally certain that there would have been some trace of this in his letter. The letter of the Secretary of the Congregation of Religious, giving the Master General written notice of the decision by the Congregation of the Consistory, is dated July 15. But again it is certain that this document was given him only later, when he was on the point of leaving for Marino, from where he wrote to me on July 27. P. Desqueyrous told me everything on July 30. The Master General was therefore informed only in the same way as all those concerned, in order to put into action the decree which was at the same time sent in confidence to the bishops. The decree was, of course, published in the *Acta Apostolicae Sedis* only on August 16.

The decree was directed principally against the *Special Introduction to the Old Testament* of Dr. Holzey, "in which, in accordance with the novel theories of rationalism and higher criticism about practically all the books of the Old Testament . . . most audacious opinions are put forward, which are opposed to the most ancient tradition of the Church, the venerable teaching of the Holy Fathers and the recent responses of the Pontifical Biblical Commission, and not only call in question the authenticity and historical value of the Sacred Books but practically destroy them." This book was not to be allowed inside seminaries, even for purposes of consultation. The measure was no doubt well meant, for seminarists should have at their disposition only specially chosen books, but the reasons given were extremely serious. The decree continued: "As there exist other commentaries with the same attitude toward the Sacred Scriptures of the Old and New Testaments, such as several works of P. Lagrange and a very recent work entitled *The Holy Scripture of the New Testament*, published in Berlin in 1912 by Dr. Fritz Tillmann, His Holiness commands and prescribes that these be totally removed from the formation of clerics, unless a fuller judgment be passed on the matter by the competent authorities." The decree given by the Pope was signed on June 29.

Submission of P. Lagrange

On that day, June 29, we were celebrating at Ain Karim—which the Eastern Church calls St. John *in Montana*—the priestly jubilee of the Franciscan P. François Darié. I was especially gripped all day by a very fervent feeling of God's presence. The following night, after a short sleep, I awakened suddenly. I was suddenly filled with a vision of death, as novel as if I had thought of it then for the first time. Unable anymore to contemplate sleep, and in the grip of anguish of mind, I spent the rest of the night in prayer, walking up and down my cell, without succeeding in calming this strange terror. Perhaps God was preparing me to care only for invisible things and for his judgment.

The decree reached me on August 5, the day after the feast of St. Dominic. My decision to submit had been taken beforehand. But I had to consult my colleagues about the fate of the School and of *Revue Biblique*. Would not both be suppressed? Would it not be worth taking the precaution of at least transforming the *Revue* before any more radical measure? We thought so, and immediately the next day, August 6, I wrote to the Master General to beg him to transmit to the Holy Father my complete submission. Firmly resolved not to continue in the same direction, which would belie my submission, I had not the courage to continue in another, for this would not be taken seriously. I therefore asked to leave Jerusalem, at least for a year, renouncing both writing and teaching on biblical matters. Not being anxious to run the same risks, my colleagues proposed with me to transform *Revue Biblique* into a *Revue Palestinienne et Orientale*, which would have nothing to do with the Bible. I have not kept a copy of this letter; I can find only the resume which I have just produced.[d] There were therefore no grounds for the claim that I was dismissed from office of prior and removed from Jerusalem against my will. In this excessively narrow circle my position be-

---

d. This letter, which must have been found later, is quoted in full by P. F.-M. Braun, *L'Oeuvre du Père Lagrange*, pp. 124–125. We reproduce it as Document No. 28.

came extremely painful, and I did not wish it to be possible to attack the School on the grounds that I was still part of it.

The Pope received my letter and replied to it in Italian on August 16 to P. Hyacinthe Cormier, wishing him a happy feast: "I have read with the greatest satisfaction (*compiacenza*) the fine letter of P. Lagrange, and you will be kind enough to reply to him that I am fully assured of his state of mind and that I congratulate him on his full submission—it also seems to me that it would be possible to substitute *Revue des Études Palestiniennes et Orientales* for *Revue Biblique*, and that the School should also busy itself with the study of Palestine and the East. Your most reverend paternity will have to see whether it is right to give him leave of absence from the moment that he suggests it without rancor."[61]

Letter to the Pope

At this I thought I should write to the Pope directly. Nevertheless on August 17 I got up in the morning with a letter which emerged from my heart ready-made, and in the course of the day I sent it off. I transcribe my rough copy:

"Most Holy Father, prostrate at the feet of Your Holiness, I have just affirmed to you my sorrow for having offended you, and my obedience. My first thought was, and my last thought will be, always to submit myself heart and soul to the orders of the Vicar of Jesus Christ. But precisely because I feel that my heart is the heart of a most submissive son, may I be permitted to communicate to a father, the most august of fathers, but nevertheless a father, my sorrow at the grounds which seem to be given for the condemnation of several of my works, incidentally not named, which are held to be tarnished with rationalism? That these works contain errors I am prepared to admit, but that they were written in a spirit of disobedience to Church tradition or to the decisions of the Pontifical Biblical Commission, deign, most Holy Father, to allow me to declare that nothing was further from my thoughts. I remain on my knees before Your Holiness to beg your blessing."

Letter from P. Cormier

The Master General wrote to me on September 5: "I yesterday had an audience with the Holy Father, who spontaneously expressed to me his great and complete satisfaction with your letter, and encouraged me to publish it." This was done, with the widest publicity, echoed in newspapers and Catholic weeklies. If the Holy Father was satisfied,[62] not everyone was, not even among those closest to the Master General. One person complained that "a careful reading of the act of submission reveals that it does not link together sufficiently clearly the disavowal of ideas."[63] But since it was the rationalist spirit of my writing to which attention had been drawn and not a particular work or a particular idea, there was some fear that this reproach of rationalism, which I denied vigorously, would stick. This is what the Master General thought, and he raised the matter with the Holy Father: "I added that you had been hurt that some people had called you a rationalist and insubordinate." Nevertheless the School was still threatened. After having said to me (September 8): "I approve that you continue or rather that you take on the editorship of the transformed *Revue*," P. Cormier added: "As for the School, the Holy Father is of the opinion that it would be a good thing to give it also a different name; but there is no hurry," and he envisaged the situation in which we would not have "formal classes" anymore.

Departure from Jerusalem

At this moment I could stay at Jerusalem no longer. P. Vincent accompanied me as far as Jaffa. I embarked on September 5. This date alone shows that I should have had no place in the article of September 7 in the *Journal des Débats*, an article which created so much stir and made my situation worse, as could easily have been foreseen. No Dominican was so tactless as to provide any of the information, which nevertheless betrays someone very well informed. It is also true that M. Maurice Pernot, the author of the article, had long ago made up his mind about the political intrigues of P. Fonck—that at least is how he qualified his behavior in the *Journal des Débats* of August 21, 1909. I could not fail to recognize the sympathy which made *Bulletin de la Semaine* (September 25, 1912) speak in the same way. But the old saying was verified anew: "Deliver me from my friends; I will deal with my enemies." When I begged the political editor of the *Bulletin* not to aggravate a situation which was already so unpleasant, he answered me that I had no right to prevent him defending French interests and organizing a committee of patronage for our establishment. It was only with difficulty that I persuaded him to spare us this fatal blow.[64]

The Line of Attack

The mother house was upset by all this fuss. There was some hesitation about allowing me to accept the heartfelt and generous hospitality of P. Faucher at Sèvres, which was thought to be too close to Paris. In fact I hardly had any visitors other than P. de Grandmaison, who brought me his condolences and the assurance, which I did not need, that the French Jesuits of his group had nothing to do with my disgrace. P. Cavallera—for I recognized his hand—was less successful in an attempt to clear the whole Society. When he complained that "every religious Order and even the tiniest congregations were able to have at least a pied-à-terre in Palestine, and only the Jesuits were excluded,"[65] he forgot that we were asking only that the Jesuits should come and do a work other than ours. Obliged to cast a stone at me in order to acquit the Society, P. Cavallera recalled numerous attacks which had been made on me before the foundation of the Biblical Institute. But with the exception of Abbé Dessailly, an ill-equipped and clumsy sharpshooter, who had made up the battleline if not P. Méchineau, P. Brucker (a little) in France, P. Schiffini in Italy, P. Delattre in Belgium, P. Fonck in Germany, P. Dorsch of Innsbrück in Austria, and P. Murillo in Spain? In expectation of some last minute reverses . . .! When P. Cavallera pointed out the cooperation we had received from fourteen Jesuits, would it not have been worth mentioning that we were deprived of this cooperation at a critical moment? If it proved anything—as I had shown in the same report—it is that there were Jesuits in both camps, a truth pleasant to state, but hardly controversial because nothing new. It is therefore not surprising that the Reverend Father abstained from signing his article, which in the last analysis was aimed at a fallen ally, since he concluded with a sympathetic thought about "the pain that I feel at the measure which has struck P. Lagrange and my desire to see

granted to Catholic scholars all the liberty and all the honor owed
to their task and their deserts." And of P. Fonck: "You know
enough history to be aware that the best intentions do not rule
out clumsiness and even indelicacy." I could have intervened,
but I did not breathe a word in any newspaper, and no stir about
me occurred. As I could not go on forever tramping the woods of
Saint-Cloud, which winter would soon strip of their melancholy
autumn splendor, I was allowed to settle in Paris and preach at
Saint-Séverin. I cannot sufficiently thank P. Boulanger, the provincial, and the fathers resident in Paris for their generous and
heartwarming welcome.

The Future of *Revue Biblique*

But on every side I was reproached for being too hasty. I had
given up the title of *Revue biblique* and they were asking for the
sacrifice also of the Biblical School; why not suggest to the Jesuit
Fathers that they settle in instead of us? The publisher, M. Gabalda, who had succeeded his father-in-law, M. Lecoffre, was
distraught. *Revue biblique* had never had so many subscribers. *Revue des Etudes Palestiniennes et Orientales* threatened to be a fiasco.
My well-known hastiness had ruined things. I could only put forward as an excuse that I had merely returned to an idea which I
had long matured and had submitted to the Master General on
the morrow of the preventative prohibition of the commentary
on Genesis. It had seemed to me obvious that we could no longer
continue critical study in the way we had previously done. I had
begged the Master General to dispense me from biblical studies.
Thus I could not forbear pointing out to him that my prognosti-
cations had been verified. But, for his part, he persisted in his
plan and asked that biblical questions should not at all be excluded from the new *Revue*. Well then, why not keep the title *Revue biblique*, since the public had no inkling of what was going on?
I allowed myself to be convinced, but a similar about-turn
seemed more difficult for the Master General, forced to confess
our hesitations to the Holy Father. He made up his mind on the
spot, much earlier and with much more conviction than I would
have believed possible, and sent off the following letter to Pius
X.[66]

Letter from P. Cormier to Pius X

"Most Holy Father, Your Holiness must permit me to have recourse to you as Father, Protector, Counselor, Guide. The steps to transform *Revue biblique* are meeting with difficulties. The contributors who could be counted on are very few, and the character of the subjects put forward very narrow, so it is impossible to hope for a large enough number of subscribers to cover expenses. On the other hand, many priests, religious, Catholic professors of distinction and even bishops have been contemplating the prospect of the disappearance of *Revue biblique* with a secret sadness. In accordance with the instructions of the Holy See it was improving from year to year; it had refuted in a masterly fashion numerous heterodox exegetes, winning the esteem of many scholars, even rationalists among them; it has succeeded in dispelling their prejudices and bringing them nearer to the true faith. It does not appear that it would be dangerous to allow it to continue as an experiment, at least for one year. It could even be hoped that the Holy See might be ever more satisfied by its tone and its results. For the Order of St. Dominic and for its poor old Master General this would be a new and important pledge of good will on the part of Your Holiness, who would not find us ungrateful. In any case Your Holiness gave no command but simply accepted our proposal for a transformation. If, therefore, there is no difficulty about this proposal that we are making after a more prolonged investigation of the circumstances, and taking into account the admirable conduct of P. Lagrange, who has made an excellent impression everywhere, then we shall take the appropriate action, etc."

The letter was written on October 8. The Pope wrote at the bottom *iuxta preces in Domino, die 9 octobris 1912, Pius P.P.X.* This quick answer seems to indicate that he consulted no one—only his own generous heart. The Master General had thus repaired and prevented the tiresome consequences of my overhasty reaction.

Encouraged by this success on the part of the Master General, I made strong representations to him, in spite of my humbled situation, how important it was that our School should give absolutely no impression of being in competition with or even opposition to a Pontifical Institute which was forthwith to be founded in Jerusalem. P. Cormier did not perhaps appreciate sufficiently the difference between Jerusalem and Rome, where there was plenty of room for both Jesuits and Dominicans. And in the last resort there was the decisive reason: "To this is added the censure lately inflicted, which hardly allows us to show ourselves aggressive or exclusive."[67] After the censure the Master General could not decently set his face against the foundation at Jerusalem. There could never have been any doubt of that.[68]

Intervention of Cardinal de Cabrières

I must, out of gratitude, here mention the kindly intervention of Cardinal de Cabrières, bishop of Montpellier. He wrote to me from Rome on November 10: "I shall see Mgr. de Lai and also the Pope, the same day. I shall make representations to the former that you should be given precise and complete indications of the complaints against you; and I shall ask the latter to embrace you and give you his blessing, when P. Cormier invites you to come to Rome." But the Master General did not consider that this would be appropriate. As for Cardinal de Lai, he said to Mgr. Sevin that he was quite overcome by my letter (to the Pope), but nevertheless he charged a distinguished canonist, P. Ojetti, S.J., to give some explanations to the archbishop of Siena, who wanted to know why some of my works had been sandwiched between the two condemnations without any further indications. The good father found especially in the commentary on St. Mark what he judged most horrific, and it was laughable.[69] Nothing has been so useful in forming opinion in my favor as that list of charges. Unfortunately I have not been able to find it again in the periodical which contained it. Furthermore, the authority of the Congregation of the Consistory was not implicated in it, let alone that of the Pope.

Rue du Bac

The little apartment of the Rue du Bac where P. Séjourné took me in was, by its warm welcome and its memories, and also by our hopes in spite of everything, a little Saint-Etienne. Our conversation was about our beloved priory where our brethren were doing their duty so valiantly. Before I left, P. Gardeil had been appointed prior, but he thought he could be more useful in Paris, and the Master General had no wish to force him. So P. Raymond Crechet whom I had had as sub-prior was elected, in an election to which I united myself in heart, and which was confirmed.

IN THE SERVICE OF THE CHURCH (1913)

Return to Jerusalem
The year began with sadness. I was so ill with influenza that I was unable to complete my course of Lenten sermons at Saint-Séverin. But the *Revue* continued to run to the satisfaction of the Master General, and the School of Saint-Etienne had not cut back its program in any way. My stay in France was a consolation for the saintly soul of my sister Pauline, the best friend of my childhood, because her son Albert Rambaud was killed in Morocco, heroically guarding the honor of the flag. This delayed my return to Jerusalem. The permission from the Master General, who certainly consulted the Sovereign Pontiff, is dated June 4. On July 4 the funeral of my nephew took place at Royton (Isère). The same day I left for Marseilles, where I arrived at midnight, and on the morning of July 5 I embarked for Jerusalem with orders to take up again the course on exegesis.

Prize of the Académie des Sciences
The Académie des Sciences Morales et Politiques had awarded P. Lagrange and the Biblical School a prize of eight thousand francs. A Jerusalem correspondent to *Unità Cattolica* suggested that we were considering this well-deserved reward as a reply to the Pope![70] But truly it is wrong of me to drag up this insinuation. When will clumsy political maneuverings be banished from the Catholic press? I would rather reproduce the flattering words of M. Fagniez, the president of the Académie: "The other half (of the Lefèvre-Daumier prize) is awarded to P. Lagrange and the Biblical School at Jerusalem of which he is director. In so naming his office the Académie has wished to do justice

to that institution and to the particular merits of all those who have brought it honor, to P. Lagrange for his directorship and his own publications, to his colleagues P. Dhorme, P. Jaussen and P. Vincent, and finally to the work in its totality as an institute of learning, on which depend a periodical and a collection of works, as a practical laboratory and center of explorations by the position it holds at the crossroads of Hebrew, Arab and Phoenician civilizations, and by its contacts with the heirs of those civilizations, and finally as a monument of faith, of scholarship and of patriotism, which preserves the ancient renown of the Franks among peoples less forgetful of the benefits we have conferred than we ourselves are of the glories we have won."[71] It will not escape notice that the distinguished M. Fagniez held anything to do with theology at arm's length.

The Work Continues

I returned to Jerusalem at vacation time. I used the vacation to write a little life of St. Justin. There was a theory to be clearly found among our opponents that a lack of theology spoiled my learning. It was therefore with some satisfaction that I heard it said of me by the Master General that the examiner had been "delighted not only by the facts but by the competence in philosophy and theology which you show. I said so to the Holy Father in my audience this morning."[72]

I too was delighted at this appreciation, but nothing equaled the unalloyed joy of having resumed my shared labors with my dearest brethren. However I was compelled to admit that since the publication of *Bethléem* and the first fascicles of *Jérusalem* by P. Vincent and P. Abel, of the *Samuel* of P. Dhorme, and the new *Mission en Arabie* of P. Jaussen and P. Savignac, all my former pupils had overhauled me, and I could now say my *Nunc dimittis*.

Nunc Dimittis

All the more is this true today in 1926, after they have not ceased to grow greater, and I grow weaker, to such an extent that I am no more than a useless cog. Human nature has sometimes suffered from it, but I rejoice about it in the Lord. My only desire is to die in communion with the Catholic Church, and in the grace of Jesus Christ my Savior, with the Immaculate Virgin at my side. My intention has always been to serve the Church, and so I bitterly regret having troubled so many souls. Once more I submit everything I have written to the judgment of the Vicar of Jesus Christ, from whom I humbly ask forgiveness and pardon.

M.-J. Lagrange
of the Order of Preachers
Jerusalem, April 10, 1926.

Notes on My Life

NOTE BY P. LAGRANGE

I have long hesitated to write these notes, until the day has come when I am seventy-five years old. I have taken the decision because if someone takes it into his head to speak about me, I should like it to be done correctly: a recent example has shown me that the best informed people can unwittingly distort the truth. And further I am determined that my debt to my parents should be known; I can hardly hope to make this convincing, for they gave me so much solid teaching and good example which I did not follow. I use the first person singular. I do not see that there would be any gain in modesty or humility if I said: "N. did such and such."

4. Formative Years
(1855–1873)

ROOTS

Birth and Origin

I was born at Bourg (Ain) on March 7, 1855, on the first feast day of St. Thomas Aquinas after the proclamation of the dogma of the Immaculate Conception. On that occasion a statue of Mary had been erected on the Renaissance façade of the fine gothic Church of Notre-Dame, at that time the only parish of the town. Following the pious custom of the country, after the christening on March 12, the feast of St. Gregory the Great, the baby was carried to the altar of the Black Madonna, so much beloved by the Bressans, to consecrate it to Mary, while the beginning of St. John's Gospel was read.

Neither my father nor my mother belonged to Bourg. My father, who was then forty, had been born at Prat, in the commune of Saint-Romain-sous-Gourdon at the entrance to the Charolais, six kilometres from the present industrial town of Montceau-les-Mines.

My grandfather was a peasant who by unremitting hard work had succeeded in acquiring a reasonably good property. He had enough influence, as mayor of the commune, to get the parish re-established at the Restoration. He remained very attached to this regime, and when political events were not to his taste, he liked to say so—that things are not what they were under good old Charles X. My grandmother was called Cléot and her mother Aumônier. The family held that these Aumôniers were the family of the Aumônier who married Chrysostome Alacoque, father of St. Margaret-Mary.

One of my childhood memories is their golden wedding celebration. What has remained most vividly in my imagination is the never-ending chiming of the village bell, kept in motion by the young men who constantly took turns to climb the clock tower to swing the bell. The only mental image I have kept of my grandfather is that of an old man still gathering sticks on a sunny hillside. My grandmother lived on after him, and I can still see her cutting a figure as a little old lady, merry and active. I was taken to her deathbed—my first contact with the mystery of death.

The Minor Seminary of Autun

My father was educated at the minor seminary of Autun. That remarkable institution owes its success to two of his fellow pupils. One of these, though considerably older, was Cardinal Pitra; he was a master at the minor seminary before entering the Solesmes Congregation of the Benedictine Order. My father's classmates, whom I knew because they remained friends of his, were Mgr. Landriot, bishop of La Rochelle, then archbishop of Rheims, who put up in a most dignified manner with the outrages of the Prussian occupation of 1870–1871, although his heart was broken by them, and Abbé Farges, his faithful helper, who lived and died a teacher at the minor seminary. The bishop of La Rochelle's *La Femme forte et la Femme pieuse* is still read, and his *Christ de la Tradition* puts him in the first rank of the rare French theologians of his day, although he has been accused of pantheistic tendencies! He conceived the audacious plan of making the minor seminary of Autun a school second to none and felt that the study of modern languages must be introduced. M. Farges and he split the task between them: one went to Germany, the other to England. It was important to be up-to-date with science; nothing to this end was neglected, not even a room for physics and chemistry, something quite unheard of in those days. Botany and entomology had a special attraction there, in the surrounding woods and tall forests of the park of Montjeu. Geology, then in its infancy, had its place of honor, also helped by the varied terrains of the countryside. Archaeology had been introduced there by Cardinal Pitra; it springs naturally to mind in a region where Mount Beauvray on the horizon recalls Bibracte, the so-called Temple of Janus, and the Stone of Conart, the supposed site of Divitiacus' tomb. The old gates of the town date from Roman times, and the memorial of St. Symphorian, an inscription of the Ichthys from the early Christian centuries. The Middle Ages are represented by the cathedral, while the minor seminary itself, magnificently located in an area adorned with trees as old as itself, has something of the magnificence of the age of Louis XIV.[1]

I must admit that the minor seminary as it was in my father's time, and as I myself knew it, had a quite different air from the clerical schools of today, dedicated solely to the formation of future ecclesiastics. At that time there were no Christian colleges, nothing but lycées or university colleges, or minor seminaries. These therefore opened their doors wide, and there was no need for boys to profess an intention to become a priest before being accepted; and, once accepted, they stayed till the end. The choice was theirs. However, right up to the expulsion, the minor seminary of Autun never failed to provide a large and fine contingent for the major seminary. Mgr. Landriot had been at the receiving end of attacks by the Abbé Gaume who, seconded by Louis Veuillot, so violently championed classical studies. He maintained them with unshakable resolve. But less in order to yield at least something, than from an equally burning conviction of the wholesome beauty of the Fathers of the Church,[2] he arranged the studies in such a way that classical and patristic literature held equal prominence. The homilies of St. John Chrysostom, the sermon of St. Basil on reading pagan authors, at the beginning the Acts of the Martyrs, then extracts from St. Jerome and St. Augustine—all these accompanied the great classical authors and were no obstacle to success in the baccalaureate; the demands of the syllabus guaranteed first place to Demosthenes, Cicero, Tacitus, and Sophocles.

Having once mentioned the name of the minor seminary of Autun, I have written of it as I knew it. In my father's day all this advance was no more than embryonic. But a friendship linking him to such spirits is sufficient evidence for me of his elevated tastes. Alas! Like all young people, I thought only of the future. How often I have regretted not having asked him about the days of his youth, and his studies! But he never spoke of himself and I thought only of myself.

Departure for Lyons

Once he had finished at the minor seminary, my father entered the major seminary also at Autun. It was not long before he realized that he had no vocation to the priesthood. Then he headed for Lyons to make his career there. That was still the normal course of action in my day. Those who did not enter the seminary, and did not return to the plow because they felt called to a higher purpose, made for Lyons, most frequently to study medicine. Of this period I know nothing, except that he found there one of his fellow pupils of Autun. After first being a curate at Chalon-sur-Saône, P. Souaillard had followed P. Lacordaire, not as one of the very first but at any rate immediately after the restoration of the Order of St. Dominic in France. He had had great success as a preacher at Lyons. He was a true son of Bourg: passionate, spontaneous and spirited. P. Lacordaire hovered in regions where admiration followed him with a respectful astonishment. P. Souaillard had a great attraction, and played his part as a disciple in the effect produced by the great orator. With my father the old friendship blossomed into a very close relationship.

One day they met on one of the river steamers which ply the Saône even today. After their first words, P. Souaillard, following a sudden inspiration, said to my father: "I am on my way to the Falsan family. Our meeting is heaven-sent. I am convinced that you should marry Elisabeth.[3] I will speak about you, plead your cause, and hopefully succeed."

My Mother's Family

My father protested. This union seemed to him badly proportioned. His peasant origin, even if veiled by his distinguished personality, was not such as to fit him for a family who held an honored place in the bourgeoisie of Lyons. They had no pretensions to nobility. My mother's father proved that. The emperor had made General Maupetit a baron. At his death the title came to my grandfather Pierre Falsan, who had little taste for commerce, though he had been forced by his father to follow this family career. He refused the title, thinking that a noble title demanded a noble way of life. But they stayed in the bourgeoisie. It was not forgotten that the head of the family before the Revolution had been known throughout the town as Chevalier Falsan.

On his side, my father had no intention of rejecting or even of neglecting his own people. His wife would enter into the family, would be close to his elder sister, married to a peasant, to his other sister, a nun of Saint-Charles, to his younger brother, a priest and science master at the minor seminary of Autun, and later parish priest of his native parish. The plan conceived by P. Souaillard seemed doomed to certain failure. Dr. Potton, married to the elder Mlle. Falsan, and a member of a family which at that time belonged to the highest stratum in the structure of society at Lyons,[4] was by no means the least opposed to this alliance.

A Vocation Opposed

It seemed that a still more decisive obstacle was going to arise from Mlle. Elisa Falsan's very firm leaning toward the religious life. But it was precisely this which provided the solution. She was born after my Potton aunt, the daughter of Pierre Falsan's marriage to a young lady of the Chavanis family, which still has a very honorable name at Lyons. Her mother having died in giving birth to a third child, my grandfather remarried Mlle. Therese Nièpce, daughter of Colonel Nièpce, commandant of the garrison of Lyons. Enrolling during the last period of the Napoleonic epic, sent to serve under Jerome of Würtemburg, a colonel at the age of twenty-seven, Nièpce had married a girl from Zandt, a member of a noble Bavarian family. But once the empire came to an end, he never rose higher than colonel. In my childhood, I knew this venerable old man, who passed his enforced leisure by carving ivory in delicate filigree-work. My mother therefore never knew any other mother than this stepmother, who nevertheless gave her an affection which is rarely encountered between blood relations. On each side there existed an impassioned tenderness with, on my mother's side, the most touching trust. It was, I think, to this mother she had made her own that she owed the fervent piety which was the mainspring of her life. Mme. Falsan was under the spiritual direction of the Jesuits, and they were also of great help to her daughter, who remained always most grateful for this, and used to speak of them to me with great reverence and enthusiasm. All the same, she confided to me that she never felt completely at ease because she was kept on too short a rein, and rather than thinking of the nuns of the Sacred Heart, among whom the spirit of the Society was dominant, she had resolved to seek admission among the Sisters of St. Vincent de Paul. The matter was practically decided. Sister Marchand, who at Lyons was just such a popular figure as Sister Rosalie at Paris, presided over a house popularly known as "The Soup Kitchen" and already my mother was allowed in to distribute soup to the poor.

But her family totally blocked this vocation. In vain did my mother beg, beseech, weep, pass whole days in prayer; nothing could overcome the opposition of her parents and all the family, united against her desire. The Falsan family and the Nièpce family were Christians, friends of the clergy. My grandfather had a Mass said on Sundays on his estate at Saint-Cyr. But they would not allow a young girl to break the bonds of family and enter religion.

Gentle and docile, very affectionate, herself wrapped in the conception of family ties which meant so much to the people of Lyons, my mother was exhausted by a struggle of which the outcome could only be violence or submission. She protested at least that if she was required to marry, she could accept only a thoroughly Christian young man, who made a point of showing himself to be such, who shared her faith and would continue at her side the practice of the sacraments she had never left.

My Parents' Marriage

When, therefore, my father came on the scene, she took to him and made the solemn statement that if he was not accepted, there should be no further talk of marriage.

The wedding took place on May 1, 1850. I wonder whether the Falsan family was influenced by the political situation. Their ideal was the government of Louis-Philippe. When that fell, the revolution, especially at Lyons, was a bitter social upheaval. There was fear that the town would be sacked. There was fear in my grandfather's household. They remembered a great silver tureen which was sold, and my mother told me of her sadness at seeing it represented by nine hundred francs in brand new crown-pieces. Perhaps they were attracted by the thought of entrusting the frail Elisa to a resolute man, who owed his position to his own hard work and would know how to defend and protect her.

The marriage was a happy one. Bourget had not yet laid down that it was a mistake to rush into a marriage. I do not claim that my mother never suffered in her relationship to her husband's family. But her delicacy prevented anything being visible. My father behaved with equal tact. Besides, my Lagrange grandparents had that inborn nobility of sentiment which was characteristic of the Christian peasant of France in the old days—to the extent of striking Young, the English traveler. As a child I never noticed any difficulty in family relationships. Burgundy was more distant—the journey from Macon had to be made by coach; we saw each other less, but that was all.

Incidentally, my parents did not remain at Lyons, as my father had bought a solicitor's practice at Bourg-en-Bresse, and their life together began, soon to be completed by cradles.

A Christian Couple

I feel slightly shy in saying that they were a Christian couple, although I am the product of their moral union no less than of their blood. My father was truly head of the family. But there was still a hint of deference, a checking of his energetic nature when dealing with the woman who had chosen him and who was his model. He was always the one to make important decisions, but his glance always asked a question, and he often had no need of explicit advice. I will recount the traits of his truly incomparable and upright character. Christian to the marrows of his bones, he went beyond the norm of Christians at the time by receiving Communion four times a year; in everything he was scrupulously faithful to the Church. While I was still a young man, I observed his truly astonishing lack of tension. When we used to go into his office, it seemed as though he had no work on hand—no files on the table, no long interviews with clerks or clients. His clear mind saw to the bottom of the most complicated cases: then he wrote them up clearly, without any erasures. Business never dragged!

It is understandable that my mother never felt the slightest temptation to interfere at all. She had no taste for it, nor, I suspect, any talent. Her spirit, certainly typical of Lyons, was nevertheless a practical one. In the household everything ran smoothly, thanks to a tradition to which she remained faithful; but my father kept the accounts for her. Before her marriage she had passionately loved painting, but she put her easel aside. Her spiritual life was everything to her, although she entertained as she should, with a preference for those of a lower stratum in society: in small towns rank is, or at least was, extremely important. Prayer was a refuge for her. In one very trying time of trial one of my cousins saw her go into a church utterly shaken and emerge transfigured. Perhaps she lacked judgment of others; she was incapable of seeing their faults. That was one aspect of her generous idealism; she was attracted to everything beautiful and good, and was not capable of stopping short at anything else. This was not that tendency, sometimes rather sickening, of making excuses; she truly did not see evil. She herself saw what was lacking to her in life's bitter struggle, of which she really had no clear idea; so she relied on her husband in complete confidence. As he spent the day in his office, I passed most of my childhood with her. I had learned needlework to gain the right to work with her and my sister Pauline, my junior by nearly four years. There were gentle conversations, gentle thoughts kept in the heart, constant influence and frequent unspoken calls toward a life where the good assumed the aspect of the beautiful.

The moment came when my mother was compelled to give up this delightful intimacy in circumstances especially hard.

EARLIEST FORMATION

A Question of Principle

My father would never have consented to sending me to the Lycée even as a day boy. His determination on this point was inflexible. Today the situation has totally altered, and there are not lacking Catholic teachers at the university. I do not know how good the teaching was at Bourg, but it was a question of principle. To avoid my being too cut off, a teacher at the Lycée was asked to give me lessons at home. In summer we were in the country, a kilometer and a half from the office, and that year my mother, who was often unwell, had had to take the waters at Plombières, not for the sake of fashion, but perhaps because it was fashionable.

My teacher, M. David, whom I name with gratitude, nevertheless made the mistake of flattering himself on a flair which he considered interesting. This enabled me to take things easy. I gave up work, and one day, to avoid his complaints, I decided to take to the neighboring woods.

When my mother returned, there was no alternative to begging pardon. The experiment was considered sufficient, and it was decided that my laziness could be corrected only by a boarding school. My brother Louis, my senior by three years, had already had one year at the seminary of Autun. I was to join him after the summer holidays of 1864. My mother would find herself cut off from both her sons by a cruel separation.

She had chosen Oullins, where the Dominicans of the Third Order had just founded a private school with P. Captier (the heroic martyr of the Commune) as headmaster. It was near Lyons, near her family and near herself. This was, I think, the only occasion in which my father demanded a sacrifice from her. I have said what the minor seminary of Autun was, what it had meant for him, and what it still meant because of the presence of his friend Farges. For him there was nothing to equal this simple, sturdy and very academic education. The pupils at Oullins, belonging to rich families, went without that activity which was not yet called sport. They went down to Lyons in hordes and made merry, but they did not go without winning brilliant success in examinations. At Autun the uniform was blue smocks except on Sundays, and in winter they wore clogs. But study was taken very seriously, and my father knew that his former fellow students, M. Farges and M. Lequin, would watch over his son. M. Duchêne, the superior, had the reputation of being an excellent educator of the young.

The Rigors of Boarding School

Of this primitive severity my mother could at first see only the thorns. Never a day off school except in the long vacation. The journey was long; it was impossible to get to Autun by train. Being always of delicate health, my mother could undertake this trek only two or three times a year. Unbelievable though it may seem, the discipline of the minor seminary was so strict that she was not even allowed to take us out for a meal in a hotel. She brought food in a great hamper, and we ate with her in a wretched little parlor. What wonderful days, all too short, spent chatting under the great trees in the garden! Each time she left, it was for our mother a separation as though for life.

This, obviously, is the bad side of boarding school; it separates a child from the family. But what right have we to add that it is against nature, especially at a time when vacations are, in the eyes of parents, all too frequent? Family affection is sacred; the family itself is the basis of human society. Everything that weakens it or lessens the rights of parents is a blow struck at the human community. But clearly parents are exercising their rights by choosing a boarding school for their children: they deprive themselves of the sweet presence of their child on the assumption that it is for the good of the child. It is a matter of forming future heads of families, and, if possible, leaders of groups of people. Obviously boarding school develops a sense of responsibility: the child is obliged to act, to take up a position, and immediately feels the consequences. In a situation where his little friends are chosen for him, he follows and perhaps corrects his first sympathies. A schoolmaster will not always have the indulgence of a mother or the partiality of a father for him; he must make his own way. The pain of separation, the longing, in all kinds of circumstances, for the dear nest of the family can but increase the attachment of child to family. He will be glad to find it again as a young man, at the moment when the day boy is longing to be emancipated from it, without having learned to act for himself. In a word, boarding school creates stronger and more independent personalities. Is that not just what we lack today?

But this is no place for me to discuss that thorny problem. My own observation—and no doubt this fault will diminish with the general elimination of Greco-Roman civilization—is that at boarding school as it was, the child was dedicated uniquely to classical studies, without any dedication to the practice of the faith. Instead of looking around and dreaming of a middle position, or, for the more ambitious, aiming at earning a good salary, the ideal put forward is an image of glory: military glory, the glory of the forum, the laurels of a poet. The best among the ancients were consumed with this desire of glory. For them it became a reality, the great reality. The purpose of life was to leave a name in the memory of men.

Well-born children long to imitate great figures of the past. I remember my amazement when a good preacher showed us that saints are greater than heroes. Must I admit here that as a theological student I had difficulty in understanding the Christian concept of vainglory? I no longer refuse to confess this fault. But in the last analysis, is this the most dangerous temptation for the youth of today?

A Precocious Liberalism

Obviously I anticipate a little. At the age of nine and a half I was hardly advanced enough for this. Nothing happened to increase my homesickness; there was no unpleasantness toward the new boy. If such barbarous treatment had been the norm at the seminary, the presence of my brother would have sufficed to protect me from it. We were always very attached to each other, never leaving each other during the holidays, sharing the same enthusiasms, the same recreations, the same affection for our parents. At the seminary, true, each went his own way, a member of his own group without any restriction.

I began in the seventh class. My first beginnings were undistinguished. I have never been what is called a good pupil, for I unreservedly followed my own interests instead of concentrating on doing the work set—a little enthusiast who hid away to read *The Last Days of Pompeii* by Bulwer Lytton, or *Ivanhoe* by Walter Scott, and neglected his Latin exercises. From time to time the teacher blew me up fairly roughly, but not unkindly.

It went less well with the master in charge of the junior school, the only one of my masters whom I do not remember with great gratitude. I reckoned that in him I met a cold hostility. If I had earned good marks in class (what was called "a pink ticket") he used to mention it in public, adding that I had lost it because of my bad spirit. Unable to handle this treatment, which seemed to me despotic, I had asked him to read us the rules, because I was perfectly prepared to obey rules, but not whims. This lad of ten demanding a constitution seemed to him grotesque. He countered by accusing me to my father of neglecting my studies and using my time to versify the *Télémaque*. My father's consternation may be imagined, but it was certainly from him that I had learned this precocious liberalism, which I have never renounced any more than did P. Lacordaire. My father was a legalist, so he did not like the absolute power of the empire. He told me that in the plebiscite of 1851 there were only two of them at Bourg who voted against. Together with the name of Albert, that of my godfather, and Mary, out of devotion to the Most Blessed Virgin, he had given me the name Henry at baptism, out of respect for the Comte de Chambord. But in character he was liberal, and read *Le Correspondant*. This time I had no difficulty reassuring him about a poetical vocation which went no further than doggerel rhymes. I gave it up unhesitatingly, which shows clearly enough that I was not a poet born.

The Call of God

Another incident was more serious. The master in charge of the dormitory was absent and the pupils realized soon enough that he had not been replaced. There was a rumpus during the night in which I took only a small part. But the ringleaders put the blame on me, and I was removed from the class of preparation for First Communion. This time it was my mother's turn to express touchingly her deep sorrow. I was so moved that I soon got myself reinstated, and made my First Communion on May 27, 1866. My mother was prevented by her health from coming. My father was at his father's deathbed. My uncle and godfather, Albert Falsan, stood in for them, and ever afterward showed an affection toward me of which he has since given so many proofs. My childish contrition brought from me floods of tears; my comrades claimed that I made my confession at the top of my voice, and that they heard every word. I can still see myself among the others, in that chapel which has been converted into a barracks room. In the evening the First Communicants went to the foot of the Lady statue at the end of those spacious walks which could almost be called esplanades. As after my baptism, Mary took me under her protection. She has played her part of the faithful Virgin. I am certain that on that day I heard the call of God. I acknowledged it to my mother, who came as soon as she could, under the great tree at the end of the garden. To hear this was bliss to her. At that time I was thinking only of being a priest, without thinking of any special vocation; she blessed God, though without giving the impression of attaching too much importance to this effusion of a child's piety.

Simply Idle

However, these good intentions did not last long. I became simply idle, to the great scandal of M. Lequin, the form-master of the fifth class and a former fellow student of my father's, who made a point of rubbing my nose in the reminder of this. Uninventive as he was in his teaching, he had a passion for Greek and insisted at all costs on our remembering Greek roots, of which more than one was quite fanciful. There was no escaping this, but it turned out to be the only subject which I enjoyed. Studies as a whole I detested. My father wrote that he would not come to the prize-giving, as he did not wish to feel ashamed in the house where he was brought up. It needed a good deal of courage for me to point out to him that I had at any rate won a *proxime accessit*. That was not much, and he left me in no doubt of the fact. The following year everyone was astonished to see this little dunce up with the leaders. I never came first; this place was reserved for Xavier Cornu, the perfect pupil, intelligent, serious, quick to learn, open to all academic subjects, both arts and sciences. He died as a young master at the minor seminary; beyond the shadow of a doubt the Church of France lost in him a true light. Second place belonged almost as regularly to Etienne Bonneau, who was brilliantly gifted at poetry and wrote Latin verse in the meter of Sappho and Alcaeus as easily as Virgilian hexameters or Ovidian elegiacs. At most I could compete for third place with Louis Bonnard, who died very young, serving the university.

I could not even keep up this pace. From the third class onward frequent illness prevented me taking part in prize compositions. Anyway, even if I still cherish these memories, they can interest no one but myself. I am practically the sole survivor of my contemporaries.

Care for the Future

In spite of having sent his sons away, entrusting them to kindly and experienced teachers, my father took a keen interest in their future, and made sure of sounding out our feelings in the matter. It seemed to be taken for granted that my brother would take over from him as solicitor, so that his path was already mapped out. Had I not some taste for industry? To make sure of it, my father took me to the mines of Montceau and especially to Le Creusot, proud to show me the impressive advance of metal-working in his own country. I was struck by the power of the machinery and especially by the chain of processes which made a finished implement out of molten metal. The lava of iron pouring at boiling point out of high furnaces amazed me. But I was more bewitched than seduced, for the haunting thought of that furnace horrified me. I was not made to be an engineer.

UPHEAVEL OF THE WAR

Anxieties

At this time my father took me to Dijon, where an important case was in progress for which he had prepared the brief. I followed the pleas without understanding them, but with a longing one day to speak with such fluency and with the straightforward tone which appealed to me more than the incantations of preachers. But all these preoccupations were to be shattered by the agony of the war. On our way back from Dijon we could hardly find a seat on the train crammed with soldiers. "To Berlin!" was the cry. The officers kept opening maps of the war zone, running from the Rhine to the Spree. My father was less confident. This time he had voted for the empire, on May 8, 1870, a day of noble light whose brilliance still shines in my memory, because he feared social upheaval. But he had no doubt that the empire would make this confirmation of its power the occasion for completing its ruin. The *Marseillaise*, forbidden till now, was let loose upon France, and seemed to be a call to demagogy. The memory of the volunteers of 1792 had no message of hope to anyone who knew his history. The Prussia which we found facing us, armed to the teeth, had little similarity with the Prussia of Valmy, which had no real desire to make a thorough attack on the Revolution that had destroyed the French monarchy.

So my father was anxious. So much I understood that night of the return from Dijon to Bourg, the night when I really began life.

A Collapse

Since the Great War my younger contemporaries are apt to smile at the mention of the campaign of 1870. It was short but tragic. France thought that it could dictate laws to the whole of Europe. Mexico had shown a few cracks to those who could see clearly, but it was so far away, so ephemeral! On its own borders France would be herself once again. It was a collapse. Blow after blow, usually on Sunday morning, the terrible news struck. After Sedan it was clear that the empire was at an end. More recently, and with some semblance of truth, it has been judged that a revolution in a country under enemy occupation cannot be justified. But the empire was not overturned by a revolution; it simply collapsed! All France was waiting for the signal which Paris did not fail to give. In the provinces this signal was received in the morning of September 5. The population of Bourg immediately rushed to the parade grounds. The empire was declared to be at an end, and the republic was proclaimed without any great enthusiasm. Then a dried-up prune of 1848 called Puthaud was installed as prefect, which gave some wags the opportunity of calling the government Putrid. And it was really the court of King Pétaud. Like all the young who did not like the empire, I was a Republican. The Comte de Chambord was still thought of only by the aristocracy, withdrawn onto their estates, and brooding till the day when France was seen to be threatened. But the choice of leaders which was in fact made quite upset my religious convictions. Everyone knows today that Gambetta was the incarnation of the National Defense movement, so all is forgiven him.

But even then there was no secret about the alacrity with which he settled himself on to the throne of power as though he naturally belonged there, and felt totally at ease. Babble about liberty though he might, everyone saw him oppose free elections after the capitulation of Paris, while Jules Simon himself, later so discreet and deferent in the choice of bishops, was at that time known only as hostile to any positive religion. When Jules Favre, after emphatic declarations on territorial integrity, was seen to forget to include in the armistice the army of Bourbaki, which had been irresponsibly launched against the Prussian rear, disillusionment became general. I do not intend to move here into the field of politics or strategy; I am simply explaining how my republican convictions of an ideal of liberty gave way before the brutal reality. Nor was I the only one, as the February elections for the National Assembly showed.

Day Boy at Bourg

But to return to more personal reminiscences. At the declaration of war I was hardly more than fifteen, and of such delicate health that I had been compelled to leave the seminary; I could not think of joining up, or at least I understood the impossibility of realizing this burning desire. So at the beginning of October I again took my place in the seminary. We did not stay there long. Garibaldi had come to help France, less to pay the debt which Victor Emmanuel refused to pay than to lend a helping hand to the revolutionary cause! In his legion were a large number of Spaniards. These were at first fitted into the seminary by our squashing together a little. One night the foreign volunteers were so many that the older pupils were thrown out of their beds. The next day we all left, sent home to our families. What should be done now? My father bowed to the demands of the inevitable. My brother and I were enrolled as day boys at the Lycée of Bourg. Then I could judge the high academic standards at the minor seminary. There I had hardly been tenth in the class, but at the Lycée I found myself first. On his side my history teacher was astonished at my Catholic protestations against the treaty of Westphalia. What louts! There was soon to be an end of the malaise caused by this situation in a period of sharp opposition between free instruction and the university.

A Delicate Humanist

As a sequel to a sleigh-ride in the snow I caught erysipelas of the face, a complaint which became chronic with me, and I was obliged to leave the Lycée. When I was able to return to work, my father asked the form master of the class of rhetoric, M. Fontaine, to tutor me. He was a delicate humanist, who scarcely took the trouble to stand in the way of my own tastes. He liked to contrast the poverty of the Latin traditions with the brilliant imagination of the Greeks. Soon all my tutorials were whittled down to being translations from Greek; he first gave me Pindar. However, at this time I was already much enamored of Cicero. But I read him on my own. I have always found his own eloquence less to my taste than his views on eloquence. If he is not the first of orators, no rhetorician is comparable to him. The historical procession of Roman orators in the *Brutus* confirmed me in the view that the most enviable way of life was to be found in public speaking. It was no longer possible to conceive a future government of France without a parliament where orators would first rise up and later guide the country. I here leave my illusions, both those shared with others and those peculiar to myself, open to severe judgment. I also made the acquaintance of Molière, for whom I had had little taste at the minor seminary. I was staggered by the forceful realism which asserted itself with the authority of a penetrating common sense; but in the long run, however much I admired him, I have not so much taken him to myself, because this natural genius, for all his usefulness at the time of *Les Precieuses*, has a certain pedestrian quality, often devoid of poetry.

The Epic of Defeat

Nevertheless France continued the unequal struggle; in the last analysis it served no purpose, for France's honor had never been compromised. So strong was the conviction that France could never be finally conquered that in the provinces no one appreciated at first that the armistice meant the capitulation of Paris. The question was seriously asked what unheard of and still unknown disaster could have befallen the Prussians; it was known only that they had sent to the rear three coffins covered by a golden flag. Such moonshine and prophecies of unknown origin served the credulity of the man in the street. But there was no holding out against the evidence. In the street the soldiers were raising their rifle-butts in the air. The Départment of Ain being included in the armistice, one of them told me how he had fled desperately from the Jura as far as the boundary stone, against which he had fallen asleep. But it was sheer relief after a superhuman effort during a freezing winter, when food was short and clothes and even shoes were torn to shreds. For a long time it was the regret of my life that I had not taken part in this epic of defeat.

The Paris Commune

We must admit that the Paris Commune was a lunacy, a delirium of the siege. But it was a bloody delirium and a fiery lunacy. Let the young of today try to empathize—to use their own terminology—with our state of mind when we learned that the supporters of the Commune had fired in cold blood on the peaceful deputation in the Rue de la Paix, that they put before a firing squad the hostages they had procured, that they set Paris on fire, not only the Tuileries, in their determination to respect neither our national glories nor the works of art in the Louvre, nor the sanctity of Notre-Dame. Their delight was in destroying every man's right to live in an ordered society. However, after this explosion of savagery the second round of elections took place. A reaction was expected. They were unequivocally radical. That was my first lesson in politics. The first round of elections had raised the highest hopes. Thenceforth I was convinced that there was something rotten in the state of Denmark. Someone had read his Shakespeare!

And I remained convinced that, if France has not since then been engulfed in the revolution, it is because the Commune was checkmated—too roughly, some say, but it has not yet been forgotten!

AFTERMATH OF THE WAR

After these unhappy events, my dear mother took me to the waters at Uriage to ensure my health for once. Then I returned to the seminary, which had cancelled the vacation to make up for a lost year. It took place all the same! During the night of August 15, fire devoured the roof of the seminary. The pupils, hurriedly awakened, were co-opted to make a bucket-chain to halt the fire, but there was no avoiding a second hurried departure. I was wholly at sea, prostrate with shock.

Sons of René

What were my thoughts on that day of the Assumption? Certainly I had received Communion with devotion in the chapel of the infirmary. But why, all that day, did the lines of Tasso in the *Gerusalemme Liberata* keep running through my head? I was in the grip of a very special affection for this poem, but it did not last long. Already Dante had claimed me for his own, and he has kept me.

The damage from the fire having been repaired, we returned in autumn. There remained that last year, which was a considerable strain because there was the baccalaureate to prepare, which in those days was taken all at once. I was less than ever in a state to keep up a regular stint of work. I abandoned myself to daydreaming, which our teachers used to anathematize, but whose charms the youth of today does not seem to appreciate; deceptive and deadly, no doubt, but delicious and even intoxicating. Without knowing, we were sons of René. Besides, I had to return to my father's house. Were these illnesses not to some extent imaginary? Today I would be tempted to think so. Certainly I made no attempt to combat this tendency to follow only my own whim, and others indulged me. In such conditions what would happen to the baccalaureate at the end of the year?

(Added on, September 22, 1936): When I am dead people will say how active I was. This began only at the seminary. My mother well understood how soft my character was. She wrote to me, I think in February 1869, "Congratulations on winning first place. It was high time, for I had the impression that you were going downhill fast. I am well aware that in winter you have to look after yourself; but with your soft character you must be careful, my friend, not to get into the habit of listening to yourself too much and becoming slack and idle—faults which I noticed in you during the vacation."

The Delights of Daydreaming

I already had, certainly, a fair amount of intellectual curiosity, but all this kept turning into daydreaming. I had certainly not read *René* when I wrote to my friend of seminary days, Ravel-Chapius, these words whose sole interest is to show the state of mind of adolescents of that era! I wrote to him on May 8, 1872, a few days after passing the baccalaureate: "I shall spend the coming winter at home.[5] I shall give myself up wholly to literature, history and the arts. To an increasing extent poetry and eloquence are steadily mounting in my estimation. They all unite together for me in one aesthetic pleasure. I want to get to know the arts and Paris. After that, what will become of me? I tell myself sometimes that if I ever was ambitious, I am so no longer. This is perhaps the effect of the collapse which follows a violent passion.[6] In any case, behind my carefree and happy exterior I have known and suffered the whole range of hidden suffering, of melancholy regret, of yearning for an ideal unknown or only vaguely sketched. I have never opened my heart to anyone, and perhaps even this letter will be burned before I send it. You perhaps think of my old vocation to be a Dominican, and laugh. All right! It is precisely to renew this and to come nearer to making up my mind that I am waiting for the First Communion. I hope that among those children I shall be able to hear and see. Perhaps not all their hearts are pure, but they are all loving. They will all pray for me and their prayers are all-powerful. As for making a good speech, I know that this is quite beyond my powers. My actions always fall short of my dreams. . . ."

This light came, as clear as I could wish, as I shall explain later.

The Baccalaureate

But we must return to the year 1871. I went back to Bourg in February, I think, in poor condition, in the grip of this deadly daydreaming. My father then took a decision which made me take myself in hand. He proposed to me that I should sit the examination for the baccalaureate immediately without further preparation. It was a challenge. (End of addition of September 22, 1936.)

At that time there was an examination session for the sake of candidates for the schools of government. I need only give this reason and I would be in luck. This was what happened, and I passed without difficulty in the examination run by the faculty of Lyons. French composition did not get a very good mark. I had read Auguste Nicolas and Balmès, the bright lights of Catholic apologetics at that time. Without any anti-clerical prejudice and perfectly correctly, I was considered too traditionalist. Science was not brilliant. In a room of the palace of St. Peter, the examiner said that I gave the impression of falling from Fourviére, whose little church sparkled across great tracts of ice.

In response to this quip of good M. Dieu, we climbed up the next day to the sanctuary of Mary, to thank the immaculate patron of all citizens of Lyons, my friends full of merriment and myself tasting bitterly the emptiness of this little success. it was a touch of your grace, my God!

The Examination of Saint-Cyr

My father, at first delighted with the success of his expedient, was immediately brought up short by a scruple: "You gave your word that you would present yourself at Saint-Cyr: I do not want you to begin life by being untrue to your word. You must present yourself at Saint-Cyr." I had no desire to be accepted, and I was afraid of making a fool of myself by sitting a special examination for which I had made no preparations at all. My friends thought my pretensions ludicrous. But soon, now that the crushing weight of worry had been lifted, I felt ready to prepare for this laughable examination. I returned to Autun covered with laurels but a prey to the merry mockery of my friends. To avoid being exposed to turning in a blank paper I took some classes in design and in technical drawing; I went riding a few times; the rest would be of a piece with this. My father had always made us learn fencing during the vacations, since this sport had no place in the seminary.

The examinations took place at Lyons during the summer: four days of written papers, two each day. The number of candidates was considerable, and all were keenly competitive. My carefree attitude did not fail to shock them. They talked over their results uneasily. I was always content—with very little. This freedom of spirit was no doubt an advantage. I got on the short list, to the great amazement of my teachers, who had a more exalted idea of Saint-Cyr. But I refused to contemplate the ridiculous possibility of finally getting in. If the impossible had happened and I was offered a place, I would have refused it, so infatuated was I with my aim of a profession involving words. My father thought that since everyone was going to be a soldier, it would be an advantage to do military service as a member of Saint-Cyr; therefore he insisted that I enter for the oral examination. I beg the reader to believe that, if I insist on these tiresome details, it is to give a scrupulous conscience its due. During the oral examination my father had another scruple. He went to find the president of the board, expressing to him the fear that my admission would deprive another candidate of a place he could count on. If this were the case, he would immediately withdraw my candidacy. M. Favre—if I remember rightly—answered him that supernumerary candidates were always offered places, in the expectation that unexpected gaps would appear, and besides, looking up my marks, he assured my father with a smile that he had nothing to fear. To the honor of the school my name did not figure among those of the successful candidates.

Archaeological Excursions

My last days in the region of Autun have left me the most delightful memory. M. Bulliot, the distinguished president of the Aeduan Society, had long been alone in holding that the Gallic Bibracte had not been replaced by Augustodunum, but had been perched, in the fashion of other cities, on the summit of Mount Beauvray. Excavations had proved him right. He had had built there a few small houses to direct the excavations, and was going to lay the foundations of a chapel dedicated to St. Martin. He had invited me to spend a few days there with his son Antoine and a few friends. We slept on matting, rushed all over the woods, and the healthy old man—he was, Homer would have said, on the threshold of old age—took a very well-meaning pleasure in proving to us that his legs were still more supple than ours. These were my first archaeological excursions. M. Bulliot challenged us, on the rocks where—so he thought—a great assembly of the Gauls had taken place, to pronounce a Latin harangue for Diviacus on the glories of Roman civilization, and for Vercingetorix on the sacredness of independence. We had no intention of taking up this challenge before a master who knew so well the commentaries of Caesar.

The Decision of the Comte de Chambord

Mgr. Landriot came up to bless the first stone of the little building. The sorrows of the occupation of Rheims still weighed heavy on his mind. As long as hope remained of a restoration of the monarchy, he was convinced that the Comte de Paris, with his noble adherence to the principle represented by the Comte de Chambord, would not gain the allegiance of the army. But had not the claimant to the throne given them more than one excuse? On this matter I remember that my father also did not share the general conviction that the king, in order to save France, would give up the white banner, which had never formed part of the national flag under the old regime. The naive M. Chesnelong made himself the bearer of this good news. But Lucien Brun, his companion at Frohsdorf, said not a word. And my father always said: "Wait till Lucien Brun speaks." He had good reason to keep silence, even though the prince spoke. And it seems to me that he did not adequately appreciate the effect his word would have. I was only eighteen years old. One morning, October 5, if I remember rightly, I bought a newspaper and read it. I realized that it was all over, and this intuition was shared by every Frenchman, young and old, except a few charismatic figures like the venerable religious who said to me at the death of the Comte de Chambord: "Now I can no longer understand the plans of Providence." Who can ever flatter himself on being able to read them in advance? It is quite enough to work out what human intentions make plausible.

Youth Conquered

I dwell on this point because I do not think that the generation, aged from fifteen to twenty after the war, is fairly judged. Literature, and M. Paul Bourget more than anyone, has represented them as a generation of defeatists, demoralized in advance in the struggle of life, taking refuge in an ivory tower because they could not face the coarser reality. Defeatists! Defeated by what? The resistance to the Prussians had been heroic, not inglorious; there was no bombast in saying with the sculptor, Mercié: "Glory to the defeated!" And the hope of a reversal was the spur to a prompt recovery with such elasticity that the Germans regretted not having crushed us more thoroughly. Yes indeed, this youth was defeated politically, imbued as it still was with those old principles which it identified with the good of its country. Insofar as the elections gave a stronger majority to the left wing parties, the watchword was to avoid all external difficulties in order to concentrate on the progress of the revolution. The saying of Gambetta which is still considered sublime, "Alsace-Lorraine, think of it always, speak of it never," was no more than a slogan to drive home a patriotism profoundly linked to the France of ancient times. When one thinks of a great cause, a full heart cannot but overflow. And in the assemblies of which even Gambetta was not proud, anyone could see a wave of incompetence breaking, leaving no other function to speech than empty protestations. Before the inevitable victory of force of numbers, a force which cannot be considered very rich in intelligence, those who considered themselves an elite were judged powerless and became discouraged—or else shifted their position. After the royalists had been checkmated, the empire—can there now be any doubt?—regained popularity. The tragic death of the prince imperial completed the discomfiture of those who ineptly called themselves conservatives.

To many fine spirits the advent of a more extreme socialism seemed inevitable. It could not be foreseen that anti-Catholic forces, attached nevertheless to material prosperity, would turn the blow by throwing the prosperity of the Church to be dismembered by the poorest elements in the population.

I wanted to have done with politics, insofar as I am here giving my personal testimony. I had become sincerely royalist, but not militantly so, nor enrolled in right-thinking circles in order to gain a position in good company.

Worldly Temptation

In this I was also kept safe by an example given me by my father. At this time the minor seminary of Autun contained scarcely any sons of the bourgeoisie. Most of the pupils came from the countryside, minds barely refined but vigorous, judiciously chosen by the clergy from among those who were most gifted and were sons of sincerely Christian families. In addition, the landowners of Morvan, some of them belonging to the high nobility, avowed themselves satisfied with the education at the minor seminary. I always had friends in both groups. But at the end of my studies I was invited to a chateau, and it seemed to my father that I was unduly inclined to look for connections above myself. I never met in him the least trace of socialist jealousy. Following his example I have always refused to snipe at aristocracy, to pick on certain absurdities, the inevitable withering away of a class which no longer fulfills its proper role, when it does not seek to adapt itself to new circumstances in order to perform services as valuable as those given in days gone by. But my father knew by experience—that of others rather than his own—that the false glitter of being part of a closed world is often won only at the expense of the dignity naturally deserved. He gave me the names of young people who were allowed into this world only as squires to carry ladies' cloaks. I have since come to know that as one climbs toward the highest ranks of the aristocracy—I mean the French royal family—courtesy is so perfect that one feels oneself to be on an equal footing. But this is the product of an exquisite generosity and cannot be taken for granted. My father was, then, very wise to give me this advice, and it has served me well. I did not canvas for the loan for Don Carlos, to be repaid when the king was in Madrid, nor did I even subscribe to it except to annoy some of my comrades.

Balance Sheet of an Education

At the moment of leaving the seminary or rather after such a long passage of time, I can ask myself what was the result of this education over the period of eight years, though it is true that the last years had been considerably curtailed. I will leave aside the studies. They were very strong, especially in Greek. In the fourth class anyone who was smart could recite the passages of Homer set for the examination and explain them without opening the book. In the class of philosophy when discussion came to an end, we opened Demosthenes or Thucydides without preparing it. Science comprised trigonometry, mechanics and cosmography.

If I had attended to the classes as I should have done, I would have acquired an excellent grounding for future work. But my own lack of solidity deprived me of what was most important. More than once I reported sick to escape unpalatable work knowing that I would be able to take to the infirmary the books I liked. I have never stopped paying the penalty for this lack of regard for grammar; it took a cruel vengeance, until I finally understood that it always has the last word. Invent the most fantastic critical systems: that is your particular choice and others will be indulgent toward you. But a grammatical fault is inexcusable. I have said to young religious, with excuses for the irreverence, that in studies a grammatical fault is the equivalent of the sin against the Holy Spirit in the religious sphere.

I have never been able to fill this gap, and this is why I never dared later to take the degree of *Licence ès lettres*.

Religious Formation

But basically what is essential in a seminary is religious spirit. How far had I gotten in this? What had been done to develop this?

After having said so much that is good of my beloved seminary, I think I can make this reservation that not enough attention was paid to religious instruction. This care fell on each master, who had a special class for his pupils every Sunday. The pupils attached no importance to it at all. Officially the prize for religious instruction was at the top of the list. But it happened only too frequently, except for our impeccable Cornu, that the prize-winner appeared nowhere else on the list. The smart pupils gave up this prize to the wiser ones, who were not always the most intelligent. Were the teachers themselves adequately prepared for this subject, which is more delicate than others? For them too it was an extra which many regarded as a burden. I think that it represents noteworthy progress in the minor seminaries of today that a spiritual father is appointed whose sole care is to form solid Christian convictions in the hearts of the children. Spiritual reading—such was the name given to a chat about virtues and vices, obedience and breaking of rules—occurred almost every evening and was the duty of the director of each division of the school. When Monsieur le Supérieur was seen approaching, not a word was spoken and grave statements were expected, some people bowing their heads already in advance. He rarely intervened, but his authority was supreme. No one had ever stood against him.

Everyone went to confession to a priest of his own choice. Communion was not daily or even frequent by today's standards; but feasts were marked, even in our studies, by some composition or other, often Latin verses on the theme of the day. When a child took a wrong turning, the director of the division tried in a fatherly way to put him back on the right path. I had experience of this.

On the whole it was a regime rather of trust than of severe discipline. Care was taken to feed the flame of the vocation to the priesthood, especially in the higher classes, but the children who were heading for the priesthood were assumed to have good will. On their part there was no concealment: when we were discontented, we did not hide the fact. This was all to the good.

One day on a boat I met one of my fellow students, older and holding an important office in an Order rightly famous for the excellence of its teaching methods. After some opening remarks he said: "You remember how badly looked after we were at Autun. No discipline. In our houses it is a very different matter. We lose sight of the children neither day nor night; they are watched over ceaselessly." "I certainly have no memory of such slackness," I replied, "but under a regime of suspicion, I think I would have withdrawn myself from it." If anything held on to me in my extracurricular fantasies, it was certainly the trust shown me by M. Duchêne. It might well be said that he was wrong, and I admit that his trust could have been better placed, but he was not wrong in thinking that nothing has more effect on the heart and character, and that is what needs to be formed.

Among the most efficacious means of touching the hearts of children, of combating their egoism and the lure of pleasure, long before public or private verbal instruction, I would place visiting the poor at home. There was at the minor seminary a sodality of St. Vincent de Paul, very regular at this duty, and it was an honor to be a member of this.

The Dominican Ideal

My director, M. Duchêne, did nothing to steer me toward the priesthood. At times I am surprised. No doubt he considered my thoughts too profane and my desires already too worldly. It had always been taken for granted that neither my brother nor I would enter the major seminary. To make us good Christians in the world was the aim with us. The good seminarian who passed unhesitatingly from one seminary to the other, had no preferences, no pretensions, no tendencies. That was the judgment of my comrades, except Ravel-Chapuis, who always maintained that I was the only survivor among them who had failed to respond to my vocation.

In fact, however, I was not wholly without some call within me. Since I had read the Conferences given at Notre-Dame and the *Life of St. Dominic* by P. Lacordaire, the Dominican ideal quite dominated my thinking. I had given myself up to St. Dominic, less after the reading of his work than by the seduction of the luminous image imparted to the saint in the Coronation of the Virgin by Fra Angelico. I had no doubts about the exactitude of this portrait: it is in fact just what one would imagine the loving vision of a pure soul to be. Long before entering the Order I was his son, and prayed to him every day. A letter from Abbé Auduc, when he had entered the major seminary, reminded me that, in the second place, on the day of the Annunciation, I had received a revelation that I would enter the Order of St. Dominic. I have only the vaguest memory of it. But at the moment of leaving the seminary I clearly heard a new call. I had been charged to accompany everywhere the little children who were preparing for First Communion as an elder brother helps his father in forming the little ones. After Communion, which always took place on Trinity Sunday, I went out briefly into the cloister. I was told without any possibility of mistake that I would take the black and white habit of the Order of Preachers.[7] I even vowed, without telling anyone anything, that I would do so, though I remembered this only later, when I had already fulfilled it.

But all that belonged to the future, a future which did not press. I was younger than all my comrades. I had time to think about it. Why not spend a whole year at last in my family, in the calm of the home I had so long missed, and in peace?

A Year in the Family

My father was entirely in agreement, this time with the joyful assent of my mother. I could well prepare for the examination of the first year of law at home. A barrister, still young but brilliant, M. Chanone, was kind enough to coach me. My father, intending to send me next to Paris rather than to Lyons, had me entered at the faculty of Dijon with permission not to attend the lectures.

This year was delightful, and was the time when my intimacy with my mother became complete. One day she opened her desk for me and showed me a little box full of faded white flowers, medals, little toys, souvenirs of her children who had died young. "Poor mothers," she sighed, "this is all they have left to them." I was amazed that I still had not known her whole heart, for I thought that her whole affection was lavished on us, whom she cherished so tenderly. My uncle and godfather, Albert Falsan, willingly took me with him on his geological walks. His skill lay in practical observation rather than in theories, and he would offer no explanation that he did not recognize on the spot to be the case, hammer in hand. It was he who proved the presence of the ancient Rhone glacier, by the moraines at its edge on the plains of La Bresse and the foothills of Le Bugey. He was also every inch an artist, and I loved to listen while he talked about his stamp collection or the art books of his library.

I wanted to have books for myself. My father agreed and told me to submit to him a generous list. My taste was for the classics: Orelli's *Cicero* had pride of place. But when he saw arrive, among the works of Montesquieu, the *Lettres persanes* he immediately ordered me to send it back to the bookseller, not wishing, he said, to have in his library books hostile to religion, even indirectly, and especially sarcastic ones. Anxious as he was to develop me, he wanted this to be in a Catholic direction. Lessons in drawing and cello satisfied my artistic leanings.

This year of rest, or so to say of preparation for life as an independent person, under the most tender and enlightened care, was very dear to me, and consequently passed all too quickly.

5. A Fresh Start

THE STUDENT

My father had decided that I should continue my legal studies in Paris. It was not, therefore, his principles to put the advantages of a superior foundation before family life. Lyons was nearer, but the Catholic faculty did not yet exist. It was considered that the Catholic students there were not grouped together to form a body where their convictions might grow roots and become springs of action. Being from Lyons, they lived at home. It was quite natural.

Paris, apart from the reputation of its schools, had enough attractions, enough useful secrets to impart to each individual whatever his tastes and preoccupations for the future required; so students flocked there from every direction. Also Catholic life was, like everything else, more developed there. The Catholic club of the Luxembourg especially had a good reputation, and there legal or medical students, those who were preparing for the *Ecole centrale*, found a real meeting place, under the direction of M. Eugène Beluze, who had used up all his financial resources to set up the buildings of the club and a hostel adjacent, in the interests of the students. There was no annoying supervision, but it was taken for granted that the strictest good behavior would always be observed. My father knew that I would be well received by the foundation and its administrator, whom he had known. He had decided to present me there toward the end of October 1873.

Retreat at Autun

Fond memories still drew me to Autun. There at least was a boarding school which had managed to inspire love for itself. Before leaving for Paris I asked to make a three-day retreat there, with my beloved P. Duchêne, and at this crossroads of life to ask myself seriously which way I should follow. It seems to me that he could have resolutely taken hold of a hesitant will and directed me toward the priesthood. He did not. No doubt his judgment was correct, and without a more definite attraction it would have been wrong for me to leave the beaten track. I had plenty of time before me. To see Paris, to sit at the feet of the best masters, to see the museums, to hear the great symphonies and operas, to see Racine and Molière at the Théâtre-Français—all this seemed to me both infinitively attractive and wholly innocent. I was certainly not attracted by the pleasures of evil temptations.

Part of my strength came from the conviction that there was no danger of my falling away from this healthy state; was there any need to shake it pointlessly by making me apprehensive of an unavoidable fall? To be persuaded that escape is impossible is the most dangerous force to drag someone down. M. Duchêne made no attempt to shatter my illusions; he strengthened my good intentions, and with my father still more confident, we reached Paris.

A Faithful Friend

M. Beluze gave us a most cordial welcome. Indeed this was the experience of practically everybody. If being a saint means being animated by the purest and most all-embracing charity, consecrating all one's life to the good without every judging those who do evil, and that for God alone, then M. Beluze was simply a saint. No one living in the world has so fully given me the impression of an existence consecrated to God. At first charity appeared more fully than piety, but piety was at the root of everything.

His son Paul had just completed his studies at Arceuil, under the Dominicans of the Third Order. He was beginning law. Without any suggestion on the part of our parents we linked up, and M. and Mme. Beluze opened their house to me as though to a son. I can easily explain how Paul Beluze became my friend. Friendship was one of my classical traditions. Montaigne and Boethius had kept the tradition fresh, and certainly Paul had some delightful qualities. This first movement of fellow-feeling became a solid friendship, for it lasted until his death. Everyone around us was surprised, for we were not like each other in any respect. I was often moody, morose, always in a dream, worried about the future; he was a man of the moment, taking everything in good part, quick to follow distractions without becoming attached to them. One day he astonished me by his answer to my uneasy question whether he did not have any ambition. No hunger for power was all right, but no desire for glory, the idea that his name should be on all men's lips, as the Romans used to say? No! He had never thought of it. He loved literature, but music more, and preferred visiting a friend's studio to the Louvre. It was not, therefore, the desire to exchange with him my most secret thoughts that constantly drew me to him, just as he was always coming to me, and there was never any coolness between us. I now suppose, for at that time I did not reflect on it—was this a matter for analysis at that age?—that what most drew me to him was the straightforwardness of a generous and faithful character. I have always put character far higher than that which is nowadays called intellectualism. Also Paul had good taste in everything balanced as though by instinct. He always passed his examinations without even trying. Everything was full for him of promise of the unworried life to which he was tending so effortlessly, with an optimism which dissolved my melancholy. Perhaps also—I must tell the whole truth—his obliging nature gave some scope to my desire for domination: in all the arrangements to be made between friends I had his consent beforehand.

Study in Paris

I did not go with him to the law lectures. He went to satisfy his father and in fact to meet his friends and read *Le Figaro*, which it was necessary to have read in order to escape the bores who recited it aloud. Practical law has never had the slightest attraction for me; it would be enough to cram for the examination during the last month. Later I became attached to Roman law as an historical study. At that time I was envisaging above all the *Licence ès*

Lettres. I enrolled at the Sorbonne for the practical course in higher studies. M. Tourmier, the director of Greek studies, would not allow anyone to attend the lectures unless he had the *Licence* and he told me so. I went to see the manuscripts in the Bibliotheque Nationale under the guidance of Ch. Graux. This is what later inspired me to found a practical school of biblical studies. In fact I pretty soon fell back on the school of the Carmelites, where the saintly bishop of Valence, Mgr. de Gibergues, was my fellow student. But I lacked the groundwork: Greek held no great promise for me. The *Licence* in history did not yet exist, and the *Licence ès Lettres* presupposed to good pedagogical formation. In philosophy the situation was worse. The tone was set by a Kantianism softened in the Catholic schools. M. Graux revolved his Ego for an hour with ludicrous seriousness. He was the only lecturer with whom I could never take notes, for there was nothing precise on which to fix the attention. Lastly, and perhaps this was the main reason, the lectures were early in the morning: at eight o'clock! It would have been necessary to go to bed early, and the evening was the most agreeable time to go for a walk.

The Program of a Dawdler

The legislation natural in a sensible democracy of closing shops in the evening to enable the employees to spend the evening with their families had not yet occurred. At this moment the boulevards were at their most animated. One was not inconvenienced either by harsh noises or by evil smells or by danger from cars. One simply dawdled, which is, I imagine, no longer possible in Paris. Having read Toepffer, who was then in fashion—*La Bibliothèque de mon oncle*—I kidded myself that a great deal was to be learned in this way, that dawdling provided the best spiritual formation. So we dawdled. This consisted in attending a few lectures: I heard Taine lecture on *Le Centaure* of Maurice de Guérin at the Ecole des Beaux-Arts, once or twice P. Monsabré; at the Chambre the Duc de Broglie revealed to me the aristocratic eloquence of Shakespeare's *Coriolanus*, with a tone the more eloquent because it was very French. The theater was more attractive to us. Sarah Bernhardt in *Andromaque* or *Phèdre* was beyond the dreams, but Delauney in *Le Menteur* of Corneille was a surprise. What sparkle in the lie which was created at that very moment—it was visible in the expression, first uneasy and then wreathed in smiles, of that brilliant improviser of fairy tales. And the same author was the creator of old Horace and Polyeucte! The opera came back too often for our taste to Gounod and Ambroise Thomas, but there was also Mozart's *Don Giovanni* with Fauré. The conservatoire was quite closed; one could listen to the great symphonies only on Sundays with Pasdeloup. But on Sundays students limited themselves to the most frugal meal in order to savor more profoundly an emotion which kept them out of breath till the next concert. We went often to the Louvre, to churches, to Versailles, to Saint-Germain, to Les Salons, but also to Longchamps and even to Chantilly for the races. With this program of dawdling, the days passed quickly. There can be nothing difficult about wasting time in Paris for someone who has an inquiring mind and is open with joy to an unknown and seductive world.

There was even a little time, not much, set apart for good works. Paul and I always remained faithful to visiting the poor in the Society of St. Vincent-de-Paul. I also used some Sunday mornings to teach the catechism to a few young chimney-sweeps who recruited each other and came to us of their own free will. Their First Communion took place in the Franciscan church, at that time Rue des Fourneaux, and in the evening the children, no longer black with soot but clad in their First Communion garb, were invited to eat by M. Keller, the great patriot of Alsace.

An Apostolic Soul

P. Dulong de Rosnay had been kind enough to take my spiritual life under his charge. He was an apostolic soul in the fullest sense of the word, looking after his spiritual children with boundless devotion. One day as I was arriving to see him, I was astonished to see him pick up his hat to go out. "My dear Albert," he cried, "I have forgotten to do what I promised you. I will run and do it now; wait for me."

He was an inspired orator, and then it seemed that his hair stood up on his high forehead like the flames of a Giottesque archangel. He used to preside over the Ozanam conference where we made our first attempts. His authority, it must be admitted, came less from the extent than from the depths of his teaching, from his spiritual quality and his personality. He insisted above all on courtesy in discussioin, and this word was frequently on his lips. He was on his way to God, and he carried others with him. His widespread action and his influence on the youth who were devoted to him aroused some anxiety. One must wait and see. The surprising thing is that they made him successful in the Marianist Congregation. When Mgr. du Marais was appointed bishop of Laval (or was it Le Mans?) he asked for him to be his vicar general. We thought we knew that his superiors had not held him back, and he went. We were told that he would be replaced by another priest. No one went to see him. It was dear P. Dulong that we wanted.

Military Service

After the *Licence* in law it was necessary to do military service. At that time there existed an institution which had all the advantages except that of being democratic. Young men who had diplomas or who passed a rather testing qualifying examination did only one year and paid fifteen hundred francs to the state. To judge from the food bills of those days, the state could pocket roughly half this sum. One year was quite sufficient for instruction; the first six months were very tough, but one knew that there were only six more to serve. We made a very united group. Besides Paul Beluze, Georges Holleaux, the elder brother of M. Maurice Holleaux, director of the School at Athens, became a very dear friend of mine. His style was impeccable, and, what to me was more interesting, he was fascinated by the question of our destiny, so that our conversations easily took a religious turn. Georges Malézieux, a member of the Paris bar, who died recently, was the fourth. Money was held practically in common between us; when we ran out, we drew lots to see who should ask his family for a loan. All this helped the profession of soldiering to pass quickly. This tough year was located at Soissons. When it was over, I returned to my legal studies, aiming at a doctorate. But I entered the Catholic University which had just opened.

Return to Study

I had always been passionately concerned for academic freedom, especially as a Catholic, but also as a liberal of the school of

Lacordaire. For me the most noble episode of the religious struggles of the century was always the initiative he took with Montalembert in opening a free school, and their noble pleas at the
court of Paris. Free secondary education had been begun by the
Falloux law in 1850, and the persevering efforts of Catholics, led
both in the country and in the National Assembly by Mgr. Du-
panloup, had won a moderate liberty which has in fact been further reduced. So I enrolled for the lectures at the young Catholic
University of Paris: the examinations occurred before a mixed
board presided over by a state teacher, but at the Carmelites'.

My faith, then, was unharmed, and had an aggressive fervor, roused by the threats which were already piling up on the
political horizon.

Until then I had been supported by an unyielding logic
which was a great help. I was afraid that if the integrity of my
morals gave way I would lose also my faith, since I considered
faith incompatible with failure to observe the laws of God.

Since I have made the decision to write these pages, I must
here tell the truth. I fell, not often, but profoundly, and this created in me a new situation, in which faith could have been compromised. I say no more, because I do not want to give this
account the attraction of an unhealthy curiosity.

The Return of the Prodigal Son

As for a vocation, there was no question of it. But all the
same God was waiting for me there, waiting to exercise his infi-
nite mercy, unworthy of it as I was. He seized me, as so often, by
means of suffering. My parents, whom I loved with extraordinary tenderness, were having to put up with painful trials. I was
sick at heart. One day I was at the races at Longchamp, when a
friend told me that a telegram was waiting for me at my lodgings.
I went straight back. Saddened to the depths of my soul, I in-
stinctively set off for Saint-Sulpice. I entered and went right to
the end of the church, at the feet of Mary. I prayed for a long
time, and fervently. When I came out I was no longer the same
man. I bought a rosary, having mislaid my own. I returned to the
catechism. When I got back to Bourg, I was overcome by the
sense of a wasted and empty life, of an ideal sacrificed. Should I
come back? I had made myself unworthy of it. What spiritual di-

rector would hear such a proposal without a smile? What mockery from my friends! But I learned then that there is no struggling against God when he wishes to draw us by his grace. Conquering all shame, I unburdened myself of my desire on the eve of the Assumption to my erstwhile confessor, the chaplain of the Convent of the Visitation. He welcomed the prodigal son with kindness; he even told me he had been waiting for it. In a few minutes everything was settled. I had decided to return to my former way of life.

Would my parents be convinced so easily? The person they most trusted was M. Duchêne, who was still superior of the minor seminary at Autun. He was kind enough to make the trip to Bourg. He acted as an intermediary for an avowal which to my mind must appear laughable by being so hasty. Judging only by my external appearance, which had always been correct, my father showed no astonishment and made no opposition. It seemed to him only that since more than one year would be required for me to obtain my doctorate in law, I should continue my legal studies. That title could be useful when the juridical situation of the Church was so threatened. I consented to everything, being myself so stunned by my change of life that it seemed to me sensible to bow to experience.

An Extern Seminarist

I cannot remember how I came in contact with Fr. Hogan, the Irish director of Saint-Sulpice, who later published a book on the training of the clergy which was considered a shade too liberal. The priests of Saint-Sulpice were entirely devoted to their holy task, and had no outside ministry. He accepted me on sight as a seminarian, in extraordinary harmony with my own dispositions of which not even I was aware. He advised me to read St. Paul, not at first to penetrate to the depths of his teaching, but in chronological order, beginning with First Thessalonians, which is so natural, so moving, such a faithful picture of the apostolate at its very beginnings.

It goes without saying that my legal studies profited from this change. Since the previous year I had concentrated on them, inasmuch as the examination for the doctorate and the thesis both required considerable effort. On the advice of M. B. Terrat, who had left the state faculty to become the leading light of the Institut Catholique, I chose as the subject for my thesis birthright from the time of Diocletian, when the Roman Empire attempted to consolidate its situation by creating frameworks which in the end produced practically a system of passes. These forcibly kept everyone in the situation into which they had been born, replacing the joyful freedom of the local patriotism of the second century by the enslavement of decurions to the city, and of peasants to the soil, just at the moment when Christianity was calling souls to spiritual liberty.

From now on I was free to follow my vocation. I was now clear that the Dominican life was my goal. But the austerities of the Order were painted in such colors that I was afraid that they would be beyond my strength. To leave the Order once I had entered it was a repugnant prospect. I told myself that at my age I must proceed with caution and not go back on my tracks. A year in the seminary would be a necessary preparation to weigh up my physical and spiritual forces in order to enable a spiritual director to make a scientific judgment. M. Duchêne had ruled out the seminaries of Autun and Bourg, where I would feel isolated among lads fresh from secondary school. He had suggested Issy, where there is always a certain number of late vocations, as well as young men who are still seeking their way.

Visit to Algeria

Nevertheless for my parents the sacrifice had become more difficult. My elder brother had never had much taste for a career as a solicitor. He had resigned himself to it, but office life did not suit him. Returning to his studies after his year of military service, he had wanted to go back to the army, and my father no longer tried to hold him back. At this time he was in Algeria, at Fort-National. That was where we, Paul Beluze and I, went to see him, to show him my affection at the moment when I too was about to leave the family home.

We were received in a very fatherly way by Mgr. Lavigerie, archbishop of Algiers, not yet a cardinal, who had the highest opinion of M. Beluze, and we met at his table the Algerian missionaries who were about to leave to take possession of the seminary of Saint-Anne at Jerusalem, where with their well-known devotion and success they educate part of the Greek Catholic. clergy.

Mgr. Lavigerie gave us some letters of introduction for his missionaries, who then lived in simple hovels where the bed was merely a sloping piece of wood such as I had known at police stations. This admirable life and primitive apostolate filled my dear Paul with enthusiasm: "As you are going to become a priest, you had better become a White Father." Indeed I was thinking of a white habit, but I kept my secret. I said goodbye to my brother, who had accompanied us as far as the sea, and a few days later I entered at Issy. You have treated me, my God, as your merciful heart allows you to treat a prodigal son. It was such a lovely year, in which I was carried along by grace, without making any effort at all.

THE SEMINARIAN

I first put on a cassock on November 21, the day when Sulpicians consecrate themselves every year to Mary. I admired their simplicity, their disregard for honors and even for outside influences, their hidden and hard-working life, fruitful because they are apostles of apostles. At one time this way of life seemed to me so useful to the Church, so safe because so devoid of external glitter, that I suggested to my spiritual director, M. Lafuge, that I go through the little door which led to La Solitude, the novitiate of the Sulpicians. He turned me away from it because he considered that my vocation to the Order of Preachers came from God. And in fact each Dominican feast increased my attraction. I could no longer have any doubts. While I waited I was encouraged to read Holy Scripture a great deal, and especially the Gospels. In the end I decided to work methodically. Those who most shared my taste were Pierre Batiffol and Henry Hyvernat, who remained friends for life, especially Mgr. Batiffol, as Hyvernat chose the United States as his study center. So it was especially with Hyvernat that I took up again the study of languages; he knew more of English and I of German: we helped each other, so enthusiastic that we even read while walking in the woods at Meudon. One day I took him by surprise with a Gaelic grammar:

every language seemed to him worth learning. Batiffol was less interested in rudiments, and also less fervent about philosophy. His vocation for history was already beginning to appear. The extent to which he was always the wisest counselor, the most devoted friend, always ready to help, I described in *La Vie Intellectuelle* when we had the sadness of losing him.

The time for ordinations arrived. On June 6 I received the tonsure, and my name was written on a heart of gold offered by the ordinands to Our Lady of Loretto. At that moment I made my final decision.

The Death of a Friend

Paul Beluze came to see me several times at the seminary, because we went out, I think, only on New Year's Day. At the beginning of May he arrived all sad, though he was normally always joyful, happy about the present and confident about the future. That future was to have its happy auspices confirmed by a brilliant marriage. Was this a presentiment? He begged me to come to Paris with him, to help him sort out a little difficulty he was having with his father. I could not indulge this fantasy. Nevertheless I went to his parents a few days later, learning that he was ill. The doctor was not worried; he was being kept in bed, but on a sort of camp-bed in the drawing-room which did not give the impression of a sick room. I went away unable to justify my unease. One Wednesday, May 29, a free day, a mutual friend came to tell me that Paul had died in the night. Without a word to anyone, I rushed off and found Paul on his deathbed. As for his parents—he was their beloved only son—nothing at all had been suspected. His parents' only consolation was that the nun who was watching at his bedside had heard him singing the *Salve Regina* as if he were half asleep. Then he lost consciousness. A priest summoned in all haste had been able only to give him the last anointing. M. Beluze was heroic. He kept an eye on everything, organized everything, a little meticulous, as usual, but like an automaton, so evident was it that his heart was elsewhere. A few days later he said to me: "God has given me the grace never yet to have complained." He never did complain. He was already a saint, but his saintliness was completed by this martyrdom.

I will not speak of my own sorrow. In his *Retractions* St. Au-

gustine accuses himself on exaggerating the expression of his sorrow in the *Confessions* when he spoke of the death of his beloved
Nibridius.

I must say that having entered upon the road to the priesthood, the absence of such a faithful friend should not have left
the same gap. We had already been separated by force of circum-
stance. The sharpest blow was the initially crushing impression
of a divine intervention, which St. Augustine would have called
a secret judgment of God. M. Beluze had consecrated his life to
helping young people toward a firmness of their convictions and
toward the practice of a Christian way of life. As far as any lay
person can, he gave them to God, he cherished them, these
young people, the strength of the Church. And God took his own
Son away. And yet, still more selflessly, since he no longer had
the hope that God would pay him back in his beloved Paul, he
went on with his task. Was that what God had wanted? A whole
burnt-offering of the affections of the family. The saintly M. Beluze bowed before this will, and his love only grew in the face of
this sorrow which would have crushed anyone else. Such are
sometimes God's ways! To me it brought a flood of light. For me
the only obstacle to religious life was the love of my parents. It
must not block the road of grace. I am sure that without this terrible lesson I would not have had the courage to break the hearts
that were so dear to me.

My Parents Under Trial

For the blow was very hard for them, harder than I could
have guessed, and even so I did not fully appreciate it. If a young
man asked my advice under the same circumstances today, I well
believe that I would advise him to wait.

For my father was undergoing a formidable trial, the only
kind of trial which one would have thought could never touch
him. Drawn on by his confidence and his uprightness, he found
himself implicated in an intrigue. When this was unmasked he
was threatened with a trial in which his professional honor was at
stake. If I heard vague talk about these things, I told myself
firmly that my father had nothing to fear. His honesty was recognized even by his political adversaries. It was inconceivable
that he should have supported any dubious venture, if only be-

cause of his professional competence. But, in the end, attacks were going on behind his back, and the more concerned he was about his honor, the more he suffered. If he had explained all this to me when I opened my heart to him at Saint-Cyr on August 30, the feast of St. Rose of Lima, I well believe that I would have asked God for a deferment, so pressing was his need. But he kept a heroic silence, and only told me to think the matter over carefully. My mother only spoke of his gentleness, and touched my heart by her tears, but I do not believe that she appreciated the seriousness of the situation either. And also I had such an unqualified faith in the duty which lay on me that I was sure I would gain God's blessing and renewed prosperity on those whom I was abandoning to him, at the altar of the Black Madonna to whom they had consecrated me.

To dwell no more on this unhappy memory, I will say only that my father was very severely censured by a court of inquiry whose chairman was more royalist and more conservative than himself, without my father ever making any hint that he was dissatisfied or that he suspected the chairman's good faith. This verdict was quashed at the court of appeal in Lyons, with a most flattering tribute to a probity which should never have been suspect. My father's joy was so great, and this time he explained to me this tiresome affair so fully, that only then did I realize what a sharp blow I had dealt to his love. Nevertheless he still never complained. He too learned from this trial. It was no longer a matter of the just man rewarded by God with temporal blessings, but of the Christian united to the cross of Jesus Christ who is transformed into him even in this life.

Contact with the Dominicans

Once I had gained the consent and the blessing of my father and mother, I set about entering the novitiate. I seemed to be walking in a flood of light, as though God was showing me the path by means of a blazing fire. Everything seemed arranged to bring me to the port which was destined for me.

Before the feast of the Assumption, I had aroused the attention of my mother by asking to go and spend the feast of Our Lady at the Charterhouse of Selignac. The prior, for whom I had the highest veneration, could give me some good advice. His first words to me were: "We have here a Dominican father, who is trying our life for the second time; he will be better at telling you what you should do. This temporary Carthusian—for he came out, and died a Dominican—was P. Doussot, one-time chaplain to the Papal Zouaves, whose gallantry at Patay, when he unfurled the tricolor adorned with the Sacred Heart, had seemed mad even to the brave among the brave. He advised me strongly to enter the province of Toulouse of which he was a member, but to make no decision before seeing Saint-Maximin. By birth I belonged to the province of Lyons, but some hard words for Montalembert and even for Lacordaire had made an unhappy impression on my inveterate liberalism, and even on my feelings as a Catholic penitent. It was doubtless the work of a single religious, but he claimed not to be speaking for himself alone. So I was not sorry to have a look at another province. It was very easy for me to go to Saint-Maximin, on my way to M. Beluze at Aix, where he had already welcomed me with his son. I there found Abbé Castellan (now archbishop of Chambéry), Paul's cousin, whom I had known when he was a student at the Rue des Postes, and who had also renounced the world. Being a Provençal and very proud of the glories of his native land, he offered to introduce me to Saint-Maximin; from there we climbed up to La Sainte Baume and came down the mountains to his house at Roquevaire.

Entry to the Dominicans

Saint-Maximin is the only ancient friary that the Dominicans have in France. Built in the thirteenth century by Charles II of Anjou, backing on to the magnificent basilica which was destined to be the sanctuary of St. Mary Magdalene, somewhat adapted under Louis XIV to a less austere ideal, it has nevertheless preserved a fine monastic atmosphere. Filled with fervent young religious, it exercises its fascination even on hearts not prepared for its influence. I was bowled over, and as soon as we got back to Marseilles, Abbé Castellan took me to the friary in the Rue Montant. There a further coincidence struck me. When we had journeyed to Algeria with Beluze we had gone into a chapel decorated with the poetry of the rosary, built by M. Bossan, the architect of Fourvière. Kneeling at first near the entrance of the church, my attention drawn involuntarily to the group of figures above the choir which dominates the nave, I was so absorbed in prayer that my friend had difficulty in tearing me away from a place where I already felt that I belonged.

P. Cormier, at that time provincial of Toulouse, and later Master General of the Order, welcomed me. He was about to leave for Saint-Maximin, where he was to preach the retreat. It was a good moment to make all the decisions. This was done. After a retreat which moved me so much that I found it painful, I went briefly to take leave of my parents and returned to receive the habit on October 6.

Today, October 15, the feast of the incomparable St. Teresa, it is just over fifty-one years ago.

"Cetera desiderantur."

The last words, "Cetera desiderantur" were crossed out by the author when he took up the work in 1932.

6. Son of Saint Dominic
(1879–1888)

NOVITIATE YEAR

Taken up again on May 8, 1932, at Jerusalem, a few days before leaving for France, finding myself unoccupied.

The novitiate is a time of hidden life. And I did indeed spend this year seeking God. Why then speak of it to others? Because I am convinced that the graces I then received provided me with such light that the faith was more firmly rooted in my spirit. Certainly also because, obscure as this area is, the good will which inspired me coupled me so closely to the service of God and to his love that it was never possible for me to renounce him.

The Father Provincial, before giving me the habit, had asked me whether I wanted any particular name in religion. I suggested Joseph, from devotion to the husband of Mary, Paul in memory of my friend, Thomas because of the attachment I already had to the great teacher Thomas Aquinas and to his teaching. The last two names were already held by two religious who had recently entered the Order. So a halt was called after Joseph. All the novices received first the name of Mary, but their second name remained the only one in use, except in the case where both patrons were Mary and Joseph. That is why I have always signed myself "Marie-Joseph," happy in this double patronage, which is commemorated by the feast of the Espousals, since suppressed.

The Novice Master and the Brethren
The novice master to whose care I was entrusted was P. Albert Gebhart. His situation was unique. As his health was ex-

tremely delicate he was often dispensed from fasts, and never came to choir, even on Easter Sunday, except sometimes to Matins, which were recited in the evening, between Trinity Sunday and September 14. He never came to the public evening prayer. But he was unmistakably a man of prayer. He is the only person in the Order who shaped me to his spirit. He never suggested to anyone, I think—certainly not to me—to undertake any penitential practices other than those in the Rule or the customary ones.

He was not seen at recreation any more than in choir. He lived in a sort of atmosphere out of this world, and when I entered his cell I used to have a very real sense of entering into communication with Our Lord. Very gentle, very kindly, but letting nothing escape him, he concerned himself with the spirit, to detach it from any motive which was not supernatural, teaching above all obedience as the only sure rule, and prayer as the only active principle of sanctification. His talks to the novices, which I have never been able to analyze, were like a spreading light which bewitched us. I have never heard anything which seemed to me so persuasive by a sort of internal pressure. I have since heard it said that he used extensively P. Alvarez S.J., one of the guides of St. Teresa. He advised me to write down the thoughts that came to me, especially at the monthly and annual retreats, if only, said he somewhat cynically, to register later whether I had not been unfaithful to the grace at the beginning. As it turned out, I spent most of the year in a very happy mood, a genuine joy at being admitted to the house of the Lord, and living in his service. Everything seemed to me to be the realization of my purest dreams as a child and an adolescent. I was hardly even disappointed at finding myself amid company considerably inferior in manners and intelligence to that in which I had lived hitherto, even in the seminary. The novitiate included excellent elements, but not those of which the world is so proud, with some exceptions, such as Br. Paul Wetterlé, who afterward became so well-known for putting politics at the service of religion. But the grace which was leading me toward humility was much stronger. I liked to apply to myself the severe reprimand of M. Icard, superior of Saint-Sulpice, to those seminarians, only just clear of the mire of mortal sin, who stand so smugly in their places among the ministers of the Lord, clad in surplices for the liturgy.

If I raised my eyes to the professed novices, I saw among them some fine intellects, such as Br. Innocent Gayraud, who also later entered the French Chamber of Deputies. But I had no further thought of the studies; that could wait until the following year.

Spiritual Formation

I read spiritual authors, among others the incomparable little treatise of St. Vincent Ferrer, who lays down as the basis of apostolic work poverty, silence and the interior exercise of virtue: *paupertas, taciturnitas, interna mentis exercitatio.* St. Catherine of Siena teaches the same principles. My pious mother was not the only person to contribute to my spiritual formation. Too modest to adopt any sermonizing tone, she nevertheless wrote to me, before the autumn retreat, that ever since my childhood she had had the vision of my becoming a priest, and she counseled me to humility and obedience. This is where all the forces of grace were drawing me, seeming to come always through the hands of Mary. The novice master had the same devotion, especially to the Immaculate Conception. And it was surely through this union of our souls in the service of Mary that I truly felt myself to be his spiritual child, and that I submitted with joy to a direction which was very intensive and almost rigorous, but with the warmth of filial devotion poured into my soul by the Virgin Mary. Love also draws forcibly: *trahitur animus et amore,* said St. Augustine. I was strengthened in this resolution to do my best in the spiritual life by a tangible feeling of the presence of God in the soul, a real revelation on top of faith, which was granted me on April 6, the feast of the Annunciation (postponed that year). When I think back on everything I then lacked, I find a failure in generosity, a repugnance for the cross, and a lack of physical mortifications which amounted to a serious fault especially because of my soft and sensual nature.

Profession Retreat

When the moment came to make the retreat obligatory before the profession of simple but perpetual vows which were then the practice, I had no further thought of examining my vocation. That year an almost cloudless interior joy seemed to me a sure sign that I really was on the right path. I took as the theme of my meditations the seven words of Mary as they are commented on by St. Bernardine of Siena. The teaching of St. Catherine had taught me the immense importance of not judging others. It seemed to me that this would be very easy if I reflected that perhaps they were suffering a great deal. "Before you judge others, do you know what they are suffering?" became a brake on that tendency to condemn which we all have. Compassion is an efficacious preparation for charity.

Decrees against the Congregations

During the whole of that year I was so absorbed by the need to bring my spiritual life under control that I neither knew nor wished to know anything about what was happening outside. I noted only April 4: announcement of the decrees. That day we were wishing a happy feast to P. Vincent de Pascal, the prior of the house. He announced to us that the government had decided to dissolve religious congregations, with the possible exception of a few which would be tolerated. So in order to maintain community life it would be necessary to go into exile abroad. I left it all to God and the superiors of the Order. The prospect of suffering for Christ was sweet. I was only surprised that the public authorities, who had been utterly indifferent to my living as a student at my own good pleasure, should show themselves so determined to prevent me living a better life under monastic discipline. What was in progress was a struggle by the forces of evil against the good and against God, the great law of history which sets the two cities one against the other. This initiative on the part of evil was simply one more reason to adhere to the service of God. The whole question was one of belonging to him. The only alteration which I could see ahead at that time was the transition from a novitiate wholly devoted to the spiritual life to a novitiate in which studies took up most of the time. That was the trial, which turned out to be very hard. On leaving France I merely read in my notes: October 30, expulsion; November 1, at Lourdes; November 4, arrival at Salamanca.

The Expulsion of Religious

I would be tempted to be less reticent about that incident today. We were profoundly saddened to see France adopt an attitude toward the sons who loved her so much, but were filled with joy at being treated like the apostles spurned by the Jews. When the police, led by the sub-prefect of Brignoles, had broken down the doors and penetrated to the novitiate room where we were waiting in silence, only Br. I. Gayraud made any audible protest. Nevertheless we did not leave until the men who were so bravely putting those evil deeds into execution had put their hands on our shoulders. They certainly did it gently, not being used to hunting such game, and we in our turn showed our unwillingness politely. Carriages took us to Trets, where we took the train for Marseilles. Leaving the same evening, we stopped only at Lourdes, where we sang the Mass of All Saints in the basilica of the Immaculate Virgin. Since she had chosen the land of France to pour out her graces, we must not lose hope. We were going far away to prepare to work for the country when the time should be ripe.

THEOLOGICAL FORMATION

Salamanca

The first contact with Spain in the already cloudy days of November was not without sadness. The magnificent friary of San Esteban, long ago deserted, was hardly in a fit state to receive us. It was more than poverty; it was destitution. But there was also overflowing joy. At Salamanca we were nineteeen kilometers from Alba de Tormes, where the body of St. Teresa lay. From the very first that great saint, the *mistica doctora* of the Spaniards, opened to us her great heart which was believed to have been pierced by thorns. If the principal purpose of these lines is to express my gratitude toward those who helped me, I declare now that what little light I have had on the spiritual life came to me above all from St. Teresa of Avila. My ordination to the subdiaconate at Avila could not but increase my devotion to that noble and valiant saint. The friary itself was full of memories of her.

Below the great cloister the little window was pointed out through which P. Bañez used to hear her confession while she was in the church. To be established at Salamanca was to be plunged into the theology of the sixteenth century, for nowhere was St. Thomas Aquinas more devotedly studied—by the Carmelites no less than by the Dominicans.

Theological Studies

This was the theology which was unfolded before me, since I had been dispensed from philosophy on the grounds of the very Thomist studies at Issy with the priests of Saint-Sulpice. Already, however, my superiors, especially P. Gallais, soon to be appointed prior and regent, were directing me especially toward Holy Scripture. During the pure novitiate the taste which I had acquired for it at Issy had developed. I found it in so much light even for my personal needs, that the novice master recommended to me practically no other reading. P. Gallais, who knew a few words of Hebrew, felt some scruples at putting a Hebrew Bible into my hands, and in his own hand he copied a few verses which he gave me to study. Then he gave me permission to follow a Hebrew course at the university, together with P. Justo Cuervo. This was an encouragement, but it was not very profitable. P. Gallais also authorized me to start Syriac and Arabic on my own. Naturally the result could not have been better.

In spite of this, such studies were only sidelines. The basis of the teaching was the *Summa* of St. Thomas, studied textually, question by question, article by article. Nothing can equal in value this daily contact with the letter of the greatest of theologians. We had not only to study the article but each class had to learn it by heart, and a certain number, sixty each year if I remember rightly, were required to pass the examination. An excellent exercise. In reciting the article one was tempted to fill gaps in the memory by improvisation, and only then did one appreciate how fitting were the terms chosen by the master, how far superior to the terms one tried to substitute for them. If the text was sometimes difficult, the commentary of Cajetan in the edition of St. Pius V, easily found in Spain, took pleasure in bringing out the puzzlement of the reader, the objection of Aureolus or Scotus, to throw light, by means of a precise distinction, on the exactness of the expression. It was an admirable mental gymnastic, which made the mind supple, supple enough to rule out approximations, confused generalizations, and no erudition could replace it. If criticism is not crisp and clear, it is merely a collection of observations without any relevance. The best weapon is exact distinction, which can be learned only by logic. For me Cajetan has been the king of distinctions, and if I read him very attentively, my theological learning has not extended much beyond him, that is, beyond St. Thomas himself, studied with the help of such an intelligent interpreter.

Spiritual Trials

How was the intensity of these studies to be reconciled with care for the spiritual life nourished by prayer? This was the delicate and often painful crux of my four years as a professed novice. Does not the concentration on the intellect alone, so necessary for the acquistion of theological knowledge, tend to clog the flights of the will? In theory, the more one knows God, the more one is drawn to love him, and theology is a more perfect understanding of that economy of salvation which reveals to us the goodness of God. But the more one seeks to know God, the more one understands how inaccessible he is to our spirit, and that the best way to draw near to him is to go to him by the way of love. Is not putting all spiritual energy into intellectual research tantamount to the renunciation of union? And this is the case even without bringing into consideration a whole clutch of secondary sciences which really must be acquired, such as those of languages and history which clutter up the memory, instead of emptying it of everything apart from the remembrance of God's generosity. It is true that strict Dominican observance, as it was practiced at Saint-Maximin, gave an important place to spiritual exercises. But between the pure novitiate and the way of life of study there was a marked contrast. This was all the more so because that outpouring of tangible graces, that joy, that intoxication with the things of God had to be limited in time. Powerlessness in prayer, a painful dryness, the feeling of being a stranger in the house of God, of having vowed uselessly the pur-

suit of an impossible ideal—these are some of the causes of bitterness and discouragement that the novice is tempted to
attribute to his preoccupation with studies. During these trials,
which can be compared to a real agony, and which are certainly
much more torturing than illnesses and many extremely sharp
physical pains, God supported me, as I now understand. On the
morning of September 28, 1882 I went to pray briefly in the oratory of the novitiate and understood, with surprise, what I had
so often read in St. Paul, that Jesus Christ is truly living in us,
that grace is his grace, given to us by him and in him, as the supreme gift. It seemed as though I had never heard anything like
this before, but I knew that it was true. I was amazed at all the
applications of this fundamental principle which occurred to me:
"If Jesus Christ is present in souls, he is doing all the good there."
The novice master, to whom I communicated my discovery, approved and sent me back to St. Paul and St. John, and among
modern writers to P. de Condren. It is, in fact, the spirituality of
Cardinal Berulle, but founded on St. Paul. I lived for several
days in this light: "Jesus Christ in prayer, Jesus Christ in my
brethren, Jesus Christ everywhere" (Saturday, October 30).
Then I fell back again into the night: "God alone! O painful
death" (December 20). *Adhaesit pavimento anima mea* (January 25,
1883). Not long after this desperate collapse (February 10), the
prior, P. Gallais, told me to prepare myself for the priesthood at
the end of that year, 1883.

The Death of My Father

Before then I was to undergo another painful trial. During
the summer it became clear that my father's health was rapidly
declining. I was sent to see him in Bourg, and my presence
seemed to rally his strength. He immediately made plans to return with me to Le Prat, his birthplace. But this was only an ill-
fated hint of his fast-approaching death. The thought that he
would not be able to be present at my Mass hurt me considerably, since he longed for it so ardently! After a few days, since his
death did not yet seem imminent, I was recalled for the community retreat. I saw him for the last time on the morning of August
8, when I went to his bedside to say goodbye and ask his blessing.

I loved him so much, with a deep respect which did not exclude tenderness. He was never very communicative, but we could feel that he was so devoted, so absorbed in affection for his family. And I knew that I had a special place in his heart, that he had counted on me to sustain my mother and sisters, and that I had disappointed this hope, but nevertheless he had withdrawn not an iota of his affection. Although I was not told the whole truth lest the sacrifice become too hard, I understood that the doctor, who had come from Lyons on some pretext or other, had little hope. When I got back to Salamanca my anxiety took the form of fervent prayer at the feet of Mary. To an extraordinary degree I joined myself to the interior dispositions of this great Christian. From what my youngest sister wrote to me in a letter bedewed with tears, the last twenty-four hours formed one continuous prayer. He lovingly kissed the crucifix, and when it was taken from his hands he remained restless until it was given back. He made the sign of the cross continually, and when he had no more strength, he marked it on his chest and asked for help by signs. At one moment he seemed to be a prey to terror, but when the priest came his calm returned and remained until the end. At the moment of death his face seemed transformed by a ray of happiness, and his features remained simple and firm. It was two hours after noon on September 21, 1883.

Ordination

The same evening, at meditation, I had a sure presentiment of this blessed death, and, after so many anxious hours, consolation, a hope assured, was the feeling which dominated. The next day, I was ordained a deacon at Salamanca, and on October 6 I made my solemn profession. In normal circumstances the prior would not have put me forward for the priesthood so soon after the diaconate, and the bishop of Salamanca did not want to perform two consecutive ordinations. But my mother, in her grief and with an overwhelming sense of emptiness, had resolved to come to her Dominican son at Salamanca, and it seemed hard to refuse her the consolation of my priesthood. So I was ordained a priest at Zamora on December 22 and said my first Mass on Sunday, December 23, at the altar of the Holy Rosary, with the un-

speakable joy of giving Communion to my mother and my sister
Thérèse. There ensued a great calm, a great silence, and my
notebook remained closed until the following September.

The Lectorate in Theology

I have not mentioned my examination for the lectorate,
which I took on July 14. So I had completed my studies of Scholastic theology. Without any scruple but with a firm conviction I
swore the oath not to diverge from *solida S. Thomae doctrina*, by
which I understood a doctrine which was incontrovertibly part of
the theological edifice of the holy Doctor. I never had any taste
for the discussions between modern theologians. As early as my
first year of theology (June 11, 1881) I wrote: "In a word, consider St. Thomas as the harmonious conclusion of all Catholic
doctrine, not the starting point of every kind of quibble. O my
most pure Soverign, grant me in the search for truth a serene
calm, a profound peace. O most pure Mary, be my teacher of
theology: teach me dogma; teach me to combat heresies, not
Catholics. Receive my spirit no less than my heart; all is yours;
deign to treat it always as you wish." I must admit that I was
afraid of a sectarian edge consisting in an excessive attachment to
a particular teaching which could then become imperceptibly a
motive of self-glorification. If this conviction was borne in upon
me as the result of a personal incident, it was no less deep-rooted
as a rule of life. All around me I heard that Thomism agrees better with probabliorism or at least with equiprobabilism. I admit
here that equiprobabilism seemed to me a chimera, and I held to
solid probability as a rule of action. The haphazard quotations of
St. Alphonsus de Liguori are infuriating and I liked to find
cleaner and more critical solutions in P. Ballerini, S.J. This was
the frame of mind in which I took my examination for confession.
As there was no alternative to applying probabilism in the confes-
sional, why not adopt it as a principle? This does not amount to
siding with concupiscence against grace, since it is perfectly simple to rely on a probable opinion which is favorable to piety and
charity. It involves laying down a juridical principle which is perfectly reconcilable with seriously striving for perfection. And
this principle of moral theology cannot be held responsible for
my too frequent failures.

First Teaching Assignment

My superior had always expressed the intention of consecrating me to the teaching of Holy Scripture. But I was not ready. To tell the truth, I did not know the history of the Church, which I was given to teach, any better. But the responsibility was less heavy. So for two years I lectured in Church history, with five classes a week. Events had less importance for us than ideas; it was primarily a study of controversies from the first century till the present, with emphasis on the teaching of the earliest Fathers. Now was the time when I concentrated on Syriac and Arabic. It was two years of very hard work which above all put me in contact with Origen and St. Augustine.

In August 1886 we returned to France. The school of theology was established at Toulouse. Three weekly lectures on Holy Scripture and four on philosophy were my portion. My taste for the Bible was fostered, or rather I was initiated into critical questions by Abbé J. Thomas, professor at the Institut Catholique, whom the relentless progress of tuberculosis prevented from lecturing. He received me at his home with the liveliest friendship. We made plans. I felt the gaps in my knowledge most painfully. I was getting older, and I no longer saw any possibility of starting all over again studies that had been badly begun. My poor notebook is heavy with this dominant preoccupation with philology and criticism, recalling memories of the novitiate and enlivening them with appeals to St. Teresa. I began to preach. In the end I felt pulled in so many different directions that I felt that I should explain my difficulty in a very filial way to P. Colchen, our holy provincial.

TOWARD THE DEFINITIVE ROAD

I truly put myself in his hands for him to do with me as he wished. Let me be used to respond to any need that occurred, as I had been at Toulouse for two years, if he wished. Master of lay brothers, confessor of nuns, occasional sermons during Lent, talks to a Catholic club, classes in philosophy and Holy Scripture—I had refused nothing. But it was my duty in conscience to inform the provincial that with this program I could make no serious progress in that vast ocean which is the study of the Bible. If he abandoned putting before me this path which had always been intended, I would renounce it too. This would be better than the pursuit of a chimera. His answer was that he was so far from renouncing it that the moment had at last come when he could devote me solely to this task, starting by putting me back on the schoolroom bench.

Vienna and Philology

A few days later I left for Paris where I received a very fraternal welcome at the friary of Saint-Jacques, then located in the Rue du Bac. There I met P. Scheil who for a year had been following a course of Egyptian and Assyrian, that is, studing hieroglyphic and cuneiform, not yet having opted, as he was soon to do, for the Mesopotamian branch of study. His example and his friendly encouragement opened to me new horizons by strengthening me in the enterprise already begun. Nevertheless various circumstances prevented me settling in Paris. P. Colchen, whom I went to see at Prouille, was not deflected from his project, and sent me off to Vienna, where I arrived on Saturday, October 27, 1888.

It seemed to me that I would gain little from following courses on Holy Scripture. What I most lacked was a philological basis. I knew enough German to follow courses in that language, and it was an excellent opportunity to initiate myself into the German methods which held sway in Vienna. So I enrolled at the university for the course in ancient Egyptian of M. Reinisch and the courses in Arabic and Assyrian of M. D.-H. Müller, who was never a well-known Assyriologist, but who was an excellent Semitic scholar, and who was kind enough to initiate me particularly by several tutorials in the rabbinic writings. I had thrown myself fervently into these purely technical studies with all the more concentration because it was too late, when I learned of the proposal for a biblical foundation in Jerusalem.

Here begins the story of that School, which I have already told.[1]

Liberty in the Faith

From the old man immersing himself in old memories. At the age of seventeen, under the influence of my parents and of the minor seminary, my intellectual temperament was already shaped, and I had a clear idea of how to view life.

The modern masters were Lacordaire, Montalembert, Ozanam: struggles for Christ and for the Church. I loved liberty, not as an achievement of the revolution, but, following Montalembert, as a last glimmer of Christian institutions. And the struggle I envisaged was, following Ozanam, by the weapons of the spirit, through historical work, prepared by linguistic study. Though I was no genius at study I had a genuine passion for Greek literature, especially Plato and Euripides. My mother had noticed my fascination for history. I had no imaginative originality. If I brought together a group of friends, it was not to swap poems but to read authors who were a little out of the ordinary, like Shakespeare, whose bizarre name amazed the nurse. For it was not unkown for me to imagine I was ill in order to gain more freedom to read my favorite authors. Attachment to pure Christian truth seemed to me compatible with a certain tolerance; even freedom in the defense of the faith seemed to me an essential condition, for had not Montalembert adopted the slogan of St. Columban in something like these words: *Si tollis pugnam, tollis et coronam; si tollis libertatem, tollis dignitatem?*[2]

Liberty, Property of the Christian

This liberty is not merely a property of human nature, but above all a property of the Christian. My antipathies also date from this time. I could not bear Louis Veuillot, whose poetry my history teacher praised so much to me; I have half-remembered only one line: *Il faut'être un Havet pour estimer Renan.* ("Only a Havet can assess Renan.") Later I came to understand the purity of his language better. But if in the *Odeurs de Paris* his polemic is to be found in the satirical tone, in his letters his flirting with ladies of quality has always seemed to me most exaggerated beside that of Musset, who alone has retained even in our democracy the atmosphere of the old days. As an old liberal I find myself quite at sea in a world which veers between a dictatorship of the right and one of the left, which are basically the same, both being restrictions by a socialist state on liberty of the individual. And I add, sadly, that certain tirades against liberalism make me fear a dangerous hankering after militarism among us.

The masters at the minor seminary of Autun, without making a fuss about it, brought us up by a traditon of simplicity and straightforwardness, and, by avoiding too strict a surveillance, in an atmosphere of honor and honesty. Their piety was sincere, and they promulgated it gently. It gave a depth to their love of literature. May they be held in blessed memory!

(September 17, 1936)

I am glad to bear witness to my gratitude to them by dedicating to them my *Critique textuelle du Nouveau Testament*.

Notes

FOREWORD

1. Cf. *L'Oeuvre exégétique et historique du R.P. Lagrange* (*"Cahiers de la Nouvelle Journée"*, 28), Bloud et Gay, Paris, 1935; L-H. Vincent, O.P., *Le Père Lagrange*, in *Revue Biblique*, XLVII, 1938, pp. 321–354; F.-M. Braun, O.P., *L'Oeuvre du Père Lagrange, Etude et Bibliographie*, Editions Saint-Paul, Fribourg, Switzerland, 1943; P. Benoit, O.P., *"L'Exégèse et l'Ecole biblique de Jérusalem,"* in *Ecclesia, Lectures chrétiennes*, April 1965, pp. 129–136; R. De Vaux, O.P., Introduction to the re-edition of *La Méthode historique*, Edition du Cerf, Paris, 1966, pp. 4–22.

1. FOUNDATION AND DEVELOPMENT OF THE BIBLICAL SCHOOL

1. Letters were received from Fathers Nespoulous, Chocarne and Ruby in 1889 and 1890. See copies in the French edition, pp. 295–298.

2. This was in a letter of February 2, 1889 (French edition, 299–300).

3. I described the journey in *La Science catholique*, the only magazine available to me at the time.

4. This appeared in the *Zeitschrift für Assyriologie*, whose pages were made available to me by P. Scheil.

5. He sent a second letter on September 16, 1890 (French edition, pp. 300–302).

6. At least this was P. Luc Marquet's impression.

7. They since have been (in 1936).

8. Paris, Bureaux de la Revue, 44, Rue d'Assas, 1892, Published fortnightly.

9. As a footnote: "The first number of *Revue Biblique* has just been published by Lethielleux."

10. *La Biblia y la Ciencia*, Madrid, 1891.

11. *R.B.*, 1892, pp. 13–14.

12. Letter from a prelate of our Order, October 11, 1891: "Il vostro articolo, sebbene gia stampato, non ebbe l'approvazione del P. Maestro del S. Palazzo, che non vuole in nessun modo la responsabilità delle idee del Card. Gonzalez." Translation of the above text: "Your article, although already printed, has not obtained the approval of the Master of the Sacred Palace, who wishes to take no responsibility whatever for the ideas of Cardinal Gonzalez." [They might have remembered the occasion in Rome when Leo XIII gave his own direct authorization for the publication of M. Hyvernat's book, *Actes des Martyrs coptes*—"Actes" which were manifestly monophysite—and appointed as archbishop of Florence the then Master of the Sacred Palace, who had been opposed to its publication.]

13. In a letter of April 13, 1893.

14. I cannot think now why I attached so much importance to P. Delattre's collaboration. The fact is that I made a fresh attempt, and asked Fr. Van den Gheyn, S.J. to help. He wrote to me on July 14, 1899: "I have passed your letter on to P. Delattre and he has returned it to me without saying what he proposed to do. . . . I like to think that your kind invitation pleased him and that he will send you some worthy contribution."

15. This broadmindedness was misinterpreted by one Catholic journalist who was guilty of a mistranslation into French—in order to safeguard the orthodoxy of the Pope—making him say: "only for Catholics."

16. That report, very brief, contains, I believe, the first proposal to devote the best minds within the Order to special studies: "Special studies need what we would call today colleges of further education. They could cover, for example, the relationship between theology, philosophy and science, Christian apologetics, the history of social sciences, and biblical studies." See the French edition, pp. 302–306.

17. Acta Capituli Generalis . . . celebrati a die XIX ad diem XXVII sept. A. D. MDCCCXCI . . . (p. 43). ["This project will be greatly served by the priory which has recently been founded in Jerusalem under the title of Saint-Étienne, and which we commend especially to the paternal care of the Master of the Order."]

18. On the intervention of Mgr. d'Hulst in favor of the "liberal school" for which he took no responsibility, see *Vie de Mgr. d'Hulst* by

Mgr. Baudrillart Vol. II, pp. 129ff—in particular the following letter (p. 172) from Mgr. d'Hulst, December 7, 1893: "I learn that Cardinal Mazzella has been making great scenes in front of the Pope to have my name put on the Index, and that the Holy Father has strenuously refused so to do, for which I bear him affectionate and filial gratitude." [On the intervention of Mgr. d'Hulst and its consequences, cf. M.-J. Lagrange *M. Loisy et le Modernisme*, pp. 50–61.]

19. *R.B.*, 1874, pp. 387 and 605.

20. *R.B.* 1893, p. 634.

21. In any case it was only the first exploration; cf. *R.B.* 1896, p. 618; 1897, pp. 107 and 605; 1899, p. 369.

22. In a letter of July 22, 1894 (see the French edition, p. 307).

23. It can be found as an appendix in the French edition, pp. 307–316.

24. Letter dated November 10, 1894.

25. Pp. 536ff.

26. *L'Enseignement Biblique*, 1893, No. 8. In an article entitled "La Question biblique et l'inspiration des Ecritures" M. Loisy wrote (p. 14): "But it can be stated, without fear of error, that this special assistance so guided and enveloped the entire activity of the sacred writers that it is impossible to distinguish in their works that which comes solely from God and that which comes solely from man. Everything comes from both at once." Then he added: "This (divine) influence even extends in a certain way to those imperfections which we call errors, but which the sacred writers and those who first read their works definitely did not judge to be so."

27. *Revue Thomiste*, March 1895.

28. *R.B.*, July 1895. [Eugène Lévesque (1855–1944), student of Saint-Sulpice, taught Holy Scripture, first in the seminary of Orléans, then from 1893 at the seminary of Saint-Sulpice in Paris. His exegetical works deal above all with the Gospels. Part of his work was also dedicated to publishing some of Bossuet's writings.]

29. *R.B.*, October 1895, but the first indication appeared in *R.B.*, 1893, p. 639: "Here again, I should like to insist upon a total inspiration, embracing the whole book, even the words, without involving divine responsibility more than necessary. . . ."

30. P. Jacomé, P. Vosté, etc.

31. "L'inspiration et les exigences de la critique," *R.B.*, 1896, pp. 485–518.

32. Tome 1, pp. 474ff.

33. Abbé Loisy has often been reproached for his lack of theolog-

ical knowledge. His adversaries made the fairly naive assumption that one could not know theology without accepting fully all its conclusions; this is not always so.

34. *Op. cit.*, p. 482.

35. *Op. cit.*, p. 491.

36. M. Batiffol, letter of November 23, 1893: "I have just been to the funeral of M. Icard. . . . Leaving the church I went to visit poor Loisy and express my sympathy. . . . As for collaborating with the *Revue Biblique*, he seems little inclined. "I would only compromise you, that's all," he told me gloomily, He is right. His own *Enseignement Biblique* will carry on in 1894." In fact the *Enseignement Biblique* appeared no more. A new approach from me made Loisy's mind up. I cannot find the letter in which Mgr. Batiffol spoke to me about it in terms more than skeptical about the end result. What I am saying here is a reply to those who reproached him for having launched me into "*loisysme*"; nothing is more contrary to the facts.

37. M. Batiffol, February 5, 1895: "As proof of our sympathy I sent him a book, the Hebrew Bible of Haupt, for him to review. He sent back a short and inoffensive assessment."— Letter from M. Loisy, December 9, 1894: "I have been meaning for a long time to tell you how grateful I am to you for sending me your *Revue Biblique* all this year after the closing of the *Enseignement Biblique*. I was very touched also by the gesture of sympathy which M. Batiffol came to make me on your behalf in November 1893. On that occasion M. Batiffol had suggested a collaboration with your *Revue*. I think it advisable not to publish anything for the time being."

38. *R.B.*, 1896, p. 341. Letter from M. Battifol, January 20, 1896: "I received this morning word from Loisy in reply to the letter you sent him. Instead of writing an answer, I am going to see him this afternoon, and have a gentle chat with him about possible modifications. . . . Whatever happens, I shall do everything I can to ensure that you have the corrected proofs in Suez; we shall send them registered to the Poste Restante in Suez."—Since the article was not written by one of the fathers in our Order, the General's Curia was not then in the habit of taking responsibility for it. A further letter, undated: "The end of the Loisy piece has been set up in print with the N.D.L.R. which you yourself edited.—I am handing the fellow over to you and no longer wish to have him hitched to my carriage." Our initial plan had been that the first article should appear in January, the second in April; hence our concern in Suez on February 13.

39. Letter from M. Loisy, dated April 16, 1896, complaining that M. Batiffol had modified his article without consulting him, although it

was merely suggestion, since the proof was submitted to him. "This incident really did distress me, even more since I sincerely intended to collaborate with the *Revue Biblique*. My participation in the *Revue d'histoire et de littérature religieuses*, which has just been founded, was not an obstacle, for the space reserved for biblical questions in this review will of necessity be limited. But my collaboration must not be a source of anxiety and trouble for you, nor must it expose me personally to vexatious proceedings, not to mention anything else."— It can be seen that by inviting M. Loisy, I was not becoming a *loisyste*, but it was pure fantasy to hope that he would cease to be so.

40. I saw him only one other time in Paris.

41. 1912, p. 478.

42. The widespread and persistent nature of this rumor would suggest a combined effort in this direction. From Mgr. Batiffol on September 25, 1894, writing about the Catholic Congress in Brussels, we have: "The 'loisytes' were numerous there, and these unfortunates were convinced that Loisy owed his downfall to the Dominicans."

43. By hand from P. Beaudouin (see French edition, p. 317).

2. FROM LEO XIII TO PIUS X

1. *R.B.*, 1897, pp. 165ff.

2. See *Dictionnaire de Théologie catholique*, Part LX–LXI, p. 588.

3. It was certain that nobody had us in mind as the target, for the question had not been raised in the *Revue Biblique*. However, Mgr. Granello, who represented the Holy Office, mixed admonition with encouragement when he acquainted me with the decree: "Siffatta riposta recherà conforto a quanti deplorano le intemperanze di una certa scuola critica, che qualche volta pare di soverchio carezzata da alcuni scrittori della R.B. Nel resto Ella non è affatto in colpa, né io intendo di muovere rimprovero. Continui, mio caro p. Maestro, a honorare coi suoi lavori e colle quotidiane fatiche il convento di Gerusalemme dove conviene stabilire una tradizione di forte e perseveranti studi biblici a difesa della Verità. La Provvidenza ha preparato la P.V. a questo scopo, etc."—An undated letter, but evidently later than the decree. Translation of the above text: "Such a reply will bring comfort to all who disapprove of the intemperances of a certain critical school which sometimes appears to be cherished to an excessive degree by a few writers of the *R.B.* Besides, you are in no way at fault, nor do I intend to rebuke you. Continue, my dear Maestro, to honor with your works and daily effort the priory at Jerusalem, where a strong tradition of perseverance in biblical studies

must be established in defense of the truth. Providence has made you, Father, worthy to carry out this work, etc."

4. Appeared in an anonymous report in the *R.B.*, 1897, pp. 634ff. I cannot remember who the author was—perhaps P. Rose.

5. My report in *R.B.*, p. 638.

6. *R.B.*, 1897, pp. 643ff.

7. Lagrange, "Phounou," *R.B.*, 1898, pp. 112ff; "Recherches épigraphiques à Petra," pp. 165ff; Vincent, "Notes de voyage," pp. 424ff.

8. M. Musil came here after us, even though he has suggested that he had seen the site before from a distance.

9. *Loc. cit.*, p. 167.

10. The *Corpus* of Semitic inscriptions has not accepted my interpretation of "Alimithras" (p. 177), giving as their reason the fact that Mithras was unknown in Semitic lands. But cf. Wellhausen, *Heidentum*, p. 50, and other observations.

11. Letter of March 20, 1898.

12. The copy of the Italian text is included as an appendix in the French edition (pp. 318–320).

13. Supplied by Canon J.M., a subscriber to the *Revue Biblique*. It was the *Revue* in the end which footed the bill, for P. Lagrange made haste to replace the number in response to the request of the good canon who had "mislaid" it and did not want to spoil his collection.

14. *Echos d'Orient*, Year 1, pp. 130ff, "*Edomites et Nabatéens*." The author, P. Simeon Vailhé, of the Augustinians of the Assumption, made no reference to *Revue Biblique*. An editor's note (p. 130) said: "This historical study is a continuation of '*Voyage à Pétra*' which we have just published, and are happy to complete." It was thus clear that the Assumptionists and not the Biblical School were responsible. Fr Vailhé was in Constantinople at the time and does not seem to have gone out of his way to claim the title of pupil of the Biblical School.

15. See his letter of August 2, 1898 in the French edition, p. 320.

16. I.e., to Father Esser (French edition, pp. 321–22).

17. *R.B.*, 1898, p. 13.

18. "La thèse de l'origine mosaique du Pentatenque," pp. 220ff.

19. *Revue du Clergé français*, February 15, 1899, under the pseudonym of Isidore Desprès, p. 534.

20. Ed. de la Bonne Presse, *Lettres apostoliques de Léon XIII*, Tome V, p. 287.

21. Encyclical letter *Spiritus Paraclitus*.

22. Before I even knew what was in the encyclical of Benedict XV, I had practically renounced this interpretation, which was also

that of Cardinal Satolli; cf. *R.B.*, 1919, p. 598. [On the position of P. Lagrange vis-à-vis the theory of historical appearances, see the restatement of the question by P. de Vaux in his preface to *La Méthode Historique* (collection *Foi Vivante*, No. 31), Paris 1966, pp. 19–20.]

23. *Le Péril Religieux*, translated from the German by Abbé Louis Collin, Paris, Lethielleux, 1906.

24. *Etudes*, pp. 655–674.

25. He used to write to me in German, French, Latin or Italian.

26. See the French edition, pp. 322–328.

27. This letter was perhaps an account of which I have found the rough draft; it is unaddressed and undated, but does in fact relate to 1899. See the French edition, pp. 328–334.

28. Letter dated February 16.

29. *Op. cit.*, Tome VI, p. 101.

30. *R.B.*, 1898, p. 13.

31. A. Firmin and Is. Desprès wrote for the *Revue du Clergé français*. M. Loisy himself acknowledged his identity with Jacques Simon, Jean Lataix, Francois Jacobé and Jean Delarochelle in the *Revue d'Histoire et de Littérature religieuses*, 1901, p. 278, note.

32. *R.B.*, 1899, pp. 50ff.

33. *R.B.*, 1899, pp. 493–509; 1900, pp 30–44, 354–377. (Albert Condamin [1862–1940], Jesuit, exegete, specialist in the Old Testament, was professor at the Institut Catholique de Toulouse from 1899 to 1901, afterward at the theological college in Canterbury from 1901 to 1918, and then at Fourvières. To him we owe numerous articles and several books, among which is a commentary on Isaiah [1905].)

34. *R.B.*, 1899, pp. 369ff, 532ff.

35. *R.B.*, 1899, Pl. III.

36. See above, note 18.

37. P. Esser who, having become the Secretary of the Index, had ceased to be examiner of what I wrote. That painful responsibility had been imposed upon P. Kaiser, a man of admirable devotion and self-sacrifice.

38. *Itinéraire des Israélites du pays de Gessen aux bords du Jourdain* (*R.B.*, 1900, pp. 63ff); *Débora*, *ibid.*, pp. 200ff, etc.

39. *R.B.*, 1901, p. 609.

40. *R.B.*, 1901, pp. 110–123.

41. February 16, 1901, p. 471. Without mentioning the step-by-step refutation of Harnack's theories, the author, after a few lines on Harnack and his party, added: "E nondimeno vi sono dei cattolici che trovano nell' *Essenza del Cristianesimo* del Harnack 'l'accento sincero di un' anima profondamente religiosa' " (*R.B.*, 1901, p 110). ("And none-

theless there are some Catholics who find in Harnack's *Das Wesen des Christenthums* 'the true stamp of a deeply religious soul.' ") This line, skillfully extracted, was, I admit, sufficient to make me an accomplice. But was it not necessary to indicate that the book's attraction lay, in short, in that undeniable stamp of religion, while at the same time rejecting the doctrine it contained? Harnack faced up to the denials of the radicals as Rousseau did to the authors of the *Encyclopédie*. Thus I said: "For us Catholics, this book is merely a device for the almost total destruction of radicalism, but the intention of the author is certainly to edify."

42. A card from P. Angelo de Santi, on behalf of the management of *Civiltà cattolica:* "Abbiamo ricevuto, etc. (We have received the letter from Your Reverence of the 2nd inst., and are sending it on to P. Léopold Fonck, who since January 1, 1901 has had charge of the biblical reports for our periodical. He will most certainly take note of it, since we all have but one single desire: the defense and total triumph of Catholic doctrine.") This was most often their way. Very kind words in private, but attacks in public.

43. Pp. 450–463. This article was perhaps not from the pen of P. Fonck. M. Minocchi believed there was evidence that Cardinal Parocchi was behind it.

44. *Revue d'Histoire et de Littérature religieuses*, 1901, p. 278.

45. *R.B.*, 1901, p. 631.

46. Found in the appendix to the French edition, pp. 334–335.

47. Ed. de la Bonne Presse, *Lettres Apostoliques de Léon XIII*, Tome VII, pp. 132ff.

48. *Ami du clergé français*, October 15, 1900.

49. *Les Mythes babyloniens*, Preface, p. v.

50. *La Question biblique au XXᵉ siecle*, p. 72.

51. *R.B.*, 1903, pp. 292–313.

52. By kindness of P. Boggiani, cousin of the cardinal of the same name.

53. See the letter and French translation in the French edition, pp. 335–338.

54. The original document is found in the Appendix to the French edition, pp. 338–342.

55. Not without twisting it a little way from the original sense.

56. Undated manuscript note of P. Lagrange: Fr. Fleming, consultor to the Holy Office; P. Gismondi, consultor to the Index. Cf. *R.B.*, 1933, p. 160.

57. *R.B.*, 1904, p. 454.

58. *R.B.*, 1903, pp. 632ff; cf. 1904, p. 155.

59. In the French edition, pp. 342–343.

60. So favorably received by the Canon Maisonneuve that it had surely to be with the agreement of the archbishop. (*R.B.*, 1903, pp. 134ff).

61. Houtin, *La question biblique au XXᵉ siècle*, Paris, 1906, pp. 120f.

62. Houtin, *op. cit.*, pp. 60f.

63. Houtin, *op. cit.*, pp. 159–167.

64. Cardinal Rampolla, president of the Commission.

65. The only change was the division of the bulletin by subjects.

66. It did come on March 2, 1904. See the French edition, pp. 343–346.

67. Letter from Fr. Fleming, secretary to the Commission, dated August 31, 1904.

68. *R.B.*, 1906, p. 149.

69. The excellent P. Lepidi once asked me: "What does *Toledoth* mean exactly?" "It is a thing," I answered. But before I had finished he replied "And what do you mean by 'thing'?"

70. The preface to the second edition of *Etudes sur les religious sémitiques* is dated May 24, 1904.

71. A letter from Mgr. Bressan informed P. Cormier that his Holiness would read the little work willingly, *col vivo desiderio*, etc. ("with the fervent desire . . . that from his reading of it he should be convinced, not only of the good intentions of the author, but also of his fitness to be a spirited apologist, as he is also a very good religious"), dated February 11, 1905 (French edition, pp. 346–347).

72. I was informed of this decision in a letter dated November 17.

73. He is named in 1905, p. 620, quite coincidentally, although he saw this as an attack.

74. *Divinitas*, etc., Turin, 1905, pp. 58f.

75. P. 162: *an haec*, etc. Cf. p. 175, note, where *Revue biblique* has *patrocinium*, etc. (Translation: "has assumed patronage and as it were the government of the disciples of the broad school.") Brief mention of P. Schiffini's pamphlet in *Revue biblique*, 1906, p. 322.

76. *Loc. cit.*, p. 94. Review in *R.B.*, 1906, pp. 148ff.

77. Reviewed in *R.B.*, 1904, pp. 612ff.

78. Pp. 242ff.

79. Pp. 390ff.

80. Pp. 266ff.

81. P. 448.

82. See the French edition, pp. 347–348.

83. Letter dated May 9.

84. One member of the Commission wrote: "During the session

which followed your departure, P. Delattre arrived loaded down with books to prove that he was right in what he had said against you. As it was made clear to him that the Commission did not have to attend to private quarrels, he returned to his charge at the next meeting, but, being nonplussed once more, did not come back again." See the letter of Fr. Fleming, March 17, 1905 (French edition, pp. 348–350).

85. Extract from *Revue apologetique*, July–August 1908.

86. Perfectly sound information on the prohibition I had received of publishing my pamphlet. But what could one say about this suggestion of a private understanding between Minocchi and me!

87. The brief allusion of October 1905, p. 620, appeared intolerable to P. Delattre. He wrote in *La Lumière:* "The *Revue Biblique*, when *L'Eclaircissement* was already circulating in the shadows. . . ." Really! Check the dates!

88. Pp. 323ff.

89. In *La Quinzaine*, April 1905.

90. Cf. *R.B.*, 1905, p. 652.

91. I give my personal impression. Others have thought he was basically very hostile toward us: nothing has proved that to me. P. Esser accused him of duplicity.

3. THE UNREST OF THE MODERNIST CRISIS

1. Letter from P. Cormier, July 22, 1906: "How sad but significant it is to see twenty students from our seminaries leave as one man rather than make the profession of faith required by their archbishop."

2. *R.B.*, 1906, p. 196, letter of January 11, 1906.

3. *R.B.*, 1906, p. 193.

4. *R.B.*, 1906, pp. 533ff.

5. Dated September 28, 1906.

6. Therefore Pius X was apprehensive for us rather than strictly dissatisfied with us.

7. Letter of September 24, 1908.

8. I was able to base myself on Fr. Kennedy's written statement of opinion: *"Post immensum, etc.* Once the course of studies has been completed, all students should have one more year during which the student follows a course of study appropriate to himself in the judgment of the rector and moderators, with the previous permission of the provincial."

9. In which I could appeal to the Louvain Schema No. 34: "To the deeper and more profound study of the Bible should be directed

those fathers who have already completed the course of theology wholly and creditably, or indeed if possible have already received the title of lector." But far from having in view only our own biblical and Oriental specialty, we proposed to set up elsewhere other similar institutes of higher education. And it is precisely this that the ratio of Rome indicates—an entirely new point! No. 35: "Studies preparatory to the teaching office comprise four branches: philosophy, with mathematics and natural science, the study of the sacred books with Oriental languages, patristic theology with history, canon law with legal and social sciences." No. 36: "No lector may undertake the teaching office unless he has completed those complementary studies for at least two years."

10. Without insisting upon the abolition of the distinction between formal and material students of St. Thomas, I did press that the immense benefit of studying the text of the *Summa Theologica* should be extended as widely as possible. "Those who are not taught St. Thomas do not even attempt to use the *Summa* for preaching. They will not open it and will not understand it, and thus will be deprived of a treasure incomparable and unique, not only for the great professorships but also for retreats and missions. It is an extremely serious matter to deprive a Dominican of this nourishment for his intellectual and spiritual life, for no one gives the taste for things divine as much as does St. Thomas. The only reason for the existence of this material is that the presence of less intelligent students makes the class overweight and prevents the lecturer from discussing difficult questions. The lecturer must tackle such questions unhesitatingly. . . . But ten, twenty or thirty hours thus lost (by weaker students) per term or per year will be amply compensated by the important benefit of studying St. Thomas."

11. Letter of Cardinal Rampolla of January 10, 1906 on receipt of the proofs. P. Lagrange here quotes in Italian the second paragraph of the letter. The translation runs: "As for your letters of August 21 and October 13, having spoken to one of my colleagues on the Biblical Commission, I see no reason to depart from the normal practice of leaving to the Order of which you are a member the responsibility for the writings of its subjects. Furthermore, the impression I have of your very sincere piety and excellent religious spirit leads me to believe that you will accept with a holy resignation all arrangements which your superiors will make on the subject of your publications and of the *Revue Biblique*." See French edition, pp. 350–351.

12. On February 9, 1907, he wrote to me exactly what he had written to the Master General: "I have had occasion to read P. Lagrange's commentary on Genesis. I am sorry that the commentary must remain in manuscript form. P. Lagrange's explanation is faultless and in

my opinion its definitive publication would bring great honor to the Order and to the School at Jerusalem, etc." He means, of course, Genesis 1–6:4. (Undated manuscript addition by P. Lagrange: I think it was at this moment that I suggested to P. Cormier the transformation of the *Revue biblique* into a *Revue Orientale* I would have abandoned all work on the Bible.)

13. At that time I wrote to the Holy Father a letter the rough copy of which I find among my papers: "Jerusalem, June 9, 1907. Most Holy Father, prostrate at the feet of Your Holiness, I have just accepted with the most filial obedience the decision which Your Holiness has caused to be communicated to me by the mediation of the Most Reverend Master General of our Order, forbidding me to have printed in any way at all a commentary on Genesis. But it is not sufficient to obey the orders of Your Holiness. I am determined to consider even your wishes as orders. If, therefore, Your Holiness would prefer me to abandon biblical studies, I unhesitatingly and instantly renounce them; I am not one of those who submit . . . and then continue. I only beg Your Holiness to deign to believe in the good intentions which have hitherto inspired me. The steps which your Holiness has taken in my regard make me fear that I have been in error, and it would now be impossible for me to write the least line in the knowledge of disobeying Your Holiness. I have the honor to be, etc." (Undated manuscript addition of P. Lagrange: Letter of P. Cormier, in his own handwriting, February 25, 1907: "The Procurator General, having had an audience before his departure for America, has given your letter to the Holy Father, and I expect that you will receive a paternal response, capable of consoling you and giving you a lead." Such presumably was the impression of P. Desqueyrous.)

14. (P. Lagrange adds, August 14, 1934, without quoting any precise document, the following note:) After the decision of the Biblical Commission on Isaiah, P. Condamin hoped (October 2, 1908): "My work, I think, will finally be allowed—without too much delay—in this restrained form." The arguments were put forward merely as more likely. He continued to hope . . . he was kept waiting . . . he finally gave way . . . to death.

15. A sample: In a letter to the Master General one censor admitted that P. Lagrange has no wish to join the camp of the independent critics. He adds: "But does he consider this a gracious concession or a strict duty? It would be well for him to make a categorical statement on the matter." So it is not enough to do one's duty; one must say that one is doing it. This censor could conceive learning and progress only as weapons to defend stock positions. Pius X had opened out a wider ter-

ritory than this in his letter to Mgr. Le Camus—a sad letter for those of us who held our ground!

16. *R.B.*, 1907, pp. 543ff. (Addition of October 13, 1934): On the encyclical *Pascendi* a letter of P. Cormier, on November 11, 1907, alludes to a declaration of acceptance, "which perhaps would be a mistake." Probably none was made.

17. See p. 352 of the French edition.

18. French edition, pp. 352–354.

19. Letter of July 15, 1907 from P. Leónce de Grandmaison.

20. Incidentally I have no idea where it found this statement of M. Minocchi. Even after his suspension from the sacraments on January 24 he spoke with much greater restraint in a letter and in an interview (*Giornale d'Italia*, January 25 and 30, 1908), and also in his commentary on Genesis I-XI, published without ecclesiastical authorization.

21. (Undated manuscript addition of P. Lagrange:) According to M. David she asked at the same time that Mgr. Amette should be disgraced. M. David was with the bishop of Grenoble and Abbé Dumaine: he was therefore a first-class witness.

22. Letter of February 23, 1908 from Abbé David.

23. Letter of May 21, 1908. P. de Grandmaison speaks of a wish of his superiors; P. Condamin (May 20, 1934) of a decision; P. Mariès (October 2, 1908) of a "measure enjoining on our fathers" Nevertheless he continued to promise his book on Wisdom for three or four years. (The previous sentence is an undated manuscript addition by P. Lagrange.) The list of Jesuits who honored us with their collaboration in the *Revue Biblique* runs: PP. Knabenhauer, van Kasteren, Hebrans, Thien, Aucler, Condamin, de Grandmaison, Durand, Prat, Mallon, van den Gheyn, Mariès, Ronzevalle. PP. Cornely, de Hummelauer, and Corluy had promised their collaboration, but did not fulfill their intention.

24. Letter of December 16, 1908. (Addition of October 14, 1934.) It would have been said: "What! He has dared to praise a book of P. Lagrange, a book in which mention is made of literary genres, where it is hinted that Daniel dates only from the second century—and that in the heart of Rome, in a papal seminary!" An unpardonable crime for which I would deserve to be hanged or deported to the Congo or the Amazon, if not imprisoned in the dungeons of Galileo Galilei. Obviously it seemed more politic to launch himself into the *Action Francaise*, ready to change again at the appropriate time, and ensure himself a fine career. We must quote also this pearl: "What an unhappy situation do those who refuse to pursue pure Orientalism create for themselves! If I find something after my thesis—or even before—which could interest the

Revue Biblique (without being too exegetical), I will make it my business to send it to you." There we are again.

25. (Undated manuscript addition by P. Lagrange:) Mgr. Sevin promised that a student be sent later and concluded (being at Lourdes), "Yes, I bless you with all my heart, most fraternally. May Our Lady of Lourdes bless you, console and help you and your marvelous work." A letter which throws interesting light on Loisy's attitude.

26. (Undated manuscript addition by P. Lagrange:) The letter of the Master General to P. Boulanger is far more formal: "Most recently, the Holy Father, discussing the question with the archbishop of New Orleans, said to him of P. Lagrange: 'There are grounds etc.' " It should be noted that the thought of the Holy Father is none too developed. To the archbishop and the bishop of Grenoble he taxes my present attitude; to the Master General he says, "Now there is nothing, but it is the past." For me the past is covered by the authority of Leo XIII; it was not touched at all by the papal decrees *Lamentabili*, etc.

27. (Undated manuscript addition by P. Lagrange:) Letter to P. Boulanger, entirely transcribed by him, June 29, 1909.

28. Letter of June 28, 1909.

29. *Ibid.*

30. (Note added October 14, 1934) It was presumably the patriarchs in *La Méthode Historique* that were meant, those before the flood, whereas I was thinking of Abraham, etc.

31. The encyclical *Spiritus Paraclitus* of Benedict XV sounds the same note when it puts St. Jerome in opposition to those who "disregarding the feeling and judgment of the Church, take refuge *too easily* in what they call implicit citations or stories which are only apparently historical." The Commission itself did not consider the terms of the first three chapters of Genesis to be strictly historical (June 30, 1909). Cf. *R.B.*, 1919, pp. 593ff.

32. Good intentions did not prevent the wounds from being murderous. "The sting of the honey bee," said Our Lord to one saintly soul, "is much more painful than that of any other bee. Anyone accepts accusations made against those whom honest people condemn." (*Les saintes voix de la Croix* by Boudon, in Brémond, *Histoire littéraire du sentiment religieux en France*, VI, p. 251).

33. (Note added October 14, 1934:) The archbishop of Malines (August 26, 1909) felt that he could not subscribe, and said of the Institute at Rome: "Do not be afraid, my dear father. The Roman Institute will have its part to play, but you will keep yours, and I have every confidence that Providence in whom I know you dutifully trust—will protect you and give you in his own good time the full success which you

deserve and desire." While we wait for that good time our only purpose in existing is for our own students.

34. Letter of May 10.

35. Letter of August 13.

36. Letter of January 7, 1910.

37. (Manuscript addition of P. Lagrange, undated and without any particular attachment:) A strange letter of P. Lehu, April 2, 1910, on the conferences given by P. Fonck. The nomination of M. Ladeuze as rector of Louvain is a very important sign of calm. He is not immediately made a prelate, but Cardinal Mercier is very well received by the Pope (to whom the cardinal must have talked about M. Ladeuze).

38. Letter of January 20, 1910.

39. Letter of July 27, 1910.

40. Postcard of December 6, 1910.

41. Letter of January 31, 1910.

42. Letter of April 2, 1910.

43. Letter of March 12, 1911. (Manuscript addition:) P. Frey.

44. Letter of March 18, 1911.

45. (Undated manuscript addition, without any particular attachment:) From P. Fred Bouvier, S.J., May 29, 1911: "You mention in your letter the bias that pains you. I think it has been mightily curbed and that books like your St. Mark will contribute a great deal to removing it from any fair mind." Speaking of his review in *Recherches:* "I had a little debt of gratitude to pay you—and, also, I must say, to pay on behalf of those who have so far forgotten themselves as to treat you bitterly or unjustly." The same opinion from P. Boulanger, March 12, 1911.

46. *Bulletin de la Semaine*, October 2, 1912, p. 470.

47. The name is unknown to me; in Germany, I was often linked with P. Zapetal. (Updated addition:) Norbert Peters?

48. Letter of September 5.

49. Letter of November 22.

50. I had made a very explicit one in the *Revue Biblique* after the decree *Lamentabili.*

51. *R.B.*, 1911, pp. 440–442.

52. *R.B.*, 1911, pp. 566–591; 1912, pp. 86–111, 424–453, 544–574.

53. I am not speaking of slightly indiscreet friends. In a little broadsheet distributed at the door of Paris churches, *Le bonheur, c'est Dieu connu et aimé*, March 1912, we read: "A subscriber writes to us about the Society of Jesus; the fidelity of this Order consoles the Holy Father. It is well-known that a Jesuit was recently appointed professor

at the Gregorian University of Rome for his refutation of a thesis of Lagrange of the Biblical School of Jerusalem."

54. *Bulletin de la Semaine*, July 28, 1909.

55. August 21, 1909.

56. Imposed on the Benedictines and the Dominicans.

57. The following article from *Unità Cattolica* is found in the French edition, pp. 354–357.

58. See the French edition, pp. 357–358.

59. (Note added October 15, 1934:) Letter of P. Cormier, November 15, 1912 on the Jesuits' plan to set themselves up at Jerusalem; to ask the Pope to forbid it seemed to him to give the impression of being a protestor, and besides: "Assuming that the plan succeeds, we shall always have at Jerusalem a residence enviable and made useful by the celebration of the divine office, the edification of pilgrims, the apostolic ministry in the city and beyond, and the acceptance of clerics who wish to complete their studies with us; it will be not a large group, but an intelligent one, and devoted to the Holy See." This group decreased to vanishing point. Already on November 9: "To this is added the recent censure which hardly allows us to appear aggressive or exclusive." Fonck had foreseen everything and struck just right.

60. (Updated manuscript addition by P. Lagrange:) The Jesuits showed themselves passionately interested in the question. Besides those who made clear and public statements against me, I should mention also those who showed a real sympathy toward me: the Bollandists, PP. Delehaye and Peeters, in England Fr. Martindale, the French de Grandmaison, Condamin, Durand (Prat, a little), Fred. Bouvier, Mariès, de Tonquedec, Pinard de la Boulaye, d'Alès. Among the Dominicans no official opponents, but a number of reservations, some bad temper, apprehension about the honor of the Order. . . .Sympathetic letters from the French province from PP. Boulanger, Sertillanges, Mandonnet, Gardeil, Schwalm. The provincial of Toulouse, P. Tapie, told me that I should realize that I must take a grip on myself. . . . From Lyons nothing, apart from P. Lehu, who was in the Master General's entourage and was very sympathetic. All this was a little outside their sphere of interest. Benedictines who were sympathetic: Dom Cabrol, Dom Germain Morin, Dom Wilmart, Dom De Bruyne; the only one who openly fought for us was Dom Bonaventure Ubach, a Catalan. Sympathy among the clergy: Cardinals Rampolla, Mercier, de Cabrières, Sevin, Mgr. Le Camus, Mgr. Ladeuse, Abbé Venard and Abbé Vigouroux.

61. See Lagrange's letter of resignation, pp. 358–359 of the

French edition, and the Pope's letter to Fr. Cormier of August 16, 1912 on pp. 360–361.

62. (Undated note by P. Lagrange): I will quote only one letter, from Cardinal Mercier, October 12, 1912: "I feel the most lively sympathy for the painful trial you have had to go through, and have asked God as best I could to uphold your courage. As you yourself have declared so loyally and so humbly to the Sovereign Pontiff, your intentions have always been right, and hence, in conscience, before Him who reads the depths of the heart, your attitude and your works can never have been anything but meritorious. . . .I certainly hope that the trial into which your religious spirit has been plunged, thus giving you an opportunity to edify the Catholic world, will not break down your courage. Abbé Ryckmans has told me that you have a commentary on St. Luke on your work-bench. In my humble opinion—allowance being made for that of your superiors—I see no reason why you should not publish this commentary. This would show not only that you are not sulking—of which you would be incapable—but that you still have resilience and spiritual vigor, etc."

63. (Undated note by P. Lagrange:) A letter from P. Cormier, September 18, 1912: "A Belgian priest writing to us finds your letter not only beautiful but *clever*. I wonder what he means. Another priest said to me: 'A careful reading of the act of submission reveals that it does not link together sufficiently clearly the disavowal of ideas, which after all are the cause of what is happening, far more than P. Fonck and company.' Is that a false or forced conclusion?" This was the statement of an honest man! P. de Grandmaison wrote to me on September 18: "I have read your letter to the Holy Father with admiration." Very affectionately he came to see me at Sevres.

64. A letter undated, but certainly sometime in September or October: "We have spoken about what still seems to me the sole safeguard for the Biblical School, a committee of patronage. But no notice has been sent to the newspapers, and at the moment any agitation about the 'combinazione' of P. Fonck would seem to me inopportune. On this point we are in agreement with you, etc."

65. *Bulletin de la Semaine*, October 2, 1912, p. 470.

66. The Italian original is found on pp. 361–362 of the French edition.

67. Letter of November 9, 1912.

68. (Undated manuscript addition, without any particular attachment:) Letter of P. Cormier, January 10, 1913: "It has been claimed that the *Index* is going to raise the case of the two German authors between

whom you were sandwiched." That is precisely it, sandwiched. According to this letter it was the opinion also of the assistants to the General that no approach should be made to the Holy Father to prevent the Jesuit foundation in Jerusalem. From P. Condamin, January 3, 1913: "We have heard also, but *only from the newspapers*, that P. Fonck has at last suceeded in getting a house at Jerusalem, and even putting himself under the protectorate of France."

69. Laughable—or lamentable. One of our Fathers at Rome wrote to me on January 6: "From the very first day I said to the Master General that it was infamous; he must have heard the same also from elsewhere, for if at the first reading he was stunned, this impression did not last at all long. I was glad to relate to him a few days later the impression of P.X. whom I had met in the street: 'Such a tissue of mistakes, it is shameful!' " The document is reproduced in the *Supplementum* of P. Pesch, p. 48, with an *explicatio auctoritativa*. (Note added February 27, 1929:) Although P. Pesch's assessment seems to me exaggerated, I would no longer express myself in that way today, and I have taken account of the remarks in my revision of the commentary on St. Mark.) The objections are given in the Italian and French originals on pp. 363–368 of the French edition.

70. *Unità Cattolica*, August 30, 1913: "There has not been lacking some wag who has managed to hear somebody whispering between his teeth, 'P. Lagrange receiving a prize; it's the reply to Rome.' " Speak more clearly, please! Far be it from me in any case to intend any allusion—which would be worse—to the Society of Jesus. It is well known that at the end of the reign of Pius X *Unità Cattolica* violently attacked *Civiltà*, just as the former P. Barbier attacked P. de Grandmaison and P. d'Alès in his *Critique du liberalisme*.

71. Session of Saturday, December 6, 1913.

72. Letter of December 12, 1913.

4. FORMATIVE YEARS (1855–1873)

1. It has become a cavalry school, through a theft by the state during the episcopate of Mgr., later Cardinal, Perrault.

2. I do not know of any more solid and attractive treatment of secondary studies than the talks Mgr. Landriot gave as superior of the minor seminary to his pupils. Would they still be possible? Other teachers could learn from them.

3. Her elder sister was already married to Dr. Potton.

4. The two sons of M. Potton, the cousin of Dr. Potton, were to

become P. Ambroise Potton, a Dominican, and P. Chrysostom, a Capuchin and founder of the Third Order of Franciscan nuns dedicated to the adoration of the Most Blessed Sacrament.

5. Following my father's intention that I should do the first year of law, of which I in fact passed the first examination at Dijon.

6. There should be three exclamation or question marks here.

7. A letter to Ravel-Chapuis proves that I was looking for this enlightenment.

6. SON OF SAINT DOMINIC (1879–1888)

1. This story, written earlier, forms the first part of this book.

2. This was originally meant in connection with the assertion of the rights of the Church.